# AIR COMMANDOS
*The Saga of the Carpetbaggers of World War II*

BEN PARNELL is the president of the First Bank and Trust Company of Bartlett in Central Texas. His interest and research on the Carpetbaggers resulted from the death of his brother, S. Sgt. Garrett C. Parnell, Jr., who was killed in the crash of a Carpetbagger B-24 when returning to land in a two-hundred-foot ceiling at a British airbase. For more than twenty years he has been chief executive officer for the First Bank and Trust Company. He is very active in his profession and in civic organizations.

D1559020

## AVAILABLE NOW

# AIR COMMANDOS
*The Saga of the Carpetbaggers of World War II*

A story of the 801st/492d Bombardment Group (H)
U.S. Army, Eighth Air Force

BEN PARNELL

## ibooks
**www.ibooks.net**

DISTRIBUTED BY SIMON & SCHUSTER

An ibooks, inc. Book

All rights reserved, including the right to reproduce this book
or portions thereof in any form whatsoever.
Distributed by Simon & Schuster, Inc.
1230 Avenue of the Americas, New York, NY 10020

ibooks, inc.
24 West 25th Street
New York, NY 10010

The ibooks World Wide Web Site address is:
http://www.ibooks.net

Copyright © 1987 and 1993 by Ben Parnell
Foreword Copyright © 2004 by John Gresham
All rights reserved.

Original title: *Carpetbaggers*
Published by arrangement with Eakin Press

First ibooks, inc. mass market paperback printing: October 2004

ISBN: 0-7434-9823-2

10 9 8 7 6 5 4 3 2 1

Printed in the U. S. A.

*This story is dedicated to
the officers and enlisted men of the
United States Army Air Force
who were the Carpetbaggers.*

OSS Operational Group team to be dropped into Norway / Photo-Stroud

French Forces of the Interior / Photo-Rudolph

# Contents

Harrington from the air / Photo-Stroud

Airport at Paris, France. White airplane is General Marshall's; dark airplane is General Eisenhower's.
Photo-Rudolph

# Preface

One has to have a reason to write a book like this. It may be hope for monetary reward, a great desire to write something for publication, a burning desire to expose something or someone, or none of the above. My reason falls under the latter.

In the 1970s my younger brother visited in my home over a weekend. He had with him some of the memorabilia of our older brother, who had been killed in World War II in England, and we talked about how little we knew about the circumstances of his death. We agreed that we should look into this, then he went on home to the upper Texas Panhandle and got too busy to do anything about it. I began looking for some of our brother's old bomber crew and in time found five of the original ten-man crew scattered over the United States. I also discovered ways to locate squadron histories and accumulated a mountain of paper with bits and pieces of information about the activities of his crew and how he died.

In summary, from all this information I prepared a little book about the life and times of our brother and wondered what to do with all the material I had left over. It seemed reasonable and logical to start another, bigger book covering the Special Operations unit to which he was attached when he died. This book is the result of that decision.

I am very grateful to Mrs. A. T. Siddall and Melissa L. Roberts, who worked so hard at editing my mass of material to extract organization from chaos and to guide this story through the intricacies of authorship in order to present an accurate account.

Much of this story has been compiled from microfilm records stored at the Albert F. Simpson Historical Research Center at Maxwell Air Force Base in Alabama. For firsthand insights I am indebted to the many former airmen with whom I have spoken or corresponded over the years. They wanted the story told, and I wish each of their accounts could be published, but they provided far more material — reminiscences and photographs — than could be incorporated.

Many accounts that were published in wartime newspapers in England are included in the histories of the various units and preserved on microfilm. They painted vivid pictures of the underground war in France, the low countries, and Norway that played such a great part in the ultimate and complete Allied victory.

For background material on the OSS and the SOE, standard published sources were consulted; other works listed in the bibliography provided information about the training and work of agents sent to assist the resistance forces in Europe, as well as their delivery to the field by British and American airmen.

It was not what they were trained to do, but it was different and exciting — flying their black airplanes at dangerously low altitudes in the night to deliver agents and supplies to the underground armies fighting the Nazis. Code-named the "Carpetbaggers," they received very little recognition or acclaim for their secret and hazardous work. They thrived on an independence that was unknown by their peers in the Eighth Air Force during World War II. This story is dedicated to the officers and enlisted men who were the Carpetbaggers. For many there was no flight home.

I believe that a healthy society will remember and honor its heroes. In this book I have tried to do so. A reader must understand that the operations covered here represent less than a tenth of all the missions they flew, and the narrative describes mostly their ill-fated ones because they stand out most clearly on the records. There were other, better times — but none of the missions were easy.

It has been an interesting challenge. Regrettably, it is finished; there are so many out there I have not yet heard from. To those I never found: Let me hear from you so that the story can continue to unfold.

# Introduction

Shortly after the end of World War II, the Office of Strategic Services was abolished by President Harry Truman. Just before closing out operations, the OSS released information that revealed the extent of its involvement in the war. The agency had operated under the direction of the Joint Chiefs of Staff; Gen. William J. "Wild Bill" Donovan was the commanding general, with staff and operational personnel drawn from both the civilian population and the military services. The OSS had served as coordinator of information gathered by the military and other departments of government; it also had operated its own superintelligence agency and supported resistance forces in occupied areas.

In 1941 President Franklin D. Roosevelt had named Donovan to head the prewar Office of Coordinator of Information, charged with the task of submitting confidential information to specific government departments. After the attack on Pearl Harbor, the organization was given a new name — the Office of Strategic Services. It was to become a top-secret agency, going underground to all but a few people occupying high office in government.

OSS intelligence gathering and covert action extended throughout the world, even into the enemy's homelands. Among its members were professors, journalists, lawyers, and common laborers. Assisting resistance forces in Europe, the OSS sent thousands of tons of arms, food, and other supplies to those underground forces. More than 5,000 officers and enlisted men of the United States Army Air Force were helped by agents of the OSS to escape from behind enemy lines.

In October 1943, when the American Joint Chiefs of Staff approved the allocation of aircraft (initially for support of the Polish underground), the USAAF agreed to supply airlift. Combat crews flying specially converted B-24s, and later C-47s, A-26s, and British Mosquitos, began to carry out agent and supply drops in concert with

Royal Air Force units. These were the airmen that flew their black-painted aircraft on highly secretive nighttime missions.

For sixteen months the 3,000 airmen stationed at the Harrington air base in England mingled with villagers there without disclosing the secret of their airfield. As they made farewell calls on English families who had entertained them in their homes, the people admitted, "We never knew." A British newspaper journalist wrote of them: "Only fiction in its wildest flight of fancy could vie with the dramatic role played by the USA air base at Harrington."

Front page of leaflet dropped by 856th Squadron in November 1944 while on detached service at Cheddington.                    Photo-Beaman

# Prologue

## A Pair of Gold Cuff Links

From the control tower a uniformed captain of the United States Marine Corps watched the black-painted Liberator prepare to take off. In the night the cold, wet wind almost blew away the sound of the B-24's engines. Then the sound grew louder, the lights on the wingtips began to move, and the airplane took off with a deafening roar and was gone.

The Marine captain's job on that afternoon and evening had been to give final instructions to a young American agent leaving for sabotage work near the Swiss border in German-occupied France. At 1700 hours that afternoon the Marine had walked up the steps of an inconspicuous private house on a London side street. He was admitted and went directly to the second floor, where he asked for "Le Breton." When Le Breton appeared, the two men walked down the hall to an empty room. There the captain said that he had a present from "the colonel," and handed over a pair of very heavy, plain gold cuff links. Le Breton, obviously pleased, remarked that he never thought that he would have anything so nice. The captain told him that they would make an appropriate souvenir and they might even be useful: in France they were worth 7,000 francs ($1,400). If Le Breton got into trouble and was arrested, the police might take his money but overlook the cuff links (which might later serve as a good bribe for a guard).

"What about my commission, Captain?" Le Breton was a young U.S. Navy radio operator of French parentage whose home was in New England. He had enlisted in 1943 and had taken a radio-operator's course in the Midwest. There he was picked by the OSS, as he had language qualifications needed for dangerous duty in enemy countries. He was sent through OSS communications and agent schools near Washington, D.C., and then on to England, where he continued training as radio operator, parachutist, and agent until he was ready for the field.

Tonight he was flying to France with a British captain to become a radio operator in an underground unit. His main concern was the status of his application for a navy commission.

The captain said, "We're doing what we can. You know these things take time. I promise that we will try like hell and that we'll let you know by radio as soon as we hear. Let's get going . . . It's getting late."

Le Breton and the captain were joined by the British captain as they climbed into an American-made car painted in British army colors and driven by a uniformed British woman. The trip to the airfield at Harrington took about two hours, and the Marine outlined their schedule as they drove: they were to eat as soon as they got to Harrington, then change clothing, which would take another hour or more. The airplane was scheduled to take off at 2235 hours. Le Breton simply said that he was hungry.

The American airfield at Harrington housed the population of a small town, with buildings dispersed over a wide area of British countryside. Lieutenant Rearden was the officer in charge of liaison work between the OSS and the Eighth Air Force. As the three men waited for him at the administration building, a second car drove up with a uniformed French officer and four agents in civilian clothes. The American captain and the French officer talked together, then told the two groups of agents to keep apart from one another at all times.

The mess hall was cold, dark, and bare, but the food, served cafeteria-style, was good. Le Breton ate five desserts, knowing that the sweets he liked would be hard to get where he was going. After eating, the agents again got into the cars and were taken to a three-room Nissen hut for dressing. First in the dressing process was a security check, with two security officers searching clothing with meticulous care for evidence that would be incriminating if found by the Gestapo. Such evidence included scraps of paper like the stubs of London bus tickets or theater tickets. It is possible that a second and equally important reason for the security check was to make sure that no unsuspected double agent took with him into France written material of value to the Germans.

When the security officers finished searching the two men, the American captain took charge. First, he sealed all personal belongings, such as money, billfolds, and letters, into manila envelopes marked with each of their names. The envelopes, he said firmly, would be available to them when called for at the London headquarters. He then seated Le Breton in a chair close to him, opened his suitcase, and in a quiet voice began to explain certain items of equipment as he handed them over.

The first item was money — 100,000 francs in notes of various denominations, contained in a white cloth belt to be worn like a life preserver. The captain told Le Breton that 100,000 francs amounted to 20,000 dolars, or 500 pounds in British currency. Le Breton would never be asked to account for this money; he could spend it as he liked. However, the captain warned him to be careful how he spent it. The quickest way to get into trouble with the police would be to live beyond his means. The captain asked Le Breton, "What would you think if you were in your hometown in America and a strong young man who is supposed to be a farmer begins to flash hundred-dollar bills in the local bar? You would think that there was something wrong, and you would want to know what it was. The same will be true for you in France. Don't make yourself conspicuous by spending too much money."

Then came personal papers, necessary for any chance of survival in German-occupied territory. Each had been prepared with meticulous care to meet existing laws and fit the identity that Le Breton was to assume. The papers included an identity card, ration card, census card, occupation card, certificate of residence, and birth certificate.

Le Breton took the papers and stowed them about his person. The captain then handed him a leather wallet in which was hidden a piece of silk carrying the code he was to use for messages from the field. He was to put small-denomination franc notes in the wallet to last for a while. Le Breton must remember that it would pass casual inspection but it would not stand a real search. He was to hide it with his radio set.

A package measuring 12x6x2 inches contained the crystals for the radio set. He was to carry this package in the front of his jump suit. (The jump suits were almost roomy enough to carry a baby grand piano.) The captain then produced capsules and asked Le Breton to sign a receipt for them. The blue capsules were to be taken to overcome fatigue; the white capsules were knockout drops that would produce an almost immediate state of unconsciousness, which would last for at least six hours.

Finally, Le Breton was handed a .45-caliber automatic pistol and a small .32-caliber revolver with a two-inch barrel. Both were loaded. The captain warned that the revolver was effective only at very close range. It had no safety and would fire with the slightest pressure on the trigger.

Dressing took a while. Le Breton took off his shoes so that his ankles could be bandaged and rubber heel pads could be inserted in the shoes. A young sergeant, who introduced himself as the dispatcher, then took charge. He would tell Le Breton how to jump and when; this was the dispatcher's fourteenth trip, so he was an old hand. The jump suit, a coverall of heavy canvas, was a mottled dark green and brown; it hung in loose, baggy folds and had many pockets, into which Le Breton slipped his revolver, a knife for freeing himself if he should land in a tree, a French flashlight with two extra batteries, and a small flask of rum. A folding spade that fitted into a back pocket was removed on order of the captain, who said that Le Breton's reception committee would take care of burying his jump gear. He was then handed a jump helmet with cushions of sponge rubber, leather gloves, and goggles.

The sergeant called for help in adjusting the British-type parachute. An American Marine sergeant supplied assistance enthusiastically, adjusting each strap with care and testing the release mechanism several times. He patted Le Breton on the back. "This is one of our best chutes. Opens quick and easy."

"Yeah?" The new agent was good-naturedly sarcastic. "I know all about that stuff."

In the room by this time were the Marine captain, the British captain, the liaison officer, the dispatcher, the Marine sergeant, the pilot of the Liberator, and Col. Clifford Heflin, commanding officer of the 801st Bomb Group. The pilot told the British captain that when he got on the ground he should tell his reception committee that the Liberator would try to make two more runs to drop packages. The first would come about eight minutes after the British captain was in, and if it was safe they would circle and make another drop. The Marine officer told Le Breton that he must remember this message: "I can't let you take a thing like that with you in writing. Repeat the message to me." For the first time Le Breton appeared bewildered, stammering while trying to reply.

In one corner Colonel Heflin was talking about his men and their job. "This work is harder than bombing — trickier. You're not following a formation — you're on your own. It takes a lot of training and flying ability to hit a drop zone right on the nose. The best pilots for the job are those who have been on antisubmarine patrol. We've got some of them. Good men. We've lost six airplanes so far, but a lot of those men aren't gone for good. We know that some of them got down safely and that the underground is bringing them out."

In the colonel's mind the most difficult thing about flying a mission was not enemy flak or night fighters. "What gets to me is crossing the channel in fog or cloud, on instruments, knowing that stuff around you is lousy with airplanes but not being able to see a thing When you are dealing with flak or fighters you have so much to do that you haven't got the time to be scared. When you're waiting for a collision in the overcast there isn't a thing to do but sit and sweat."

At precisely 2215 hours, Lieutenant Rearden said, "Let's go." They moved out into the cold, damp night. The Marine captain anxiously asked Le Breton if he was sure he had the message straight and asked him to repeat it to him again. They swiftly circled the field in the same car that had brought them from London. At the dispersal point the B-24, with a big letter "D" on its side, engines idle, was waiting. The crew, in coveralls and Mae Wests, stood by. Out of its element the bomber seemed fat, clumsy, ungraceful. One of the crew drew the captain aside and pointed to Le Breton. "How old is that guy? He looks like a kid."

The captain smiled. "He is eighteen — just. How old are you?"

The crewman shook his head. "I'm nearly twenty — but that's different. Eighteen! My God!"

Le Breton and the British captain shook hands with the Marine officer, then climbed into the airplane through the Joe-hole in the bottom of the fuselage. Approximately three hours later, they would jump through the same hole into the darkness over France. The pilot looked at his watch. "Well, let's go." He nodded to the Marine. "See you at breakfast."

The young American agent left for the field.

---

Note: This account derived from *History of the 856th Squadron*, on microfilm at Maxwell AFB, Alabama.

Colonel Heflin and Staff / Photo-Rudolph

Lt. Colonel Fish (left) and Colonel Heflin / Photo-Ressler

# FOREWORD
## By

# John D. Gresham

"So just what do military analysts generate or create?" Folks in my business get that question from time to time, often leading to mumbled answers and thin answers as we try to justify our existence. However, the truth is that we are often looking for threads and connections, which can show the patterns and trends that will give an edge to warriors in future combat. Our credibility comes from making good "finds" for our customers, frequently from obscure sources or forgotten manuscripts, assisted of course by our existing base of knowledge. That knowledge, more often than not, comes from years of reading.

It goes without saying that military analysts and authors like myself are ravenous readers, consuming a steady diet of Instant Messages, email, Internet newsgroups, newspapers, and magazines with an ear and eye always attentive, keeping watch on a 24-hour cable television news channel. It is books however, that provide us with the foundations of our knowledge and expertise. Were you to walk into my home, you would find the walls covered with shelves and stacked with books, some much older than myself. Some are treasured old companions, corners and slipcovers worn by continual use and frequent readings. For me personally, each represents a piece of the knowledge base that I fall back on time and again in my work as author, analyst, and U.S. citizen.

So what makes a "really good book" that you might pick up in my library? It often varies, though "really good books" always have a timeless quality to them, even when more recent volumes have covered or replaced the same subject or time period. Often, they form the basis for an examination, or just represent the book interested amateurs should start with. Sometimes, these books are just what you feel comfortable recommending to friends and family, in the hope that what you offer in advice will not bore or inundate the reader. There also are books that provide readers with the historical basis to understand more modern systems or concepts. Such a book is *Air Commandos*.

Since 2002, following a wonderful experience helping ibooks put out a new edition of the classic book *Zero!*, I have worked to create a list of books that would be of particular interest or value to their readers of military history. Such lists are quite popular within the major military service schools and academies around the world, each having their own set of alternatives. All share a common desire to provide student readers with a broad and solid foundation of military lessons to take with them into their careers. Some books however, make a lot of the lists. Robert Heinlien's science fiction classic *Starship Troopers* is on pretty much every American military reading list I know of from the Air Force Academy to the Naval War College. *Starship Troopers* encompasses many of the values and virtues desired for good military personnel of all levels, and is a universal favorite.

It was with this same desire to provide civilian readers of military history with a similar background that I began to make up my own study list for the *John Gresham Military Library*. This series is designed to give readers a list of books that will allow them to better understand military history from a "deckplates and ditches" point of view. Battles and campaigns, the real nuts and bolts of a victorious war, are rarely won in national capitals or command bunkers. Victories in battle go to the soldiers, sailors, airmen, and marines actually in the theaters of war. They also are won in laboratories and the minds of innovative people, who see things made possible by the march of time and technology. Often, initial attempts and efforts are unsuccessful and costly in lives and treasure: such is the cost of progress in producing new engines of war. Such a book is *Air Commandos*.

Few people remember that during World War II, a time when airpower seemed to be just starting to define its roles and missions in modern warfare, that in fact it was already making decisive contributions to victory. Jobs like bombardment, pursuit, and reconnaissance had been well understood as airpower tasks since World War I, and never were questioned with the coming of another global conflict. What was in doubt were the support and peripheral missions that people tried to use airpower for, such as precision strike, anti-submarine warfare, electronic warfare, and something called "special operations support." In spite of the doubters however, each of these would become roles and missions that today are considered crucial airpower tasks.

World War II was the first major conflict where systematic, large-scale use was made of unconventional warfare troops on a strategic scale. When Great Britain was driven off of the European continent by Nazi Germany, it was the Commando units of England's Combined Operations directorate that would make the first pinprick raids back into France and the other occupied countries. What we would today call Special Operations Force (SOF) units found a willing patron in Prime Minister Winston Churchill, who created an entire department within British Intelligence, the Special Operations Executive (SOE). SOE was tasked to conduct and coordinate clandestine and unconventional warfare operations behind enemy lines with underground and partisan groups from Norway to the Balkans.

One of the keys to making such operations work efficiently was the liberal use of airpower, to deliver, resupply, and retrieve operatives from behind enemy lines. The Royal Air Force (RAF) began to use a variety of aircraft for such missions, from converted bombers deliver operatives and supplies, to the unique Lysander liaison aircraft, which could land and take off in a farmer's field in the pitch darkness of a moonless European night. The RAF, already a separate service with its own budget and procurement authority, was more than willing to create what became known as "Moonlight" squadrons, and equip the units with aircraft specialized or modified for SOF missions. However, the United States Army Air Force (USAAF) was a very different matter indeed.

When the United States entered World War II, they brought a similar set of personnel and capabilities within the Office of Strategic Services, or OSS. Headed by the flamboyant General William "Wild Bill" Donovan, OSS was the modern-day predecessor of today's CIA and Army Special Forces. Along with intelligence gathering, psychological warfare, propaganda production, and a number of other tasks, the OSS also provided behind-the-lines clandestine services like those of the SOE, for warfighting commanders like General Dwight D. Eisenhower. Unlike many of his contemporaries, Eisenhower was not a prude to the use of such unconventional warfare personnel and tactics. Fully aware of what kind of enemy the Allies faced in Nazi Germany, and looking for any edge he could find, Eisenhower found a kindred spirit in Churchill. He rapidly integrated the SOE and OSS into plans for Operation Overlord, the planned invasion of Europe in June 1944, in the hope they could help save Allied lives on the beaches and landing grounds of Normandy.

When World War II began, the USAAF was already beginning to flex its muscles in the hope and expectation that they might achieve the status of a separate service following the war. To this end, the various factions within the USAAF each sought the resources to best serve their roles and missions in the global conflict that needed to be fought. Generals in charge of the bomber, fighter, and transport communities fought tooth and nail for scarce resources and funding to best achieve their assigned missions. Thus, so-called "orphan" missions like electronic and anti-submarine warfare, and SOF support never got the high-level support they so desperately needed, and existed only because of the needs of regional commanders around the globe.

So, when OSS began to need their own dedicated force of transport aircraft to support operations into occupied Europe, it took until the fall of 1943 to convince officials of the 8th Air Force to dedicate personnel, aircraft, and resources to the job. The "Mighty 8th" was in the middle of a bloody campaign to validate precision daylight bombardment at the time, and their leadership had no interest in diverting even one plane or pilot away from their primary mission. However, with patrons like Prime Minister Churchill and General Eisenhower, the SOE and OSS soon found a new unit of the 8th Air Force being formed to support SOF operations.

What became known as the "Carpetbaggers" of the 801st/492nd Bombardment Group (Heavy) began life as a castoff collection of elderly B-24D Liberator bombers flying from Alconbury in Great Britain. Losses were not uncommon, and the learning curve steep for aircrews used to the idea that "precision bombardment" meant hitting a target city, much less the corner of a particular building. Precision navigation and deliveries of personnel, equipment, and supplies was a science the Carpetbaggers developed on their own, and paid for in blood. Eventually though, newer aircraft, better equipment and tactics, and a steady flow of personnel made the Carpetbaggers a major success story in the European Theater of Operations, albeit one little known outside the headquarters of the 8th Air Force.

However, like all SOF professions, the men of the Carpetbaggers took on the mantra of "quiet professionals," meaning their story might have gone untold but for one man interest in finding out the story of his older brother's loss as one of the Carpetbaggers. What began as Ben Parnell's personal quest for answers became a very fine book, *Air Commandos*, which tells the story of the Carpetbaggers and their service in World War II. Like many personal books, *Air Commandos* tells its story from the personal point of view of the people involved.

However, in the case of SOF support aviation this is an appropriate position to take, since in Special Operations, it's always ALL about the people. Air Commandos also tells the story of the beginning of a five-decade fight to bring SOF aviation into the forefront of airpower within the U.S. military. Orphans for the next half-century, only the creation of the U.S. Special Operations Command in the late 1980s gave SOF aviation in all the services a home, budget, and the authority to finally acquire the personnel and tools needed for their specialized roles and missions.

Today, Air Force Special Operations is finally about to take the first purpose-designed SOF aircraft, the CV-22 Osprey, into service. The story of the SOF version of the Osprey began with the story of the World War II Carpetbaggers, who struggled with obsolete aircraft, little command support, and a vitally important mission to conduct. In his own search for personal answers, Ben Parnell has gone a great service to SOF professionals everywhere. By writing *Air Commandos*, and telling the story of the World War II Carpetbaggers, Ben Parnell has helped today's modern SOF warriors obtain the aircraft that will take them into battle in the 21$^{st}$ Century. As a friend of many of the young men who will ride he Osprey into harm's way, I cannot imagine any more noble or selfless act on the part of a loving brother.

John D. Gresham
Fairfax, Virginia
August 2004

# 1 The 36th and 406th Squadrons: Getting Started

Long before the United States entered the war, Great Britain had almost completely mobilized: nearly every person, male and female, of useful age was either in the armed forces or working on farms and in factories to produce food and war materials. When American personnel began Office of Strategic Services flights (OSS) to continental Europe, the British already had the lead in the clandestine operation. The Royal Air Force proved to be excellent teachers to the Americans.

The British Special Operations Executive (SOE) began as a small research section of the British General Staff and operated under the Ministry of Economic Warfare. When approving the formation of the SOE, Prime Minister Winston Churchill exhorted the new minister, Hugh Dalton, ". . . and now set Europe ablaze." The SOE was "to create and foster the spirit of resistance in Nazi-occupied countries" and "establish a nucleus of trained men who would be able to assist as a 'fifth column' in the liberation of the country concerned whenever the British were able to invade . . . ." The American OSS, the federal agency responsible for covert operations in enemy-occupied areas, naturally worked with the SOE when the United States entered the war. In 1942 agreements between American and British chiefs of staff fused their special operations in northwestern Europe into a section called SO/SOE.

Resistance forces in Poland, Czechoslovakia, Norway, Denmark, Holland, Belgium, France, and Italy worked to prepare secret guerrilla "armies" to fight in conjunction with Allied land armies, but until the Allies arrived they operated as individuals or in small groups, carrying out tasks of subversion and sabotage. They sent out intelligence on enemy strength, activity, and movements, and they helped fugitive airmen and others to escape to neutral countries.

Throughout 1942 the SOE supplied arms and equipment to the underground forces, but logistical problems were immense, and few aircraft could be spared for the task. Nevertheless, the six sections of the SOE sent agents to France to help with the advance of the Western Allied armies, ran escape routes (working throughout occupied Europe and in Algiers), and used citizens to guide public opinion and maintain morale. Agents knew that their chances of returning safely from missions in occupied areas were no better than even. As Eric Piquet-Wicks wrote (in *Four in the Shadows*, 1957), "To be dropped in Occupied France was not a great adventure, nor was it an exciting pastime — it was a deadly struggle against a ruthless and savage enemy, most often with death as a reward."

On October 12, 1943, Col. C. S. Vanderblue, CO of the Office of Strategic Services, European Theater of Operations, posted a history-making letter to Lt. Gen. Jacob L. Devers, commanding general of the United States Army, European Theater of Operations. The OSS colonel expressed his belief that air operations to supply resistance forces on the Continent could be initiated on a modest scale. He recommended that approval be given "to the establishment of facilities necessary to supply Resistance Groups on a scope involving two squadrons of aircraft initially, with the possibility of expanding to three squadrons." He further recommended that "the details of operational procedure be determined by representatives of the commanding general of the Eighth Air Force in consultation with the SO Branch of OSS." Within seven days he had received approval of his plan from General Devers.

On October 24, Lt. Col. Clifford J. Heflin, Maj. Robert W. Fish, Capt. Oliver B. Akers, and Lt. Robert D. Sullivan were called to a meeting at Bovingdon, Hertfordshire. These officers were all of the 22d Antisubmarine Squadron. At Bovingdon they met Colonel Williamson, A-3 of the Eighth Bomber Command, Colonel Kirk, also of the Eighth Bomber Command, Group Captain Fielden, Royal Air Force Special Unit (Tempsford), Colonel Oliver of the Eighth Air Force, and Colonel Haskell and Major Brooks of the OSS. The newcomers were given a brief outline of the future duty of the 22d Antisubmarine Squadron, including a verbal description of the work, the training procedures, and the proposed modifications of their B-24 Liberator airplanes. They were told that the project required the utmost secrecy, and that their task was a radical departure from the usual duty of an American heavy bombardment group. They would work with certain British RAF squadrons in the vital and hazardous task of delivering agents and supplies to resistance groups operating in enemy-held territory.

In a few days a key group of officers and enlisted men were detailed to the SOE Royal Air Force airfield at Tempsford, Bedfordshire, to observe and receive training under the direction of Major Fish, Capt. Robert L. Boone, and Capt. Rodman A. St. Clair. Each pilot was to fly two missions as copilot with RAF crews who were flying the low-level night missions.

The first loss of American personnel occurred on November 3, 1943, when Capt. James A. Estes went MIA while flying a "buddy" mission with an RAF crew. Bestow R. Rudolph, who was selected to fly on the same night, has recalled the episode:

> As I remember, we were the first two line pilots selected. Before us, Heflin, Fish, Boone, and St. Clair went. On this night the RAF Group Captain said, "Jimmy, you go with this crew, and Rudy, you go with that one." If he had said it the other way around I wouldn't be here today. If anything was ever known as to what happened to Jimmy and the RAF crew, I don't know about it . . . . Estes, along with St. Clair, Sanders, Boone, and several others were all in the same bunch to come to Heflin's outfit at Fresno, California. Fish came before them; I came after.[1]

A few nights later, on November 11, another American officer, Lt. Burton W. Gross, went MIA, also while flying a mission with an RAF crew in a Halifax bomber.

On November 15, 1943, Lt. Wilmer L. Stapel flew his first Carpetbagger mission with an RAF crew, whose pilot was a sergeant. Stapel flew as copilot in a Halifax four-engine bomber equipped and fitted for Carpetbagger use. The drop area was northeast of Paris. Stapel would later recall the mission:

Altitude 4,000 feet. Weather was cloudy and we flew much of the time in them. Due to weather we could not spot our dropsite. Returning, as we approached Orleans, France, the clouds broke and we were over the town. Before the navigator could pinpoint our position, we were hit with flak. For a split second it reminded me of a 4th of July celebration. When I saw a shell headed directly toward me, reality set in. I leaned forward just as it burst right behind my seat; fragments struck the pilot, flight engineer, and radio operator. We lost number 3 engine and our cockpit lights. Evasive action was taken and we managed to get out of their guns' range. A quick assessment and crew check made. No other crew members were hit. The aircraft was still flying, the three injuries were not critical, and first aid was administered to them. While the pilot was receiving first aid I was elected to fly the airplane. We proceeded back to Tempsford, with the pilot landing the plane. My first Carpetbagger mission was history.

The RAF crew was put on 30 days leave, and on their very next mission after returning to duty were shot down.

My second mission was aborted about 10 minutes after takeoff. The pilot on that mission was a Squadron Leader, starting his third operational tour. The aircraft was a Lancaster. The takeoff was harrowing; just barely getting airborne at the very end of the runway. On climbout the aircraft was slow, sluggish and unresponsive. At 1,000 feet he leveled off, declared an emergency, and proceeded back to land. Ceiling at takeoff was about 200 feet. With the airplane, in the pilot's opinion, ready to crash at any time, he ordered his crew to their crash positions. I elected to stay put in the copilot's seat. One crew member (I have no idea who it was) came forward and told me to get my butt back behind the cockpit bulkhead and assume the crash position as had been ordered by the skipper. I went. I got into position and within seconds the engines started winding up, the aircraft felt like we were in a spiral. Before I could make any move (if I was going to crash I wanted to be in the cockpit) good or bad, the engine noises subsided to normal and the aircraft was leveled out. After several more minutes of flying, the aircraft hit the ground, bounced several times, veered to the left and came to a stop. The engines stopped, the escape hatch opened, and we all scrambled out. Colonel Heflin, along with the RAF Station brass came out to find out what went wrong.

I voiced my opinion to Heflin that I had had enough flying with the RAF and much preferred to make my next mission with my own crew.[2]

A second meeting was held at Bovingdon in late November

1943. At this meeting it was disclosed that the ground sections of the disbanded 22d and 4th Antisubmarine squadrons, and the combat crews of the 22d, would form the nucleus of two new squadrons. These were the 36th and the 406th, to be attached to the 482d Bombardment Group (Prov.). They were to operate from Tempsford with the RAF during the first operational moon period (those nights when the moon was out) in December and were to use their own modified B-24 Liberators on operational missions.

The air echelon of the 22d AS Squadron had arrived in the United Kingdom in the latter part of August 1943; the ground sections had arrived about September 10. The 4th AS Squadron had come over in July 1943. Both squadrons were assigned to the 479th Antisubmarine Group at Dunkeswell, Devonshire. During the first weeks of October, however, the U.S. Navy began to move into Dunkeswell airfield: the Army Air Force Antisubmarine Command was being broken up and the job of patrolling the Bay of Biscay was to be the navy's.

The 22d AS Squadron was relieved of its duties and ordered to move to a new station at Alconbury, Huntingdonshire. The combat crews of the 4th AS Squadron were severed from the ground sections; some of the combat crews joined heavy bombardment squadrons stationed throughout England, while other high-hours combat crews were returned to the States. In early November the ground sections joined the 22d AS Squadron at the large and desolate airfield at Alconbury, which was occupied by the 482d Bombardment Group (Prov.), a Pathfinder (PFF) group.

The two new squadrons were officially activated at Alconbury on November 28, 1943. Colonel Heflin, former commanding officer of the old 22d AS Squadron, assumed command of the 406th Squadron; Captain Boone was the operations officer. Major Fish assumed command of the 36th Squadron, with Captain St. Clair as operations officer.

The 406th Bombardment Squadron (H) designation had been assigned to the Eighth Air Force, First Bomb Division, on November 11. The unit had been constituted in November 1940 as the 16th Reconnaissance Squadron (M). Officially activated in January 1941 at Fort Douglas, Utah, it was attached to the 42d Bombardment Group and assigned to the 3d Wing QHQ Air Force, March Field, California. The unit designation was changed to the 406th Bombardment Squadron (M) on April 16, 1942, and to 406th Bombardment Squadron (H) on November 11, 1943.

Constituted on December 22, 1939, and activated February 1,

1940, at March Field, the 36th Bombardment Squadron (H) had been based at several stations in Colorado and Alaska. It had been assigned to the Eighth Air Force on November 2, 1943.

Heflin and Fish were relieved of their unit commands on December 14 and transferred to Headquarters, 482d Bombardment Group (Prov.). Heflin became air executive, and Major Fish, operations officer, of the Carpetbagger special project. Captain Boone assumed command of the 406th Squadron, and Lt. Lyman A. Sanders became operations officer. Captain St. Clair assumed command of the 36th Squadron, with Capt. Robert L. Williams as operations officer.

The units suffered their first combat crew loss on December 27, when Captain Williams, with full crew, was lost while on a navigational training mission in the south of England. After encountering extremely bad weather, their B-24 flew into a hillside, instantly killing all crew members.[3] After the death of Captain Williams, Lt. Benjamin A. Mead assumed the duties of 36th Squadron operations officer.

On January 2, 1944, Colonel Heflin and Capt. Edward C. Tresemer of Headquarters, 482d Bombardment Group (Prov.), received orders to report to RAF Station Tempsford "for temporary duty of approximately 30 days." With them went nineteen officers and thirty-four enlisted men of the 406th Squadron and eight officers and nineteen enlisted men of the 36th Squadron. The first Carpetbagger missions by American units, after training, were conducted from the British RAF airfield at Tempsford, and because there was a crucial lack of facilities at Alconbury the 36th and 406th squadrons were to operate from Tempsford until the moon period of February.[4] A great deal of comradeship and cooperation quickly developed between the units as they learned to work together closely.

Two days after arriving at Tempsford, Lieutenant Stapel flew as copilot, with Colonel Heflin as pilot, along with Stapel's crew, on the first Carpetbagger mission for the 406th Squadron from Tempsford.[5] A total of six missions were flown by 36th Squadron crews and nine missions by 406th Squadron crews during the moon period of January.[6]

Readers of British newspapers began to learn a little about the work of the underground patriot forces in France and Belgium, forces that were being supplied by the Carpetbaggers. On Saturday, January 15, 1944, the *Daily Express* reported:

*Patriots Wreck Railroads:* French patriots last night attacked the Ger-

man-held Annecy railroad depot and blew up several locomotives
. . . . At Rumilly, in Savoy, patriots stopped a train, forcing the
passengers to alight, then sent the train rushing uncontrolled along
the line until it overturned . . . . In Belgium, patriots, complying
with directions given them by the Allied Command, carried out 41
acts of sabotage in one week on the railway tracks in the province of
Hainault.

On the sixteenth the *Sunday Graphic,* in a brief item, referred
vaguely to "secret airmen" whose work "is a close secret and will make
amazing reading after the war."

The units, still operating on detached service from Alconbury,
flew twenty-one completed missions and thirty-five noncompleted
missions during the moon period of February.[7]

Early that month seven crews of Carpetbaggers were sent to Leuchars Airfield, near Edinburgh, Scotland, to work with the "Cold
Weather Man," the old Artic explorer Col. Bernt Balchen. Their assignment was to take part in newly activated OSS operations to the
Scandinavian areas. Captain David Schreiner was the pilot of the crew
picked for a trial flight to be made as soon as a newly arrived B-24
could be modified.

Later, in September 1944, Schreiner flew as copilot with Lt. Col.
Keith Allen on a fateful mission to drop two Norwegian agents near
Kirkenes, Finland. This was a round trip of 3,000 miles, which was
the absolute limit of the range of a B-24. At the coast they were
greeted by intensive flak, and after sustaining major battle damage
with two engines shot out, Allen told the crew that they would not be
able to make it back to Scotland. The two agents were dispatched
within twenty-five miles of the spot at which they were expected, and
the airplane headed for Murmansk, the nearest Allied landing field.
But at Murmansk harbor the entire Russian fleet — every visiting ship
in the harbor and every coastal battery — opened up at the crippled
B-24. Allen swerved to run, but it was too late. He ordered the crew
to jump, and all but Allen parachuted to comparative safety in the icy
water and on the savage rocks where Russian sentries opened fire at
them. Allen died and was buried there; the others were eventually returned to England.

Articles continued to appear in British newspapers, reporting on
the secret war going on in France and Belgium. On February 14 the
following story, by Victor Schiff, was published in London:

High up in the snow-covered French Alps cameramen recently made one of the most remarkable records of the war — a film of the "Men of the Maquis," the French guerrillas . . . .

As shown in the film record, the day of the "Army of the Maquis" begins with the traditional French military ceremony of saluting the flag. The scene is a glade in a fir forest, where the patriots have established their camp. The majority of the guerrillas are in shabby civil clothes, and shiver in the cold, but some wear their former French uniforms. They include an officer who, when unoccupied France was invaded, joined the patriot Army with a military car. This is now the pride of the camp. Somehow the partisans get the petrol to keep it running.

Another news story was distributed by Reuters on February 15:

"Parachute containers with tommy-guns, revolvers and ammunition are being dropped by the British to arm French patriots," according to Phillippe Henriot, Vichy Minister of Information and Propaganda.

Broadcasting last night on Vichy radio, [Henriot] said: "Fourteen parachutes with metal boxes containing arms and explosives were dropped in the Dordogne Department on the night of February 4. A wireless set arrived by parachute on February 9, with instructions in English. On February 11, 18 boxes were parachuted at Lacelle, containing 85 tommy-guns, 3,400 rounds of ammunition, 25 revolvers and explosives. On the same day another 124 tommy-guns with ammunition, 570 grenades, 2,000 packets of dynamite, 20 Colt revolvers and 32 Mausers were dropped in the Var Department. Yesterday 41 metal containers, whose contents have not yet been examined, were dropped in the Allier Department, while today, only a few hours ago, over 300 tommy-guns and a large quantity of ammunition were dropped in the same place. At another place today, 18 metal boxes containing tommy-guns, ammunition and explosives were dropped."

The Carpetbagger units later received a message from an agent in the field:

Please brief the crews where to drop leaflets. On Saturday they were dropped in the fields far from houses, with the result that I was among those requisitioned by the Gendarmes to pick up the tracts on Sunday after. I am now suffering from backache. This is not my idea of a picnic.[8]

In mid-February the Carpetbagger units were relieved of assignment to the 482d Bombardment Group (Prov.) and were reassigned to the Eighth Air Force Composite Command. The 36th and 406th squadrons moved from Alconbury to the "mud flats" of Watton, Norfolk, on February 17. Some personnel moved by motor convoy and some by air. Almost immediately, however, it was determined that because of the lack of concrete runways and hardstands satisfactory operations could not be conducted from Watton. Colonel Heflin made arrangements for the units to operate from Alconbury once again, and on March 1 the ground and combat crews began the move from Watton back to Alconbury. On February 27, Headquarters, 328th Service Group, was designated Group Headquarters for the units.

Operations during January had been completed at a rate of 47 percent of missions dispatched. February operations had dipped to 37.5 percent completed, which was considered an acceptable rate. In March, missions dispatched were completed at a very satisfactory rate of 58 percent. However, a new, startling figure was being discussed by the men, with grief in their hearts for their fallen comrades: three full crews went MIA from the 36th Squadron during March.

Wilmer Stapel recalls:

> On the night of March 3, 1944, Lt. Nesbitt and S.Sgt. Roettger of my crew volunteered to fly missions as fill-in's with Lt. Carpenter and Capt. Wagstad. They were both shot down; Lt. Nesbitt became a POW until the end of hostilities. I don't know what happened to Sgt. Roettger. Lt. Hal M. Harrison, my copilot, was given a crew of his own.
>
> On the night of March 5, for a mission to Belgium, Lt. Russell C. Rivers was assigned my crew as copilot. Dispatcher was S.Sgt. Charles J. Roth, and substitute bombardier for the night was Maj. Charles A. Teer, who was group staff bombardier.
>
> Takeoff 10:00 P.M. Length of mission: 4:45. Weather: Clear over Belgium. Drop zone NE of Brussels. We took off and dropped to 500 feet crossing the channel. Ten minutes before crossing the Belgian coast we started to climb with changes in heading to (we thought) confuse enemy as to exact point of crossing. As we got within three miles of coast we started a rapid descent and entered Belgium. Leveled out at 1,000 feet altitude and proceeded on course to drop area. Twenty-five miles or so into Belgium, searchlights and intensive flak greeted us. It seemed that we had just entered the gates of Hell. Our airplane cockpit was lighted up as if it was daylight. Shells started exploding all around us and we were hit several times. I started evasive action and dove for the ground. Each time I

would start a turn it seemed that we would be hit by more flak. As I approached the ground, Charlie Teer would yell, "Pull-up, pull-up!" I then would pull back on the stick until our airspeed would start dropping off and back toward the ground we headed. The tail-gunner and dispatcher began firing their guns at the searchlights and out they would go. After ten minutes of enemy fire, we ended up in the clear with our airplane out of range of their guns. An airfield showed up right in front of us and I had to literally pull up to miss a water tower and the control tower.

All was again serene and so I resumed an altitude of 1,000 feet. We reached the target area and I dropped the flaps 20 degrees when airspeed permitted and started our run. Before we could open the bomb bay doors fully, another hail of bullets and tracers greeted us. I abandoned the run and we crew members decided to head for home. The only way to get back out was to take a heading of west, pour the coal to the engines, drop down, and buzz our way out to the coast. On the way out we saw several other aircraft go down in flames but I figured we were so low and with the other aircraft in the vicinity the enemy gunners did not have time to pick us up until we were past their emplacements.

As we reached the coast of England we were not sure of our position. I continued flying on a westerly heading. Lt. Rivers kept telling me that the barrage balloon radio squeakers were getting louder and stronger. There was now cloud over England. We broke out of the clouds and could see barrage balloons dead ahead a couple of miles. I immediately turned north and missed striking any cables to which the balloons were attached. We were over London. We then proceeded back to base and landed without further incident. No one on the crew had been hit by all of the shells and bullets that had penetrated the aircraft. There were many, many bullet holes. A hole almost large enough for a man to crawl through was evidence of a direct hit on the left wing. It hit between the outboard and left fuel tanks. Inches either way would have been disastrous. Parts of the left rudder and stabilizer were shot away.

At the debriefing, the only explanation for all the heavy flak was perhaps we were off course. Several weeks later a new flak map was received by Intelligence. The Germans had moved into the whole coastal area from Holland to France with a huge number of light and medium guns to aid them in protecting the area from invasion by the Allied forces.[9]

Lt. Frank G. McDonald and crew of the 36th Squadron flew two missions, completing both, but went MIA on the night of March 2. The field reported that they had received nine containers and three packages. Whatever happened to McDonald and his crew, therefore, happened after they had completed the mission as briefed.[10]

Early in May, Lieutenant Kelly returned to England and reported that their B-24 had gone down after being hit by flak. Three members of the crew were thrown clear of the wreckage. After leaving the site of the crash, they found a shed at the edge of a small village where a young French girl brought them food and drink. Sometime later, after getting up the courage to approach on old man, they were led down the main street of the village, still in flying gear, and taken to a house where they were given civilian clothing. Arrangements were made to get them out of France. After several bad connections, Kelly was taken in by peasants who agreed to shelter him along the route, and eventually a French woman arranged for a guide to take him over the mountains into Spain.

At one point in his journey, as Kelly was being led through Paris, he followed his guide onto a subway car. He was lagging a bit behind and not paying attention, and the door of the subway closed on the seat of his trousers. Instinctively Kelly said, "Whoa, there!" loudly in English, and found himself facing a train full of raised eyebrows.

Kelly's guide on the trip over the Pyrenees was somewhat eccentric and inclined to drink too much wine. Though very grateful for the guide's help over the mountains to freedom, the American did not particularly enjoy a side trip of three miles just so his guide could show him a stone marker indicating the boundary between France and Spain.

It was believed that two others of the crew, Kendall and Ross, were captured and taken prisoner. No further information was known about the fates of other members of the crew.

In early March 1944, the first agent-dropping mission, "Bob 141," was flown, and two agents were successfully dropped. Colonel Heflin then requested that approval be given to begin dropping agents on regular missions. His request was immediately approved by Colonel Haskell, chief of Special Operations, OSS.

Lt. Wade A. Carpenter and crew of the 36th Squadron flew two completed missions but went MIA on the night of March 3.[11] About a month after the crew was reported as missing, a monitoring station of the Federal Communications System operating in the United States picked up a German radio broadcast listing the names of recent POWs. The complete list was not heard, but the name of Lieutenant Eshleman was heard, along with Nesbitt, Carpenter, Burris, and

Herdman. It was believed possible that the names of other crew members were broadcast but were missed, or that some of the crew survived, evaded the Nazis, and would eventually make their way back to England.

On the night of March 3, Captain Wagstad and crew completed their mission successfully but went MIA.[12] A message from the field confirmed the success of the drop.

Missions continued throughout the month — some with success, others without. But all were marked with the risk and sacrifice of brave men.[13]

During the last week of March, this message was received from an agent in the field:

> I visited the Maquis last week and was much impressed to be able to inspect first-class men with a wonderful morale. During the March-past, it was heartbreaking to see such a splendid body of men dressed in shabby clothes and worn-out boots, some with their toes out. I made a speech which was covered with Hurrahs for our two countries.[14]

A total of sixty-nine missions were flown during the March moon period, with forty completed.

A final move was made by the two squadrons on March 28, this time to a permanent home base at the village of Harrington, Northamptonshire. There the airfield was large, set among picturesque hills and valleys, with comfortable living sites for two squadrons. On April 4, the 36th and 406th squadrons were assigned to the 801st Bombardment Group (Prov.), which had just become operational. Colonel Heflin was appointed commanding officer, and Major Fish, deputy commanding officer, of the new group.

# 2　The Carpetbagger Airplanes

The first airplanes for the Carpetbagger special project, delivered in November 1943, were a quick modification job on the B-24D Liberator four-engine heavy bomber, and as modified they were not entirely satisfactory.

The B-24 was produced in greater numbers than any other combat airplane developed for World War II, including the fighters. A total of 18,188 were built, averaging out to cost $215,516 by 1944. This was considerably more expensive than the 12,721 B-17 Flying Fortresses built, which averaged a total cost of $187,742. However, it is difficult to compare the B-24 multipurpose warplane to the well-known, sleek, and graceful B-17. The B-17 and the B-24 were both powered by four radial-type engines of 1200 horsepower, each driving three-blade props. The B-17 engines were manufactured by Wright, the B-24s by Pratt and Whitney.

The B-24 was looked upon by some as a slab-sided monster, huge, ugly, and hard to handle; but what it lacked in appearance it made up for in performance, reliability, durability, and efficiency. Built around the bomb bay, it embodied the best features of design and construction of the day and represented a new bloodline of combat airplanes.

The B-24s were built by Consolidated Aircraft Company at San Diego and Fort Worth, by North American Aircraft Company at Dallas, and by Ford Motor Company at Willow Run. They possessed an advantage over the B-17s with larger bomb-load capacities and the ability to go farther and faster with the same ten-man crews. In March 1939, with a 3,000-mile range, a top speed of over 300 miles per hour, and a ceiling of 35,000 feet, they could outperform the B-17.

Numerous versions of the B-24 were built. As improvements were developed they were incorporated into the airplanes on the production lines and became B-24A, B-24C, B-24D, E, F, G, H, J, L, and M. The exceptional load capacity, speed, and range made it an excellent transport: the C-87 was built for the army, and the RY-1 for the navy. For long-range photo-reconnaissance work the F-7 was designed, manned by a crew of nine and carrying eleven cameras.

After several operational missions, it was found that further modification work was needed on the B-24Ds to prepare them for Carpetbagger work. Because it was believed that the navigators and the bombardiers performed the most critical job of the mission — pinpointing the aircraft on the target area and dropping loads accurately — and because their space was so restricted, most of the changes were made in their compartment areas. The problem of abandoning the airplane at low altitude was also corrected: the airplane was so cluttered with poorly installed and unnecessary equipment that on some aircraft it was nearly impossible to get out of the nose compartment with a parachute on.

The first airplane was modified in these ways in about a week, and when flown it met with instant approval. Instructions were given that the rest were to be prepared as quickly as possible. The early aircraft were all B-24Ds, but B-24Hs and Js were brought in later when B-24Ds could not be obtained in airworthy condition.

The ball turret opening was closed in with a metal shroud, with all inside surfaces perfectly smooth. This opening, called the "Joe-hole" and used by agents to parachute from the airplane, tapered from forty-eight inches at the bottom to a forty-four-inch opening in the fuselage floor. It was covered with a circular plywood door divided and hinged in the middle. When opened, the door folded back under the control cables out of the way. Two strong points for static lines were placed at the rear of the Joe-hole door, flush with the floor at the aft side of the Joe-hole, for attaching the static lines of the Joes' (agents') parachutes. Each set of strong points could accommodate eight straps, the maximum number of Joes that would be jumped in a "string" from the airplane.

One strong point was also installed for static lines in the rear of each bomb bay. One red jump light and one green jump light were installed at the Joe-hole, enabling the bombardier to tell the dispatcher when to dispatch Joes or material. Red indicated "action station"; green meant "go." Jump panels were installed at the hole, helping to eliminate projecting structures in the area and providing a device on which to attach the jump straps. Handrails were installed on the right side of the fuselage at the hole, and on the left side of the fuselage at the rear hatch, giving the dispatcher something to hold on to when the Joe-hole was opened or packages dispatched from the rear hatch.

A plywood floor was installed over the corrugated metal floor of the airplane. A strong point for static lines was installed at the rear hatch, in the aft left-hand corner of the hatch opening. A movable roller with a safety belt was mounted in the upper center of the fuselage so the dispatcher could move the full length of the fuselage without having to remove his safety belt.

The command deck was stripped of all unneeded radio equipment and oxygen bottles. Necessary units for the transmitter were moved to other areas of the airplane. The command deck and the opening over the rear bomb bay were covered with quarter-inch plywood for cargo space. Blackout curtains were installed over the waist-gun windows, and a door was installed in the fuselage with a window so that the tail-gunner could be seen.

The dead-reckoning compass was mounted on the pilot's panel and tilted so that it could be read at a glance. The interphone jack-boxes for waist-gun windows were moved to the top and front of the windows, and a fourteen-foot extension cord was installed for the dispatcher's microphone and headset. The gun mount was removed in the rear escape hatch and the plexiglass replaced with metal; flash-hiders were installed on all guns.

The first airplanes were completely painted standard black matte; later ones were given a glossy black antisearchlight synthetic enamel on the undersurfaces, with the upper surfaces left the standard olive-drab, if already so painted. For airplanes not yet painted, standard black matte was used on the upper surfaces.

Type F-1 airspeed indicators were installed on those craft not so equipped. Blisters were installed at pilot's and copilot's windows to enable them to see the ground ahead of the airplane when making low-level approaches at night. A loosely hung curtain was installed between the pilot's compartment and the radio operator's compartment to prevent light reflections in the upper turret and the pilot's compartment. The radio equipment was removed from the navigator's table and installed above the table; a Mark V drift-meter sight was installed in the navigator's compartment.

Carpetbagger airplanes were equipped to manage four general methods of navigation — pilotage, dead-reckoning, radio navigation, and celestial navigation. In addition, the airplanes had special equipment for Carpetbagger work. One addition was Radio "Gee," or "Gee Box," a radar navigational aid which picked up signals from ground stations. In England, on the ground, were a "Master" station and two "Slave" stations. These were used to send out combinations of signals which were picked up and recorded on a grid indicating the airplane's position within a quarter of a mile over England or, with less accuracy, over the Continent. The Germans had some success in jamming "Gee" signals over their own territory.

The S-phone, similar in principle to a walkie-talkie, had a range of eight to ten miles and permitted communication with an operator on the ground to direct the airplane to the pinpoint. The "Homing S-phone" used a radio compass in the airplane and enabled the navigator to direct the airplane toward the ground operator as on a radio beam.

Radio "Rebecca" was a radar directional air-ground instrument which recorded radar impulses on a grid and directed the navigator to an operator on the ground, whose set was known as "Eureka." The ground operator could transmit a signal letter to the airplane by varying the intensity or frequency of the blip.

The radio-altimeter projected a beamlike stream of radar impulses that were reflected from the ground back to the airplane. By measuring the time required for the impulse to make the round trip, an absolute measure of the airplane's altitude could be established. This instrument made dark-period flying at low altitude relatively safe. The dead-reckoning compass, used in all airplanes, allowed the navigator to apply corrections to his compass readings. Pilotage permitted fine adjustments of flight and was always used when the airplane was crossing over dangerous territory or running into the target. Pilotage was used if the bombardier had adequate visibility and could see and identify objects and landmarks on the ground.

Also in the navigator's compartment, a relief-tube was mounted on the right side of the aircraft. A one-quart C.T. fire extinguisher was installed under the drift-sight mount, and a swivel seat was added on the left side of the nose compartment. Various instruments were relocated, and blackout curtains were installed between navigator and bombardier, with the bombardier's chair in front of the curtain. On B-24Hs and Js the nose turret was removed and replaced with plexiglass.

A fluorescent light was mounted for the use of the bombardier for reading fluorescent-type maps. Another flexible light, with a reflector painted black and with a rheostat for mapreading, was mounted in the bombardier's compartment. All bombing equipment was remounted so as to be readily accessible when the bombardier was seated in the nose. A B-16 compass was mounted in the nose compartment along with a clock, and the bombardier's interphone box was mounted on the right side of his compartment. A knee-operated light switch was added (when mapreading or on a bomb run it was unhandy to use a hand switch). All metal surfaces in the bombardier's compartment were painted a nonreflecting black, and a loosely fitting curtain hung in back of the navigator's table, between his compartment and the pilot's compartment.

IFF radio, 0–400' and 0–4000' dual altimeter, Mark II Rebecca, Gee radio, and "S" phone were all installed. Flame dampeners were installed on turbo-superchargers. Tailpipes caused manifold pressure beyond the controlling range of the supercharger regulator and were not used. Finally, night-type gunsights were installed in the gun turrets.

All armament and associated equipment was removed except the upper turret and tail turret. The bombardier's windshield wiper, which did not operate well anyway, and the bombardier's heater on the right side of the fuselage were removed. The fuel transfer pump and hose on the bomb bay catwalk were removed; American bomb shackles were removed and replaced with British conversion shackles, as the containers for dropping supplies were furnished by the British and used British suspension lugs. The ball turret upper support was removed to give extra headroom. The D-12 compass, the VHF radio set, and all transmitter tuning units on the command deck were removed. The oil slick release and all bomb rack equipment were removed.

The B-3 drift meter, all interior brackets not being used, all oxygen bottles, brackets, regulators, flowmeters, and plumbing were removed, as were all rear-mounted armor plate and all radio antennas not in use.

Because the drops were accomplished visually by the bombardier, the bombsight was removed, as well as the astrograph and mount. Dome lights in the rear fuselage were painted red, restricting the amount of light but providing enough to see well. This step enabled the agents to have good night vision after leaving the lighted fuselage. The British blacked out the interior of the fuselage of their airplanes before dispatching agents. Cases of panic by the jumpers had occurred, as the mental hazard of not being able to see that their parachute straps were attached before jumping was too much for some of them to take.

Most maintenance problems on Carpetbagger airplanes were brought about because many of the airplanes were the old B-24Ds and had been allowed to deteriorate before being assigned to Carpetbagger work. However, the airplanes had no oxygen equipment, as it was not needed, and that alone eliminated a major maintenance item. Carpetbagger combat crews had very few of the usual problems with superchargers, engines, and electrical equipment encountered by units flying high-altitude operations. Ground sections had the daylight hours to service airplanes for the night operations.

New crews tended to obtain speed by using manifold pressure rather than proper trimming of the airplane, which caused many engine changes. Numerous failures, such as no compression after flight, cracked heads, cylinder assembly shearing off cylinder hold-down studs, and large amounts of metal filings and bearing material in oil screens, could be traced to excessive manifold pressure. This was finally controlled by watching the fuel consumption of individul pilots and talking to those who showed very high consumption.

Much of the maintenance was brought about by the crew-training unit in the group. This unit trained the combat crews for the Carpetbagger project, and at times the crew-training unit caused more maintenance than actual operations. It was determined that sixteen airplanes could be handled efficiently by the ground sections. At different times each squadron had from twelve to twenty-one airplanes, but eighteen or more were too many.

Fuel consumption, on the average, was low. Consumption for missions of approximately six hours was about 260 gallons per hour. On missions of approximately eight hours, consumption dropped to 220 to 240 gallons per hour; on missions from eight to ten hours, to between 200 and 225 gallons per hour. On some missions over ten hours, fuel consumption dropped to as low as 180 gallons per hour. As the crews gained experience, fuel consumption dropped and fewer engine failures were encountered. It seemed that high fuel consumption and engine failure went hand-in-hand.

Most battle damage to the airplanes was caused by antiaircraft guns of below 40mm, and no Carpetbagger airplane was known to have been hit by antiaircraft guns of larger caliber. Damage was usually minor, maybe a couple of 20mm explosives or a few .50-caliber or .30-caliber holes which were easy to repair. Usually, if an airplane was accurately hit by the fire of a small-caliber ground battery, the craft was lost.

# 3  The Crew and Its Missions

Some of the pilots in Carpetbagger work expressed a feeling of being shielded from the usual camaraderie of team-players.[1] Each mission was for a single crew, and they never saw anyone during their flights. Upon their return to base, they shared none of the joys usually associated with the successful completion of a mission; it was simply a matter of having survived. The next night, or the night after that, they would fly again. The combat crews delivering supplies and agents to the underground armies took on a certain character which set them apart from the usual combat units. The secrecy in which they operated, while the daylight bomber and fighter missions made daily headlines, emphasized that difference.

But the delivery of arms, supplies, and agents, and the successful evacuation of downed American airmen from enemy soil, were sufficient to bolster morale. There was great satisfaction in accomplishing the overall mission, which was hazardous and important, even if unsung at the time.

Each combat crew in Carpetbagger operations was made up of eight men: pilot, copilot, navigator, bombardier, engineer, radio operator, dispatcher, and tail-gunner. Upon assignment to one of the squadrons, the personnel of new crews were interviewed to find out all about their backgrounds, characters, and military records. The crew captain was instructed to select eight men from the usual heavy-bomber crew of ten; two enlisted men were to be dropped from the crew. He was told to select men, if possible, who were competent in at least two positions as a crew member of the airplane. If all men were considered of equal caliber, it was best to keep assistant engineers and assistant radio operators rather than a waist-gunner or a tail-gunner who knew only one position well.

The two enlisted men being dropped from the crew were given a special security lecture and immediately transferred out. All newly assigned officers and enlisted men were then given security lectures and required to sign a security oath not later than forty-eight hours after reporting for duty.

The crews had never before experienced such security or secrecy discipline as was demanded in the Carpetbagger project. They were told, "In no other work is the individual crew as directly affected by leakage of information as in this particular project. Also, there are hundreds of others risking their lives daily who are directly endangered by your divulging vital information. Play it smart! Your job and your life are your number one concern."

After the crew was formed, an orientation lecture was given by operational personnel. The crew then reported for physical examinations at the station hospital. There identification tags were checked and photos were made of each crew member while dressed in civilian, continental-style clothes. A lecture was given by station flying control for all crew members. A navigational aids lecture was given by the group navigator for the pilot, copilot, bombardier, and radio operator. An operations orientation lecture was given, with each crew member meeting with the corresponding member of his flight leader's crew to discuss all phases of a mission from briefing to interrogation. Prisoner-of-war and escape lectures were given by the group intelligence officer for all crew members.

The pilot, copilot, navigator, and radio operator attended a procedure lecture given by the group communications school chief instructor covering radio procedure and instrument let-downs. Radio operators were thoroughly checked out to the satisfaction of the communications school instructors. A mapreading class was held by the group navigator or group bombardier for pilot, copilot, navigator, bombardier, and tail-gunner. All crew members attended a standard operating procedure lecture, given by the group operations officer, covering filing clearances, diversions procedure, interrogation, security at other fields, checking the airplane, and taking personal interest in its care.

After the lecture on radar navigation was given by the group navigator, all crew members took proficiency tests to determine their progress and status. If they received passing grades on the examinations to the satisfaction of the operations officer, they were eligible for advancement to the general training program.

For two or three weeks new crews worked closely with personnel of old crews who had been engaged in Carpetbagger work. Pilots became accustomed to flying at dangerously low altitudes in the dark when making the run over the target. The navigator had his usual duties to perform and also worked under the additional pressure of relying upon his expertise to guide the airplane to the pinpoint and back to base in individual flight. Good navigation required teamwork among all members of the crew. The bombardier worked in close cooperation with the pilot and the navigator in mapreading so that the precise pinpoint of the target could be found promptly and surely.

The waist-gunner learned to dispatch containers, packages, and "Joes," or agents. As two gunners had been sacrificed for this work, there were no nose or belly turrets and usually no waist guns. Because combat with the enemy was discouraged and avoided when possible, the tail-gunner, the top-turret-gunner, and the pilot's ability to take evasive action often served as the airplane's only defense. The dispatcher, the key man in dropping agents and supplies, was specially trained to fit parachutes and made two low-altitude parachute jumps himself. The tail-gunner was alert to prevent a surprise attack from the rear by enemy night fighters, of which there were many, and also watched the parachutes open and reach the ground. At interrogation he reported the success of the drop.

Features of the terrain had to be learned and identified with split-second accuracy for each mission. Each man was alert to discover and identify the lighting systems used by the ground reception, and each man was alert for enemy activity near the drop site. The targets, especially those in France, were deep within Nazi-held territory and were bristling with flak installations, searchlights, and night fighters.

Combat with the enemy only endangered the success of the mission, so enemy antiaircraft installations and detector posts were skirted as widely as possible. To avoid combat with the enemy, flights were made at night and at low altitude. When it was necessary for an airplane to cross enemy-held areas protected by flak defenses, a route was chosen which was likely to expose the airplane to the fire of light guns only. The altitude attained seldom exceeded 7,000 feet, and as soon as a dangerous area was passed the airplane dropped down to 2,000 feet or lower. The low altitude made it difficult for the enemy to locate the airplane either by sound or by radar. Obstacles on the ground distort the sound of a low-flying airplane far more than they do the noise of a high-flying one because of the sharper angles of sound reflection. Radar and sound-detection devices had less time in which to focus on a low-flying airplane, and the range of effective detection was shorter at low altitudes.

The personal security of every resistance worker was considered to be at stake, and personnel to be dispatched were not allowed to carry on their persons anything that could betray their stay in England. A strict system for searching SOE/SO personnel was instigated, which was necessary because of the stringent restrictions placed upon all travel from the United Kingdom. Two officers were secured from the Customs Service to carry out their duties in plain clothes. All personnel, including those sent directly to bases from London or elsewhere, were to be searched in the presence of the Country Section conducting officer. Women were searched by a female conducting officer. After the search, each agent was asked to sign a form declaring that he was carrying nothing on his person that was forbidden.

Members of the British and Allied Special Services were not required to pass through the normal control; their passage was through special controls manned by specially chosen and discreet personnel. A thorough search was required of all ranks and all nationalities. Members of the British and Allied Special Services were also required to sign a form declaring that they were not in possession of any forbidden item.

The pilot of the airplane, or his next in command, was responsible for seeing that the airplane and all its contents were completely destroyed if a forced landing was made at any time in enemy-controlled territory. All papers, maps, and documents had to be destroyed by burning. These were set on fire in the airplane and not left to be burned with the airplane when it was destroyed, as it might not burn completely. All confidential and secret devices and equipment were to be destroyed by the detonators provided, and the airplane was burned by means of incendiary destructors, of which five or more were provided. The crew knew where the destructors were located and how to use them. Additional flame strength was to be obtained by breaking the glass fuel gauges and firing the resulting flow of gasoline. The crew was instructed not to rely on just one incendiary destructor but to use them all at various places throughout the airplane.

The principal documents and papers to be destroyed were the Gee code and information, occults and pundits, alternate Allied bases, bomber codes, signal flimsies, weather cards, and all maps and logs. If the secret and confidential papers were "rice paper," they were to be destroyed by chewing and moistening in the mouth, which could be done quickly, and then disposing of the paper.

If a forced landing was made in a neutral country, the action to be taken was the same as in an enemy-occupied country, with the exception of landing in Ireland. If the destruction was carried out on an airfield in a neutral country, the crew was to try to accomplish it at an outlying point along the boundary of the field. This would avoid the unnecessary destruction of private property, and they would probably receive better treatment in the hands of the local authorities.

The procedure for a landing made in Southern Ireland was quite different. If the landing was made in open fields, and the airplane was severely damaged, then it and all its contents were to be completely destroyed. However, if a safe landing was made on an airfield, it was not necessary to destroy any part of the airplane or its contents. Under these conditions all members of the crew were to maintain that they were on a nonoperational mission regardless of the load on the airplane or in the guns. As with a landing in enemy territory, they were to give only name, rank, and serial number to the local authorities. In neutral territory they were to further insist on seeing the American military attaché. One officer was to guard the airplane at all times. They were to be kind, considerate, and above all courteous, and in a few hours should be flying back to the United Kingdom with their airplane.

Robert L. Stroud, a major and commanding officer of "Area H," the base packing station and agent-holding area for OSS, recalls:

> One officer and two enlisted men were detailed to the Carpet-baggers from "Area H" from January 1944 until the end of the war. Certain RAF units as well as the Eighth Air Force units were involved in flying these covert missions.
>
> The major RAF unit was located at Tempsford, 51 miles due north of London. The only packing facility until the completion of "Area H" on February 2, 1944, was located at the British SOE sta-

tion "61," which trained our American personnel in packing techniques.

All initial and resupply requirements coming from the resistance underground units of the occupied countries were received by SOE headquarters at 62 Baker Street in London. Here it was determined which were acceptable and which aircraft (RAF or 8th AF) would execute the mission, and orders were sent by motorcycle courier to Harrington and Tempsford for implementation.[2]

A mission began when a request was received from the field for agents or supplies. The request also might be made by a Country Section at SOE headquarters at 62 Baker Street. There was a Country Section for each of the countries in which resistance operations were being carried out. Priorities of the missions were determined by the chief of Special Operations, OSS, and the chief of SOE.

Locations of drop pinpoints were determined and sent to Eighth Air Force headquarters, where factors such as terrain and enemy defenses were considered. If approved, the Air Operations Section was notified, a number was assigned to the mission, and the Country Section was notified of the approval and the mission number. The British air minister was also informed. When all was ready at Harrington an operational order was made up and the resistance group in the field was told when the reception committee should be ready to receive the drop and what code phrase would be used in a BBC news broadcast. These phrases were called "crack signals."

Day-to-day priority of missions was determined by the CO of the Carpetbaggers and sent to 62 Baker Street each morning; that office in turn advised the Country Section of the missions coming up that night. The Country Section arranged with the BBC for the correct crack signal to be included in their news broadcast. Listeners of BBC newscasts to occupied Europe were often startled to hear announcers say such nonsense as "Tell Marie to wear her galoshes," or "Uncle Jean has two shillings in his pocket." When the reception committee heard the correct signal they arranged to be at the site of the drop at the proper time, prepared to receive the materials, supplies, and sometimes agents.

The duties of the armament-ordnance sections at Harrington were not much different from the duties of those sections in any heavy bombardment group. However, the load was quite different. Containers, which were the ordnance section's responsibility, were fitted with parachutes and loaded with approximately 200 pounds of arms, ammunition, grenades, explosives, and so on. Armament was responsible for the loading of the packages, which contained approximately 100 pounds of clothing, food rations, spare rifle barrels, magazines, field dressings, and other nonbreakable supplies. The loading of the proper leaflets and the handling and loading of the agents was also the armament section's responsibility.

A night's operations might require from thirty-five to forty-five airplanes and combat crews. Each mission called for its own load, and the loads were carefully checked to make absolutely sure that the right load reached the right place. Each airplane had to have the proper straps and lines to which the containers were attached. The containers were loaded on the airplanes by the ordnance crews throughout the afternoon, while the armament crews worked hard at loading the packages, sometimes late into the night. The word "scrub" could cancel all the work of the loading.

The male agents were called "Joes," and the female agents were called "Josephines" or "Janes." Nickels (leaflets and pamphlets) were also dropped, but their propaganda value was secondary on most supply missions; they were dropped far from the drop area to give the enemy the false impression that dropping leaflets was the prime purpose of the mission. The "farm" was the storage point for the loads to be made up, and all packages, leaflets, and parachutes were carefully checked before they were taken out to the airplanes.

The dispatcher, formerly called a waist-gunner, had been carefully trained in the procedure for dropping agents and supplies. On the afternoon of the mission he was briefed by the group armament officer. All packages and containers were to be dropped in the designated areas or brought back.

The agents arrived three to four hours before takeoff. With escorting officers and members of the armament section, they went to the dressing huts where the job of getting them ready to land in occupied territory under the nose of the enemy began. A loose-fitting camouflage suit resembling the costume of a circus clown was fitted on the Joe; there were pockets for guns and knives, a compass, money, and other articles, and a spongy rubber cushion was placed in the seat of the suit to cushion his fall. He was fitted with a rubber helmet, goggles, rubber-soled boots, and a parachute. Before takeoff he was briefed again and supplied with pills — some of them lethal, some for airsickness, some for sleep, and some to combat sleepiness. Some of the Joes took the flight as a lark, while others sat quietly, smoking and saying little.

The combat crews usually were not told in detail what they were going to drop. At briefing they were told only where the target was and what signals to use. If agents were to be dropped they might be loaded aboard the airplane after the "go" signal from the tower. Sometimes the airplane would taxi out to the end of the runway and at the last minute be given a red light by the tower. A car would then pull up to the waiting aircraft, and agents dressed in jump gear would climb aboard. Then, given a green light, the airplane would roar off into the night.

The crew was instructed not to talk to the agents for the agents' protection as well as the crew's. Packers working in the packing stations had no idea where the containers and packages were to be dropped. Their job was to place the arms and supplies into the proper packages and containers, nothing more. The packages and containers were loaded on the airplane by a separate loading crew who had no idea what was in them. The reception committee receiving the loads had no idea about the airplane's home base. They only knew that it belonged to the Allies and was helping their cause.

Most supply- and agent-dropping missions were flown during the moon period, making the ground more visible to the navigator and bombardier. Operations were also carried out in the dark, with the use of special equipment — Rebecca, S-phone, and radio altimeter. The reception comittees had to have the ground counterparts of S-phone and Rebecca and be able to use them expertly, conditions which were difficult to achieve in areas occupied by the enemy. Dark-period missions were also possible without S-phone or Rebecca if the reception committee used signals consisting of colored lights or bonfires, and if there were prominent landmarks that could be distinguished in the dark, such as large rivers and lakes.

Reception parties on the ground during dark periods used prearranged signals to guide the Carpetbagger airplanes to the target pinpoints. There were four types of reception signals, known as A, B, C, and S. The A system consisted of a triangle of three white lights, with a red light at the apex flashing the code-recognition letter. The lights were placed so that the wind was blowing toward the flashing light and across the center of the opposite side of the triangle. The B system was the same as A, except that a white light flashed and three red lights formed the triangle.

The C system was the most commonly used. It employed three torches, usually red, in a row, with a white signal-flashing light set up at the down-wind end of the line. Airplanes always came in up-wind for their drop. Bonfires were sometimes used instead of torches. Normally, the signal lights were turned on when the airplane was first heard, but sometimes when there was danger of enemy discovery the airplane was asked to give an identification signal before the lights were turned on.

In May 1944 Colonel Heflin outlined a new S system of lighting to be used in the field on some of the missions to be flown in the following weeks. With this system, two men were to stand fifty meters apart. The head man would always be down-wind, and he would hold in one hand a white torch to signal the recognition letter (which would always be the initial letter of the pseudo for that field) and, in his other hand, a fixed green light. The second man would hold in each outstretched hand a fixed green light.

The containers and packages were dropped in train over a target at a true altitude of 400 feet above the ground, at an indicated airspeed of 135 miles per hour or less, using one-half flaps. This was barely above stalling speed, but it reduced container dispersion and damage to parachutes as the shock of opening was much less at slower speed. The Joes were dropped at 600 feet above the ground, at 125 miles per hour, with one-half flaps. Blind drops of Joes and equipment were allowed only when the crew had been briefed for them by the intelligence officer in charge of the briefing. Completion of the drop depended entirely upon perfect coordination at the target between the crew and the reception committee. The tail-gunner watched the chutes open, and at interrogation he reported on the success of the drop. Until the airplane and crew returned to Harrington, and the crew was interrogated, it was not known whether the mission was complete or non-complete.

# 4 Early Missions Recounted

The 406th Squadron lost a crew on the night of April 4, 1944, when the airplane of Lt. William W. Nicoll went down on its first operational mission. At first no information was received about the fate of the crew. Four months later, two members of the crew returned to England and gave an accounting of the time they had spent trying to get home.[1]

Their target was a routine one, below the Loire River in France, but from the beginning the mission seemed to be jinxed. Takeoff was finally made somewhat later than originally planned, as Nos. 1 and 4 engines required last-minute adjustments. At 2200 hours they departed from Harrington on their first mission. At 1,200 feet altitude the Liberator's automatic pilot was turned on. Everything appeared normal as the airplane crossed the French coast at 2300 hours at 190 miles per hour indicated airspeed. There was no sign of enemy night fighters.

Suddenly, at 2320 hours, the bombardier yelled over the interphone, "Hard right!" But it was too late; the airplane was trapped in a deadly concentration of enemy flak and was doomed. No evasive action was possible, as the first burst of flak had shot off the B-24's tail, instantly killing the tail-gunner. Then the nose was hit and the bom-

bardier's voice came over the interphone again: "Get out! Get out!" Nothing was heard from the navigator.

When the fuselage became enveloped in flames at 800 feet the pilot gave the bail-out alarm. S.Sgt. Joseph Porter heard the alarm and jumped. As he descended the Germans opened up on him with machine-gun fire, but he was not hit. Lt. A. W. Kalbfleisch's hair and eyebrows were singed, and his jacket collar was burned off. Before jumping he saw the engineer having trouble finding his parachute. The pilot was buckling on his chute preparing to jump, but there was no sign of the radio operator or the navigator. Kalbfleisch ducked under the catwalk and stepped out through the narrow opening of the bomb bay door. He immediately pulled his parachute's rip-cord, thinking to himself that if he was lucky the chute would not catch on the falling airplane. Almost at once he hit the ground, and a moment later the burning B-24 crashed a short distance away.

Kalbfleisch heard German shouting and sporadic gunfire, but he was unable to run, as he had injured his ankle. He got his chute harness off and limped to a nearby creek, where he removed his Mae West and threw it into the creek. In the light of the explosion he saw that the B-24 had crashed in front of a German radio-communication station, which was well protected by antiaircraft installations. Just then, four American B-24 Liberator bombers roared low over the burning airplane on the ground, banking away, with one of them taking a flak hit in one engine.

The lieutenant set out across open country, slowly because of his injury, and walked until five in the morning. He lay down for an hour, but he was becoming colder and his swollen ankle was bothering him. Getting up, he discovered that he could not put any weight on his ankle, so he began crawling, determined to get help. As he approached a group of houses, a dog began barking at him. He stopped to make friends with the dog and was taken into one of the houses by a French man, whose wife fed him and put him to bed.

The next morning another Frenchman appeared, who told Kalbfleisch that a truck driver would drive him to the Pyrenees, where he could cross into Spain. He was given civilian clothes and a blue-patterned scarf and was told that in the course of his journey through France he must speak to no one who did not wear a scarf of the same pattern.

A sympathetic doctor treated his ankle, and the American was then taken to a nearby rendezvous, where he met Porter. Later the two men realized that it was very fortunate that they had found each other. Alone, they would have become discouraged and easy prey for the Gestapo. They spent the night buried in a haystack, lying low the following day. That night the doctor drove them for some distance to another town, where they were taken into a large house owned by a wealthy French woman whose husband was a member of the secret French intelligence service. Her job was to transmit information on German activities to London. She told them that she had on three separate occasions reported to London the position of the flak installations that had brought down their B-24, but nothing had been done about it.

Kalbfleisch and Porter stayed in this house for more than a month. Passports and identification papers were obtained, establishing them as workers on authorized leave from the Renault factory in Paris. During this time they learned of the fate of their fellow crew members. Five had been killed instantly. The Nazis would not permit a decent burial, but the French secretly carried out a burial service. A Catholic priest said a blessing over the common grave, risking his life to do so. The eighth man in the crew had bailed out and become entangled in the branches of a tree. The Nazis found him, and although he was suffering terribly from a crushed chest they did nothing to help him. For two days he lay on the ground; the only attention he received was when an officer questioned him. In spite of his suffering, the unnamed hero would not give his tormentors any information. On the third morning, when the young American persisted in his silence, the Nazi drew out his Luger pistol and shot him through the head. This incident took place at Chateau de la Rochelle on April 8, 1944.

The Germans plastered the countryside with posters and newspaper advertisements offering a 24,000-franc reward for information leading to the capture of the two men remaining, Kalbfleisch and Porter. But the French people, in their four years of experience, had come to understand the worthlessness of German promises, and no one ever came forward to claim the reward.

Several plans were considered for their escape, but all had to be abandoned. At first it was planned to contact a British torpedo boat which made regular runs to the French coast, but this became impossible when the boat stopped making the runs. The move to the Pyrenees appeared unwise because the Germans were in great strength over the route. The two Americans vetoed a plan to move them to Switzerland, as they did not want to be interned for the rest of the war. Finally, a French officer who came to the house from Geneva was given the responsibility for making arangements to get them away.

The officer told them that if they would learn French he would take them to the Pyrenees, so they set out studying, memorizing, and pronouncing the language. After weeks went by, however, they decided that the French officer simply wanted to keep them occupied. They spent a great deal of time digging a large hole in which they buried 400 quarts of champagne which their hostess wanted hidden from the Germans. A P-51 Mustang pilot joined them during this time. D-Day came and went.

At last two Frenchmen arrived from the Normandy front to guide them to the Allied lines. The three American fliers and the two French guides set out but were soon stopped by a German soldier who asked to see their papers. He expressed concern because the photo of one of the guides showed him wearing a mustache when in fact he had none. The guide was able to make a satisfactory explanation, and the soldier passed them through. They were checked out once more, when one German soldier, looking the P-51 pilot over, laughed, pointed, and said, "Schmeling!" For the first time they noticed that the Mustang pilot did bear a slight resemblance to the German boxer who had been so badly beaten by America's Joe Louis.

Their destination was Caen, near the Normandy coast. They finally entered the town, after undergoing a shelling from Allied guns and spending a lot of time in roadside ditches. The house that they were directed to was already overcrowded with refugees, so they made their way to an alternate house. Their stay in Caen was marked by discomfort, hunger, and downright fear, as the sky was constantly filled with Allied airplanes. A thousand-pound bomb came to rest, unexploded, in the ceiling of one of the sanctuary houses. Another American flier joined them, a B-17 pilot. In their group there were now five British airmen and four Americans.

Three months had passed since Lieutenant Kalbfleisch and Sergeant Porter had jumped from their burning airplane. Disagreements began to arise among the men. The Fortress pilot was beginning to show the effects of his twenty-five missions over the flak defenses of Germany and France, becoming jumpy and unpredictable. One day two German SS troopers came over the backyard wall with Lugers in their hands. When the British spotted them and yelled a warning, the Fortress pilot bolted for the water closet and locked himself in. The others were asleep in their room. The Jerries entered the house, stole whatever looked edible or salable, and looked over the house, pushing open the door where the three Americans lay sleeping. After a very brief stay, they abruptly left.

The group moved to another house. Soon thereafter an aerial bombardment began, and British troops moved up, stopping on the western bank of the river west of town, where they set up machine-gun emplacements. The Germans had guns on the eastern bank, so a constant staccato of machine-gun fire began back and forth across the river. Then British tanks started shelling the German machine-gun nests. The airmen began sleeping in a bomb crater across the street from the house, as the shelling was continuous and Allied airplanes kept up regular raids. When the barrage lifted they decided to leave the town.

Setting out, they were caught in another barrage of gunfire and decided that they had best return to Caen. The Fortress pilot became so weak that he had difficulty walking, and the others took turns helping him along. Eventually, two Frenchmen took them to another town, where they were given food, a course to follow, and arms. They soon came to a wide ditch, which they had to cross on a narrow plank. The Fortress pilot fell from the plank but was rescued by the others. At last, after crossing a checkerboard of land mines, they were suddenly told, "You can sing Yankee Doodle now." They soon found the first American patrol, a group of rough-and-ready Yanks engaged in frying eggs over a fire, their equipment-loaded jeeps parked nearby. The airmen were taken to field headquarters, where they gave the interrogating officer a great deal of information on German positions and strength. An hour later they saw a column of tanks and half-tracks moving out in the direction from which they had just come. Their thoughts were with the many heroic French people who had risked their lives to help them, and they hoped that these tanks and half-tracks would perhaps repay some of the debt owed those people.

It had taken four months for Lieutenant Kalbfleisch and Sergeant Porter to return from their first Carpetbagger mission.[2]

Lt. George W. Ambrose and his crew departed from Harrington in B-24 No. 42–40997 on their fifth mission to "Lackey 3A" in France on the night of April 27. Nothing was heard from them until May 4, when the OSS at Baker Street received a message from the field, along with a part of the airplane with the aircraft number. French witnesses on the scene said the aircraft had arrived over the target and made three descending circles. It struck the ground on the third circle, crashed and burned, killing all crew members except Sgt. George W. Henderson, S.Sgt. James J. Heddleson, and Sgt. James C. Mooney.[3]

Heddleson and Henderson made their escape to southern France and were later returned to England by British "Dakota" operations. Mooney, badly injured, was helped from the crash area by a French woman, then was taken prisoner by the Germans. Jimmy Heddleson remembers:

As I recall we were one of the first crews to fly at night without the benefit of the full moon, on the night of April 27, 1944. It was around 1:00 in the morning when we reached our target area. We made the first pass for identification and circled around for position to make our drop (second pass). The wing flaps start to come down and the bomb bay doors are starting to open. Suddenly they start back up; we don't drop and it is like we were practicing and we climb back up. As we start to circle around again, I can still see the lights on the ground in the distance on our drop area. When we start in for the third pass Sgt. James Mooney is over the "Joe hole." He volunteered for this mission (his first). We only met him shortly before takeoff, as a regular crew member, Sgt. W. Bollinger, reported off sick. I am over the smaller hole behind Sgt. Henderson who is in the tail-gunner's position, getting ready to throw some packages out. Once again the flaps start down and the bomb doors open and we are starting our approach. I can look out and see the hills, or mountains, on our left side. Suddenly, the plane shakes violently, apparently we hit or clipped something. First, I hit my forehead, partly falling out, and then I was thrown backwards toward the "Joe hole" area, with the back of my head slamming into something in the plane. Sgt. Mooney is gone; he apparently fell out of the "Joe hole." I found out later that he held onto the chutes. Luckily he wasn't killed, although the poor man must have suffered terribly. His back was broken; this I was told later. Sgt. Henderson was immediately out of the tail section. The engines were racing and the plane was climbing, seemingly straight up. He yells for us to get out. He helps me up and out, and follows very close through the window. We no sooner cleared the plane when it starts down again, only this time it is too late, because it is burning when it crashes.

I was told later that the canisters were scattered everywhere, and the French worked very hard throughout the night trying to retrieve them. Sgt. Henderson and I were apparently fairly close to each other and each of us made our way back to the plane; we found each other. The plane seemed to be . . . a real holocaust with the ammunition exploding and whatever was in the canisters also going off. We knew no one could survive this. As for Sgt. Mooney, we tried to find him, hoping he was all right. But it was night and in the mountain area and after a while we gave up. We were not only hurting physically, but also emotionally, myself being only 20 years old at the time.

We could hear noises like cars or truck engines, or so we thought. My left leg was hurt and was getting worse as it was swelling around the knee. We had no idea where we were, but the first thing we thought of was, could it be the Germans? Our plane could be seen like a beacon for miles and the noise it made in the still of the night with everything exploding certainly would attract a lot of attention. We started down the hills toward the valley, not knowing anything about the territory. We just decided to slip away in the night the best way we could. We assumed everyone was killed except Sgt. Mooney. His condition was such, I found out later, that the man whose house he was taken to had no choice but to turn him over to the Germans. He told me personally how sorry he was for having to do this. He said he felt guilty, but I tried to assure him that in Sgt. Mooney's case he probably saved his life, as I heard the Germans took him to a hospital. There was nothing this man could do, the French assured me.

It was the next day that they (the French) realized that two more Americans survived. They found the chutes, first one, then another, which they immediately buried. We moved only at night and we traveled quite a way for the shape we were in. The French started to look for us, they said, in every direction possible. We skirted villages and main roads, avoiding everyone we saw, especially the Germans. Having no idea where we were, we headed south. After several days of hiding and only moving at night, we ended up in a cemetery. When daylight came, we decided we better hole-up for the day, when we saw an old man walking toward us. We really scared him when we approached him for food or help or anything. I showed him my "wings" and he motioned for us to follow him at a distance. Eventually we ended up in a garage of a schoolhouse. We were given some bread, cheese, and wine, and after dark a group of men came in a car; it was M. Benoit, the schoolteacher. They were all armed with pistols and rifles. After a few questions and some very vague answers, they decided we were the two Americans that everybody was looking for. I also knew then that at last we had made contact with the French Underground.

We were then taken to a farm (in the car) and hidden in the barn. This place was owned by a Mme De Havrincourt. We stayed there a couple of weeks, hiding sometimes in the nearby woods and barn and house. She had a doctor come and he fixed up my forehead; he opened up the gashes and stitched them, I mean the hard way, with a needle and thread. I can still remember that.

We were spotted by the wrong person at this farm, and she told the Germans she thought she had seen "some English flyers." When the Germans came through the gate, we escaped out the back of the barn to the woods. We could see them looking everywhere, but to no avail. Mme De Havrincourt convinced them the woman was demented and they finally left. Needless to say the Maquis decided it was time for us to move on. We were taken to the Jean Crozet farm near St. Germain Laval. The main structure was walled in and a person could feel slightly safer. While here, we participated in two different nightly parachute drops. This was not only dangerous but a lot of work. The parachutes were everywhere. We loaded them into trucks and even oxen-drawn wagons. We stored them in various barns before daylight. I can still remember looking up and seeing those B-24s flying very low and turn and head back to England, Harrington, I assumed. It gave you an empty feeling in your stomach.

I spelled my name with a flashlight in Morse Code several times but I never knew if they received it. From the Crozet farm we went to the village of St. Germain Laval to stay. We first stayed at the home of René Simone for a few days, never venturing out of doors. From here we went to the home of Jean Boyer. He was an officer in the Maquis. We stayed with the Boyers the longest, about eight weeks.

It was through Jean Boyer that we participated in several raids with the Maquis. I can recall one raid in particular that involved Jean Boyer, Henderson, Joseph Tournaire, and myself. We rode (at night) on a bicycle, quite a distance from St. Germain Laval to a railroad trestle that we were going to blow up . . . . Boyer and myself went to the center of the trestle and we climbed down over the side carrying our explosives. We had a timing device for it, and we thought we had plenty of time to make our escape and would be well on our way back to St. Germain Laval before any action took place. Departing, I could look back over my shoulder and see the trestle behind us, when all hell broke loose. Obviously, our timer was wrong. (I believe these were from a parachute drop.) In the still of the night the explosion was felt from where we were.

We made our departure immediately away from there. Several times we would hide along the road as the Germans would pass us on their way to the trestle, or what was left of it, not seeing us. We made it back to the Boyers' house just as the sun was coming up. Needless to say, we were very shaken and tired.

The Boyers' house was located almost in the center of St. Germain Laval and had a small walled-in area about 25 feet by 20 feet. It was here we would spend our time cleaning and assembling British machine guns that were parachuted to the Maquis at night. Many a time we would go to the basement of the schoolhouse where the walls were about 4 feet to 5 feet thick and test-fire these weapons, always on the lookout for the enemy, because of the noise.

On the 19th of June, it was my 21st birthday and the Boyer family told Henderson and myself to get ready, on a minute's notice, to leave. We accepted our fate and after dark they led us through the back streets, often hiding in the shadows as people would approach . . . . We approached a familiar apartment; I began to get curious as, you see, it was the house of René Simone. When we went inside it was full of people and they actually had a surprise birthday party for me, with a few gifts too. The people had been planning and saving things for this occasion, such as sugar, butter, and meat. They had baked a cake and we had drinks. I had the most memorable birthday of my life. I shall never forget it. You would never believe it could happen under those perilous times.

When we left St. Germain Laval, I thought we were going to hide out somewhere else, but they took away our uniforms for civilian clothes and I was given a passport (fake of course) stating I was deaf and dumb. Henderson and myself knew what the results would be if we were caught; it would probably mean death, but we didn't seem to have much choice. Two men came in a car and, after a tearful goodbye, we left . . . . We stayed in the towns of Montbrison, Villefranche-sur-Saône, France, and many more. We would casually stroll down the street, looking very French in our berets. We were working our way to a secret landing field, near the village of Lanquait. We saw many Germans, but luckily we were never stopped. The French took good care of us. Only on one occasion we had a very close call: we were eating at an outside restaurant along the Rhone River when word came that the Germans were stopping everyone for their papers. We climbed over a wall and dropped down to the river bank. Just as we cleared the wall I spotted the Germans. We made it . . . .

We met several more French people who were also escaping back to England. The plane was supposed to come in July but didn't arrive until the last week of August. We were taken to a field before dark and hid in the nearby woods. As we heard the plane approaching, the Maquis lit several fires for the plane to land. When it came in and landed, we were waiting to climb aboard. It only took several minutes to take off. We were overloaded, but we made it. The next stop — London, England.[4]

5      Into the Darkness:
The 858th (Night Leaflet)
and the 788th and 850th Squadrons

The night leaflet operation, like the Carpetbagger special operation, was a radical departure from the usual duty of a heavy bombardment group, and the work was largely unknown by the other heavy bombardment groups. Nearly all personnel working in the night leaflet operation were taken from other Eighth Air Force Heavy bombardment groups flying daylight bombing missions over Germany. In contrast to the Carpetbaggers, their missions were flown at high altitude, from 18,000 to 24,000 feet.

In September 1943 the 422d Bombardment Squadron (H), which was until that time a regular daylight bombardment squadron of the 305th Bombardment Group (H), had gone to night operations from Chelveston, Northamptonshire. They first conducted experimental night bombing missions, then began leaflet dropping operations over enemy territory during the winter of 1943, using B-17Fs and B-17Gs.

Initially, leaflet bundles were thrown out by hand; later they were dropped in cardboard boxes from the bomb bay. Then, Capt. James L. Monroe, the 422d Squadron armament officer, invented a leaflet bomb. It was a laminated paper cylinder about the size of a medium bomb (five by one and a half feet) holding 80,000 leaflets and containing a barometric fuse set to bust at 1,000–2,000 feet altitude.

An airplane carried twelve of these bombs, and from that altitude the leaflets were scattered with great accuracy over a city.

In June 1944 the personnel and airplanes of the 422d Bombardment Squadron (Night Leaflet) were absorbed by the 858th Squadron designation, which had transferred from the 492d Bombardment Group (H) based at North Pickenham, Norfolk. The night leaflet squadron moved to Cheddington, Hertfordshire, and was established there under their new identity, 858th Bombardment Squadron (Night Leaflet).

Formerly equipped only with B-17s, in July 1944 the unit began using some B-24Hs and B-24Js. Then, late in the war, some B-24Ms were brought in. The B-17s and B-24s used in night leaflet operations were equipped with flame suppressors on the engine exhausts and flame responders on the gun barrels. The planes were painted with a glossy black antisearchlight synthetic enamel paint. The top turret, nose turret, both waist guns, and the ball turret were manned on the B-17s, and there is some indication that all gunners stations were also manned on the B-24s for this operation.

Night flying was a new experience for some of the combat crews first coming into the operation. Pilots learned to depend entirely upon the engine instruments to indicate engine problems. A close watch was kept on the instruments, as the first indication of engine failure was in oil pressure and temperature. Props could not be feathered if oil pressure dropped below forty pounds per square inch, and quick action was necessary to feather a prop. Whenever a supercharger became inoperative, the mission was aborted.

Pilots found the British "Boozer" warning system of great help when over enemy and Allied territory on the Continent where enemy night fighters and the Würzburg chain of flak and ground control stations were located. There were four cockpit indicator lights: a dim red light indicated enemy radar tracking, a bright red light indicated flak, a yellow light indicated that enemy night fighters were in the vicinity, and a blue light indicated that the airplane was caught in a cone of searchlights.

Aerial gunners beginning night combat were taught where to search for enemy night fighters from each gun position. The tail-gunner was to search from eight to four o'clock, concentrating on the high area, but not below fifteen degrees. The ball-turret-gunner covered the area below fifteen degrees, keeping his turret depressed so as not to be able to see any part of the underside of the airplane while searching low. He did not alter this angle and searched only from four o'clock to eight o'clock. It was up to the waist-gunners to search at nine o'clock and three o'clock low. The left waist-gunner searched all areas as high and as low as his position would permit between eight and ten thirty o'clock. The right waist-gunner covered all areas as high and as low as his position permitted and between four and two-thirty o'clock. The chin-turret-gunner, or nose-gunner, covered all areas between ten-thirty and two-thirty o'clock on the bow of the airplane, concentrating and varying his search between high and low areas. The chances of a head-on attack by enemy night fighters was practically nil. The top-turret-gunner covered high through 360 degrees, with particular attention to high above tail between three and nine o'clock. The gunners were to avoid searching in another gunner's area of search; in searching another man's area for only a few minutes they could easily miss the approach of attacking fighters in their own areas.

Combat crews learned that sometimes enemy night fighters dropped flares from above their airplane hoping to put it in silhouette when it passed over the plane. The flare itself was invisible, and all that could be seen was a huge area of orange light which seemed to hang motionless below the airplane.

When attacked by fighters, all gunners were to be ready to fire instantly and call correct evasive action to the pilot at the same time. If there was not time to do both at once, they were to fire first and then give evasive action directions. For dead-astern attacks between five-thirty and six-thirty o'clock, a right- or left-hand corkscrew was to be used, depending on the angle of attack. Gunners were cautioned not to waste words or time — to fire and call out, "Left-hand corkscrew" or "Right-hand corkscrew."

Some enemy twin-engine fighters used a red, green, or white light to signal another fighter to join them in the attack. If the light was sighted at nine o'clock, the gunner was to check at three o'clock for another fighter, but he must not be distracted from the proper area of search for his station. Once the fighter began the attack, the gunner who first called out his position would lose sight of him after the pilot began evasive action; he was to be certain that another gunner immediately called out the correct position. If the airplane was coned by several searchlights, pilots learned not to dive straight down in evasive action but to use full speed ahead in a gradual dive. If caught in one or two lights, they learned to sideslip, dive, or stall, depending on what seemed correct at the time.

The night leaflet squadron dropped leaflets on Norway, Denmark, Holland, Belgium, Italy, France, Germany, Poland, Greece, Yugoslavia, and other parts of the Balkans. The unit also dropped leaflets on German troops telling them why Germany could not win the war and why they should surrender. Anthony Eden, the British foreign secretary, told the House of Commons that seventy-seven percent of all German troops taken prisoner in France had one of the leaflets, or said that they had read them. The most common leaflet distributed offered German troops safe passage through the lines.

No false information was used in the leaflets, which were trusted inside Germany and in enemy-occupied territory. Dropped nightly, they included the very latest news, brought up to the hour on field printing presses operated by the Psychological Warfare Branch. Because the leaflets were successful and so widely read, the Germans began printing their own propaganda in the Allied format, pretending that their leaflets came from Allied sources. In some areas under German control, the death sentence automatically followed disclosure that a man or woman had one of the genuine leaflets in his or her possession. Nevertheless, they were read and carried for months in shoes, hats, false pockets, and other hiding places.

The night leaflet aircraft flew by instruments and seldom was grounded by weather. The combat crews were thoroughly sold on their work, having listened to eyewitness accounts by persons escaping from occupied countries who reported to them the power of the printed word under a regime whose mortal enemy was free speech.

Most crews flying Carpetbagger operations were experienced combat crews. The original crews were experienced in antisubmarine operations, and, later, new crews were transferred from Eighth Air Force groups flying daylight heavy bombardment missions. After a short period of on-the-job training, these crews quickly became old hands at the nighttime, low-level operations.

During May 1944 the personnel of two more Eighth Air Force squadrons were attached to the 801st Bombardment Group (Prov.) at Harrington, the 788th from the 467th Bombardment Group (H) based at Rackheath, Norfolk, and the 850th from the 490th Bombardment Group (H) at Eye, Suffolk.

A few days earlier, during the first part of May, General Peck, commanding general of the 96th Combat Bombardment Wing, invited Colonel Shower, CO of the 467th Bomb Group, Colonel Isbell,

CO of the 458th Bomb Group, and Colonel Pierce, CO of the 466th Bomb Group, to wing headquarters at Horsham St. Faith, Norfolk. There they were told that one of them was to give up a B-24 squadron to be transferred to the 801st Bomb Group at Harrington. They each got out a half-crown to toss: the loser was to give up a squadron from his group. Colonel Shower lost, and he chose to offer the 788th Squadron, formerly commanded by Maj. Robert L. Salzarulo, who had gone down a few days earlier on a mission to Berlin.

The 788th Bombardment Squadron (H) had been constituted on May 19, 1943, and activated on August 1. They were attached to the 467th Bombardment Group (H) based at Wendover Field, Utah. In September the group moved to Mountain Home Army Air Field, Idaho; in October they moved to Kearns, Utah; and in November they returned to Wendover Field. The group was assigned to the Eighth Air Force, Second Bombardment Division, and based at Rackheath, arriving there on March 11, 1944. On May 10 the squadron, commanded by Maj. Leonard M. McManus, was detached. Fifty-eight officers and 357 enlisted men were sent to AAF Station 113 (Cheddington, Hertfordshire), to join the Eighth Air Force Composite Command, headquartered there.

The intelligence section, headed by Capt. C. Malcolm Derry and Lt. James P. Stewart, with four enlisted men, left on May 17 for Station 179 (Harrington) to prepare for operations and the arrival of the combat crews. Lt. Carl L. Black, squadron armament officer, with twenty-five enlisted men, came along a few days later, for the squadron was to live in "tent city" once more. The entire squadron flew from Cheddington on May 27 to Harrington airfield, now attached to the 801st Bombardment Group (Prov.).

On June 13 Lieutenant Stewart, assistant intelligence officer of the 788th Squadron, flew his first mission with Lt. James F. Moser and crew of the 36th Squadron. Stewart reported as follows:

> It was a novel experience in that the work differs totally from that in which we were formerly engaged. We took off as night was falling over England and flew across country in the darkness. Visibility was rather poor at this time of the month. Occasional lights could be seen, but not much was discernible until we reached the coast. We approached the enemy coast where there seemed to be much activity. We noted flares and searchlights and other airplanes. At one time we could see another airplane caught in a cone of four lights. The flak was intense as the German gunners raked the sky for

Allied ships. Two planes, believed to be Allied, were seen to go down. Off toward the horizon we could note the flash of ground guns and what seemed to be the explosions of aerial bombing. The countryside abounded with lights. We hit our checkpoints and estimated times on the nose and waited a bit tensely for first signs of reception and calls from the target. We were "sitting on the spot" but there were no signs of reception or activity. We hovered over our target for more than 20 minutes, our margin of safety, then gunned her for home, the entire crew a bit disappointed. Activity on the part of the enemy continued, although not directed at us, and with a feeling of relief we crossed the enemy coast.

The journey home was in almost total darkness and the pilot was pushing the airplane, but the minutes seemed like years and it was cold even at low altitude. Crossing over English countryside appeared to take ages, but with early false dawn rimming the horizon and the lights of our base in sight in the distance, the tension eased somewhat and we began to talk of fresh eggs for breakfast. The mission was the 30th for over half the crew, so jubilantly we fired our "celebration flares" and started to let down. The most satisfying part of the mission then occurred, the wheels touching the runway and a few moments later good old terra firma under your feet. That's the moment you realize the tension under which the whole crew works and what it means to be "home" safely. Well, it was a long trip to find no reception, but we did our best, and all's right with the world again after a warming shot of Scotch and the appetizing smell of a plateful of fresh eggs. Better luck next time — and when do we go again? [1]

Constituted on September 14, 1943, activated on October 1, 1943, and attached to the 490th Bombardment Group (H), the 850th Bombardment Squadron (H) was based at Salt Lake City Army Air Base, Utah. The group was stationed at Mountain Home Field, Idaho, from December 4 until April 9, 1944, and then assigned to the Eighth Air Force, Third Bombardment Division, arriving at Eye, Suffolk, on April 27.

Detached from the 490th Bomb Group, the 850th Squadron, commanded by Maj. Jack M. Dickerson, arrived at Cheddington on May 11. The squadron had received a telephone message on the afternoon of May 10 directing all personnel to be ready for movement by 1000 hours the next morning: "Be prepared to move — destination unknown and secret." Airplanes were to be left behind; everything else was to go.

The motor convoy was met by an escort and rolled out of camp. At the village of Diss the squadron surgeon, Capt. Paul O. Messner, who had been away on a twenty-four-hour pass, flagged down a passing truck and climbed aboard. His equipment and baggage were all packed; he had been moved and was just now being told. Other officers and enlisted men were in similar circumstances. Upon returning to camp, many found that their outfit had gone. "The 850th, it seemed, did things in a helluva hurry!" reported one observer.

On the night of May 11, Major Dickerson and Capt. Willard H. Smith, squadron operations officer, were the first members of the 850th Squadron to take "buddy rides" on operational missions. The following night, Capt. William C. McKinley, Lt. Jack R. Sayers, and 2d Lt. Leon G. Dibble, Jr., completed their rides. Major Dickerson's flight was the only one that did not complete a successful mission in this period.

The 850th Squadron was officially attached to the 801st Bombardment Group (Prov.) on May 22, and on May 27 the entire unit left Cheddington by airplane and truck for Harrington airfield. The style of living at Harrington, in tents, did not particularly please the personnel of the unit.

The first operational missions flown by the 850th Squadron from Harrington were flown by the crews of Lt. John R. McNeil and Lt. William L. Bales on the night of May 31. Neither was completed successfully. It was not known whether the crews failed to find their targets, or the reception committees could not be present because of enemy activity.

# 6 Evasive Action in Enemy Territory

Twenty kilometers north of Cheney le Chatel, on May 6, 1944, at 0032 hours, the B-24 flown by Lt. Murry L. Simon and crew of the 406th Squadron was shot down by 20mm flak guns mounted on a troop train.[1] At the time, the train was blacked out and not in motion. Lieutenant Mead, the bombardier, bailed out at 700 feet, landing on his feet in a cow pasture. Almost immediately after landing safely, he heard an explosion and looked up to see the B-24 blow up and go down in flames.

With the help of a French farmer, Mead contacted the resistance forces. He was called for by a British agent named "Victor," and the two of them bicycled to a secret Maquis headquarters near Roanne, France. There Mead remained in hiding until late May. A wire had been dispatched by Victor to London requesting that Mead be permitted to remain and help the resistance forces in the area. In late May an answer arrived from London: "Regarding your 0733073 [Mead's AS number], keep him." From that time on, until the final liberation of France in September, Mead worked as an assistant to the British agents who were chiefs of resistance forces in the area.

Upon his return in September, Lieutenant Mead was informed that he had been promoted to captain and awarded the Silver Star for "the performance of his activities while a member of the French Forces of the Interior for five months in German-occupied France, and for his heroism in helping crew members bail out of the flak-damaged and doomed aircraft before the burning airplane crashed on May 6, 1944. The gallantry of Captain Mead on this occasion and the important and vital work accomplished while a member of the Maquis reflects the highest credit upon himself and the Armed Forces of the United States."

With the rudder control, interphone, and electrical systems shot out, and with gasoline fumes in the cockpit, Lieutenant Simon, the pilot, had sounded the bail-out alarm. Lieutenant Russell, the copilot, remained in the ship until all others were safely out before jumping, followed by Simon. The pilot landed in a tree with his feet suspended a few feet from the ground. With one hand he unbuckled the harness and fell out of the chute. Running through the woods, he found a ditch where he spent the night. There he was observed the next morning by several people passing by. Finally, a Frenchman brought him civilian clothes and took him to the home of a Maquis chief.

To avoid being spoken to, Simon feigned sleep many times while traveling on trains during the course of his evasion through France. The trains were crowded with people; many were German troops and Gestapo agents. He arrived back in England on June 1.

Lieutenant Reitmeier had also bailed out safely. After hiding for a couple of days, he approached three French boys, who led him to a safe shelter. Then he was moved to Marcigny, where he spent the night in the home of a French family. With a guide he traveled by bicycle to Loddes, northeast of Lapalisse, where arrangements were made for him to hide. He stayed there thirty-five days, while efforts were made to obtain a forged passport for him. Eventually, he decided to make his way without one.

He walked to the railway station at La Pacaudiere and, as instructed, took a train to Roanne. At the first stop a young girl got aboard, carrying the magazine which was the prearranged signal. She sat down beside him and slipped him a note in English instructing him to follow her. At Roanne she left the train, with Reitmeier following, and they turned into a side street where a man rode up on a bicycle, stopped beside them, and said in English, "How ya doing, Buddy?" He was a British secret agent known as "George." Reitmeier was led to a house owned by a man known as "Babo," who was the French intelligence agent in charge of that district. Here Reitmeier met Lieutenant Mead.

The two men lived in Babo's house for a week before Mead left to make his way to the Maquis.

Three weeks went by. One day Gestapo agents appeared and seized Babo. Reitmeier bolted through the back door, hurriedly walked down the street, and found the agent George, who took him to a house in another part of town. After two days spent there with a dentist, Reitmeier was driven up into the mountains to join the Maquis. There he ran into Mead again, but he could not work with the Maquis, as Mead was doing, as he was in pain with an injured back. He was able, however, to teach resistance fighters the use of the Winchester carbine. While in the mountains, Reitmeier learned that Babo had been liberated by the French Forces of the Interior (FFI) one hour before he was to be shot.

Reitmeier then left the Maquis, stayed for over a week near the village of Lae, and moved on to the village of St. Polgne. In St. Polgne he heard tragic news of the family with whom he had lived at Lae. A few days before, a band of Maquis had waylaid a platoon of German soldiers and killed several of them, then vanished. The survivors of the platoon regrouped and began marching toward the village. As they passed the house where Reitmeier had lived, they caught sight of the nineteen-year-old son, who was driving an oxcart out of the farmyard on his way to the village. Without provocation or warning, the Germans fell upon the boy, slashing him with their bayonets. When they left, the boy's father came out of the house and picked up his son's body, literally in pieces.

Reitmeier lived at St. Polgne for two weeks, and at the end of the time the town was liberated by the FFI. There was a great celebration at which Reitmeier ceremoniously raised a French flag in the square after the people were told that he was an American. There was much cheering, and he was the guest of honor at a large party, where all the French girls vied with each other to kiss him and give him bouquets of flowers. The next day he was freed: Mead and an English captain came in a Ford and took him back to Roanne. Shortly thereafter, Lyon was liberated, and the lieutenant went to an advanced headquarters of the American Twelfth Air Force, twenty miles west of Lyon. At the first opportunity he was flown by B-25 to Galo, then by C-47 to Italy. From there he was flown to Algiers, to Casablanca, then to England.

Technical Sergeant Latta and Staff Sergeant Collier had similar evasion experiences. Latta landed unhurt, hid his jump gear, and walked for an hour before he found a hiding place. The second night he approached an isolated house where he was fed and given a place to sleep. In civilian clothes he set out, walking for six days before he made contact with the Maquis. On May 26, he found Collier and seventeen other Allied airmen at a large Maquis encampment in the mountains.

Collier had experienced a lifetime of anxiety when he bailed out. His chute would not open. He kept pulling hard at the ripcord, and finally at an altitude of only a few hundred feet the chute opened. Upon landing, he hid his chute and began walking, hiding himself in a wood at daylight. He was spotted shortly by a farmer who was rounding up his cows. The farmer brought him food, wine, blankets, and whiskey, and the next morning moved him 100 yards to a better hiding place. Toward evening a group of Maquis appeared, carrying parts of Collier's wrecked airplane, which they asked him to identify. After several days, he was escorted to the Maquis camp where he met Latta.

Latta and Collier lived in the camp for about a week, until on June 10 two divisions of German soldiers began an attack on the position. As they were anxious to return to their units, all the Americans decided to leave, and at midnight they slipped out. The next morning the group split into units of three and four men, with Latta, Collier, and an American Eighth Air Force major forming one of the units. The major knew a Frenchman who directed them to the secret hideout of a Maquis group of about thirty men. Two days later, the Germans launched an attack, and the Maquis, greatly outnumbered, moved. They walked for three nights, sleeping during the days, blowing up bridges and picking off German soldiers as they moved. The Americans stayed with the group for several weeks. On August 12, dressed in Maquis uniforms, they took part in the liberation of a French village. More than once they were told that a guide would come for them, but none showed up.

The three Americans set out by train on September 6, and finally they were driven in style in a captured German staff car to the American lines. A few days later, they were safely back in England.

Lieutenant Russell had landed in a wooded area. He approached a French farmer and was taken in and offered food, but he was too excited to eat. Later, a café proprietress fed him fried eggs and arranged to get civilian clothes for him. After being moved from here to there, by foot, by bicycle, and by train, he was the first American airman to be returned from the interior of France after D-Day. On July 6 he returned to England by the "Dakota" operation.

Information Russell brought with him was considered of vital importance by SHAEF intelligence. He also brought word of two other members of the crew, who were taken as prisoners. Sergeant Hasty had badly injured his foot on landing, so that he was easily captured. Sergeant Dumesnil, who spoke French fluently, probably made the mistake of asking for civilian clothes in French when he approached a farmhouse. This was a mistake because Germans sometimes sent men around posing as Allied fliers in order to snare sympathetic Frenchmen. These Nazi agents spoke excellent French, and the French people were therefore suspicious of anyone claiming to be an Allied flier who spoke French. Someone called in the gendarmes, who arrested him. .

Russell was in France for a total of nine weeks and traveled 300–400 miles, about half of it on foot. He estimates that approximately 400 French people were involved in his escape. All of them placed their lives in jeopardy by helping him.

On the night of May 6, Lt. George Pipkin and full crew of the 406th Squadron went down while on a mission to Denmark.[2] After the target was found, and the load dropped, their B-24 was hit by antiaircraft fire from a single gun, probably equipped with radar, as every one of the five bursts hit the airplane. They were at 5,000 feet when No. 3 engine caught fire, spreading flames to a gas tank. At this time none of the crew were injured. Lieutenant Pipkin began violent maneuvering without success. When No. 4 engine caught fire he sounded the bail-out alarm. It is believed that all members of the crew managed to jump safely.

Lieutenant Holmes moved to the bomb bay, where he found that the hydraulic system was out and the doors had to be kicked open. He landed in a sandy area, hid his chute, and set out in a southerly direction. After walking about half an hour, he came upon Sergeant Wengert. The two of them moved on, wading through swamps and swimming canals to avoid leaving scent to be picked up by bloodhounds, which they could hear baying in the distance.

Hiding by day and walking by night, guided by their compass and the North Star, they were given food by friendly families along the way. Finally, contact was made with the underground through "Preston," which is the Danish word for minister. He arranged for civilian clothes and identity papers, then had them driven north for two days. They were smuggled into a boat going to Sweden, where they claimed to be escaped POWs and were soon returned to England. Nothing was learned of the fate of other members of the Pipkin crew.

While on a mission to Belgium to "Osric 53," the 406th Squadron crew of Lt. Henry W. Wolcott III went MIA on the night of May 28.[3] They found the target and made three dropping runs without a sign of the reception committee. Wolcott recalls that their B-24, called "Charlie," was hit by an ME-110 "Cat's Eye" night fighter.[4] "He hit the two starboard engines and we were on fire — I gave the order to bail out and followed the crew out the bomb bay. We lost our tail-gunner, Hawkins; the exact cause remains a mystery but we were later told by the Belgian people that he landed without his parachute."

Wolcott landed in a wheat field at 0230 hours. He hid for several days, then walked to the Catholic University at Enghien, where he was hidden in a priest's room for four days. Then, he recalls, "I moved about the environs of Brussels and Braine-le-Comte for two months with the Belgian people." In a farmhouse south of Enghien he joined another American pilot and eighteen Russians who had escaped from forced service in the German army. A treacherous escape organization, unsuspected by Wolcott and his comrades, came forward with a plan to get him to Switzerland. The men were taken to an apartment in Brussels which was to become known as the infamous "dog house," the place from which Allied fliers were funneled into German hands. Wolcott was caught by the Gestapo "wearing civilian clothes and without dog tags, so [he] was put into the civilian prison of Saint Gilles in Brussels to be tried as a spy."

Lieutenant Ryckman had twisted his knee and injured his back on landing. After walking at night and hiding by day he was finally taken in by a couple who fed him and gave him civilian clothes, then took him to a castle where Cozzens was hiding. After three or four weeks, they were taken by train to Brussels to the "dog house" then to a house where they saw a large picture of Adolf Hitler hanging on the wall. When their guides saluted the man at the desk, who was a Gestapo officer, they knew they had been betrayed. Refusing to give any information, they were moved to Saint Gilles prison. There they suffered solitary confinement in a closet-sized room, poor food, and mistreatment by the Nazis until September 1, when they were placed in regular cells. The next day, forty-two Allied airmen, including Wolcott, Ryckman, Cozzens, and Auda were locked into the baggage car of a train to be moved to a POW camp in Germany.

British armor was just beginning to come into Brussels. The German train made several attempts to break through the British line without success. Finally, after an abrupt stop and an attempt to reverse the train's direction, the baggage car became derailed and the German guards abandoned the train. Using a pocketknife, the men picked the lock on the door and slipped out of the car. They hid in the cabin of a Belgian barge until the next morning, when word was received that the British had completed the liberation of Brussels. The next day they caught a ride on a British supply lorry going to France, made their way to an airfield, and returned in a C-47 to England, arriving on September 6.

The other four survivors, Vozzella, Loucks, Deihl, and Tuttle, were hidden in various places by patriotic Belgians until the liberation of Belgium by the Western Allies. By September 11 all members of the Wolcott crew were safely back in England, except Sergeant Hawkins.

On May 30, at 2300 hours, Lt. Ernest B. Fitzpatrick and his crew of the 406th Squadron departed from Harrington for a mission to Belgium. At the target there were no lights to indicate a reception committee. Then "all hell broke loose" from a flak battery on the ground. The Fitzpatrick crew had unsuspectingly flown into a trap set by the Germans.

The night before, another Carpetbagger crew had completed a successful mission to a ground near "Osric 14," which was the target for this night. As a result, the Germans had moved in the mobile flak units and placed night fighters in readiness. The Belgian patriots, who were aware of what was going to take place, were unable to get this information to London in time to save the Fitzpatrick crew.[5] The B-24 was hit as it roared away from the area. Then a waiting JU-88 German fighter raked it with 20mm cannon fire, and the airplane was soon a mass of flames. Fitzpatrick, Lasicki, Swartz, and Schack bailed out safely, and during the next several days got together again. With the help of the Belgian patriots and underground intelligence they hid, moved, hid again, then moved again. More than three months later, they boarded a train to Liège, where they went immediately to the White Army headquarters. There they received new papers and identification cards, as well as work cards and were soon liberated by Allied forces and returned to England.

Sherwood, Theriot, and Kasza had similar evasion stories. On September 8 they were liberated, while hiding in their camp, by an American patrol of sixteen soldiers. They, too, soon returned to England. It was known that Dogrothy and Williams had both bailed out of the airplane successfully, but nothing further was known of their fate.

On the night of June 1, Lt. Richard L. Wright and his crew, of the 850th Squadron, flew a mission to "Bob 191." However, the mechanism for dropping the containers failed, and only the packages were dropped. Lieutenant Wright said that the reception was very poor; nevertheless, the field acknowledged the receipt of the packages. They said, however, that most of the material was ruined, as the parachutes did not open properly, and some of the packages were picked up by the Germans.

A crew of the 36th Squadron went down on the night of June 5, the eve of the invasion of the Continent. Lt. Kenneth Pratt and full crew left Harrington airfield for a mission to Belgium. Near Wavre, Belgium, after being hit by German antiaircraft fire, their B-24 exploded, blowing three of the crew clear of the airplane. Two of them, Lieutenant Leindorf and Sergeant Warren, were taken prisoner. Lieutenant Pratt successfully evaded capture and joined the White Army of the Belgian resistance, later joining the Belgian Maquis. In September, when American troops occupied the area in the vicinity of Sovet, Belgium, Pratt met them and was returned to England. It is assumed that the other members of the crew perished in the burning airplane.[6]

# 7     D-Day and Beyond: The Events in Normandy

On June 6, 1944, Western Allied armies invaded the Continent on the northern coast of France, supported by more than 4,000 ships and 11,000 warplanes along a front eighty miles long. The mightiest air and sea armadas ever assembled covered the landings. Thirty-one thousand Allied airmen flew operational missions over France that day.

At 0600 hours on June 6 (at least forty-five minutes ahead of the other heavy bombers), Lt. Col. Earle J. Aber, Jr., CO of the night leaflet squadron, piloted the first Eighth Air Force airplane to fly over the beachheads of Normandy. He led six crews, dropping warning leaflets on eighteen targets including Cherbourg, St. Lô, Carentan, Falaise, and LeMans, to alert the French about the impending invasion and telling them how to help the Allied cause. The other five crews were those of lieutenants Carl Clover, Fred Pugh, Evan Verle, Jerome Fallon, and George England. All returned from the mission safely. Colonel Aber had prepared for what was considered a "suicidal mission" by writing a letter to his mother, which he left with a fellow officer. Upon his return, he retrieved his letter and noted in his diary that it had been the most interesting day he had spent in the Air Force.[1]

In the days immediately preceding D-Day, and all during the month of June, articles in British newspapers reported the activities of the patriot forces on the Continent. There was no doubt that the resistance forces were to play a vital part in the upcoming invasion and the supremely critical days to follow. A "Special Communique" issued by the Supreme Headquarters on June 19 reported:

> Since June 6 the Army of the French Forces of the Interior has increased both in size and in the scope of its activities. This Army has undertaken a large plan of sabotage which includes in part the paralysing of rail and road traffic and the interruption of telegraph and telephone communications. . . .
>
> The destruction of railways has been most effective. Bridges have been destroyed, derailment effected and at least 70 locomotives have been sabotaged. It is reported that both road and rail traffic is completely stopped in the valley of the Rhone. . . .
>
> Canals have not been spared. One has been damaged, one cut, and another has been put out of action. Four consecutive locks of another have been destroyed. . . .
>
> Guerrilla operations against the enemy are in full swing, and in some areas the Army of the French Forces of the Interior are in full control.

On June 28, this article was published in the *Daily Mail:*

> From France and Poland comes news of increasingly heavy blows by the "ghost" armies of Patriots operating in the rear of the German armies.
>
> French Patriots have disrupted railway communications between Paris and Switzerland, and halted canal traffic between the Rhone and the Rhine in three spots. . . . Railway traffic between Paris and Switzerland is forced to detour through Brussels, a communique issued by the French Provisional Government in Algiers said. The communique also revealed that several hundred Nazis were killed in the Alps when French patriots threw back German attacks launched after the occupation of a locality which the Maquis had evacuated. . . .
>
> Yesterday the Polish Government in London heard how the underground fighters in Poland seized for a few hours the town of Pinezow, 40 miles northeast of Cracow. Encircling the town by night, a commando group of Poles overwhelmed the German garrison completely in a dawn attack, stormed the prison and set free 400 prisoners.

Capt. Runyon P. Coleman of the 850th Squadron made a successful drop on "Fireman 116" on the night of June 14. All containers were recovered from a wheat field close to the drop ground. The field acknowledged the success of "Donald 31" completed by Lt. David A. Michelson and crew on the same night, and also the drop made by Lt. John J. Meade on "Dick 88." However, because Meade's B-24 flew around for thirty minutes, and because the committee had to light large fires with petrol, the Germans were alerted and the reception committee was ambushed. Five or six were killed and all the material taken.

On the night of June 18, Lt. John R. McNeil of the 850th Squadron went down while on an operational mission, "Historian 14," to France. Information received from the field stated that the B-24 flew too low and hit a tree before making a drop, instantly killing all eight members of the crew.[2]

The crew of Captain Coleman, along with three other crews of the 850th Squadron, flew an operational mission, "Percy 18," on the night of June 25. One pilot said he found the pinpoint with poor reception, weak lights, and no bonfires. The other three were unable to see anything. A message was later received saying that it was impossible for the committee to light fires but did not make it clear whether or not they were out that night. Captain Coleman flew another mission on the night of June 17 to "Percy 19." A message was received from one of the dropped agents saying that they had all arrived safely and that the containers were intact.

While on a training mission on the night of June 17, at approximately 0300 hours, Lt. William E. Huenekens and crew, of the 850th Squadron, encountered a German fighter intruder near West Eaton, Socon, England. Taken completely by surprise, they were attacked and the airplane was in flames before the crew knew they were under attack. An order was immediately given by the pilot to bail out while he remained at the controls to permit the other members of the crew to jump.[3] At approximately 1,800-feet altitude the bomb bay became a mass of flames, trapping the pilot and the copilot in the nose of the B-24. Callahan and Sanders rushed for their parachutes, but Sanders discovered that his chute had been destroyed by flames and his path through the bomb bay was blocked by the fire. Returning to the nose, he found Callahan preparing to jump and explained his dilemma. Callahan, in the precious seconds left, told Sanders to straddle his back and cross his arms between the parachute harness and his body. Then, with Sanders clinging to the shoulder straps, Callahan sat down and slid out of the airplane. As soon as the tail had been cleared, he pulled the ripcord and the chute opened with a jerk. So that they might hold on to each other, Sanders crawled around to the front of Callahan as they drifted to the ground. Landing in a wheat field, both men were injured by the hard impact: Callahan had a broken ankle and Sanders a sprained ankle, bruises, and scratches.

Sergeant Sadler, the tail-gunner and the only other member of the crew to escape the burning airplane, parachuted to safety but suffered severe burns on his face and hands. Huenekens, Cronan, and Adams were not able to escape and were instantly killed in the crash. All living and deceased members of the crew were awarded the Purple Heart. For his heroism in saving the life of Lieutenant Sanders, Lieutenant Callahan was later awarded the Silver Star in a formal ceremony.

On the night of July 1, Lt. William L. Bales and crew, of the 850th Squadron, successfully dropped on "Stationer 151." Lt. William A. Jaxtheimer dropped one Joe on "Fireman 12B," and Lt. Oliver C. Carscaddon completed a drop on "Percy 13" Lt. John J. Meade made a successful drop on "Percy 10" the night of July 3. Agents in the field acknowledged receipt of the load. On the same night, Lieutenant Carscaddon, with at least one other crew, successfully completed a drop on "Hamish 1A." The field acknowledged receiving thirty-nine containers.

Enemy activity by night fighters and intense antiaircraft fire were prevalent the night of July 4, as was attested by all returning combat crews. On that night, Lieutenant Carscaddon and his crew were flying into France by a route crossing the French coast north of the Seine, commonly referred to by combat crews as the "Front Door." Approximately fifteen miles inside the coastline at 0039 hours, three JU-88s attacked at an altitude of 8,000 feet. The pilot took evasive action, but the airplane was so outnumbered that it was impossible to shake the attackers, and a number of hits were made on the bomber. No. 2 engine caught fire, forcing the pilot to feather the prop and proceed on three engines. The fighters continued the attack, attempting to drive the B-24 into flak areas where ground batteries could take up the fight. They succeeded in doing this over the town of Elbeuf, France. Moderate flak was encountered, and a fire was started in the bomb bay. With No. 2 engine still burning, and with a fire raging in the bomb bay, Carscaddon ordered the crew to bail out. All crew members jumped except Sergeant Hasty, who discovered that his parachute had been badly damaged by flak fragments.[4]

Determined to save the life of the engineer if possible, Lieutenant Carscaddon stayed with the controls of the airplane while Hasty battled the flames in the bomb bay. The sergeant finally managed to put out the fire, and the flames in No. 2 engine died down. Taking the airplane down as low as possible, Carscaddon headed for home with instruments out and exact position unknown. Evasive action was continued until crossing the French coast, as moderately light flak was encountered from time to time and the B-24 was beamed once by a searchlight.

They crossed the English coast at Shoreham, where friendly aircraft and searchlights guided the airplane to a landing at Ford airfield. With no brakes, flaps at ten degrees, and with the bomb bay doors open, the B-24 rolled past the end of the runway, struck a ditch, and came to a stop in a planted field with the nose smashed in and the right landing gear buckled.

Upon landing, Carscaddon reported that he had sighted a multiengined airplane afloat in the English Channel about fifteen miles out from Shoreham with wing lights on and at least one dinghy afloat. The RAF acted immediately on the report. Carscaddon maintained the required watch over the B-24 after landing because of the secrecy of the Carpetbagger special operations.

An examination of the airplane showed blood on the tail-gunner's seat, indicating that Sergeant Salo was wounded by a burst inside the airplane. It was also believed that Sergeant Stralka was wounded. Several 20mm cannon holes were found in engines, wings, and elsewhere; smaller holes from machine guns, as well as hundreds of small tears from cannon fire and flak bursts, were also counted. Neither Carscaddon nor Hasty was wounded. Hasty claimed one JU-88 probably destroyed: he fired approximately 400 rounds at the enemy aircraft at the same altitude, 150 yards out at three o'clock. The JU-88 fell off in a tight spin out of control, although no fire or smoke was seen. Lieutenant Carscaddon was awarded the Silver Star for gallantry in action.

Lieutenant Murphy, along with five other crew members, had jumped, on the order of Carscaddon. While dropping to the ground he could see a fighter above him on the tail of the B-24 "giving her hell," with the airplane burning like a torch. After he pulled his ripcord, one of the fighters spotted his chute floating down and came by to strafe him, then came back three more times, dropping flares and strafing him in a total of six passes. Having been hit by flak fragments, his leg was numb and he twisted it badly in landing, but he was able to run and hide, away from the light of the flares. The fighter then came by and strafed his chute on the ground. Murphy had seen the chute of the radio operator, who had jumped just ahead of him, and at least two others on his way down.

After hiding for two days and one night, he finally approached an old Frenchman who contacted the mayor of the village. They brought him civilian clothes and a doctor, who removed the shell fragments from his leg. The mayor kept him in bed for three days, while contact was being made with the underground. He was moved to another village, then moved again because the village was full of SS troops and Luftwaffe men. He was quizzed about the number of the airplane, where he had landed, the location of his base, and other details. They were pleased to find out what group he came from and seemed to be well acquainted with it. He was told that the Germans offered 50,000 francs and a two-week furlough to any man capturing an airman from this group. The man doing the quizzing was an elderly professor, a "fine old fellow." That night the Germans came to the professor's home, took his wife and daughter prisoner, and shot the old man for having a radio in the house.

Murphy was moved to the home of a civil employee in another village, where there was an important railway. Every night American B-26s and British Mosquitos came to bomb and strafe the town, but without much success with their bombs. The underground fixed French papers for him, but he stayed close to the house. One day he was hiding in the bedroom when three German officers came to the house and asked the housewife to cook a rabbit for them, saying that they would be back in an hour. The woman told him to come out and eat before the Jerries came back, and he was sitting at the kitchen table when in walked the Germans, forty minutes early. He was trapped, so he had to stay at the table and eat with them. They were curious about why a good, strong boy like him was not in the German army. The housewife explained that he was a railway employee who had been caught in a bombing raid that damaged his hearing and injured his leg. They examined his wounds and blamed the Americans for the bombing, then gave him 100 francs to give to his hostess' little girl. Another time he was in the yard chopping wood when two Germans came to the gate asking to buy some eggs. He went to the chicken house and gathered all he could find for them. He was given twenty-seven francs, which he turned over to the housewife.

Finally, the French contacted an American advanced artillery spotting outfit, who landed an L-4 airplane, taking Murphy's pilot identification and a note back to headquarters. He was then conducted eighteen miles through German lines, flown to the combat control battery, and put in a jeep to be driven to division headquarters. The driver made a wrong turn, and they found themselves driving back through the lines. When the Germans opened up on them with machine guns, they circled across a field and returned to their starting point. The next morning Murphy left again by jeep, and at division headquarters he was interrogated, driven back through St. Lô and Caen, then flown back to England from a beach landing strip, in a C-47.

While with the French patriots, Lieutenant Murphy had been taken one day to a cemetery, where he was kissed by a woman who had just lost three children when an American P-47 strafed the truck in which they were riding. The children had just been buried there the day before, but this mother had no hatred in her heart for Americans. Every Sunday the French put red, white, and blue flowers on every American and British grave in the cemetery.

Nothing further was known of the other five crewmen who had bailed out of Lieutenant Carscaddon's burning B-24.

On the night of July 4, the 850th Squadron crew of Lt. Charles R. Kline did not return from a mission to France.[5] A message received from the field said that the reception group had had to move some distance from their original drop grounds. They had contacted the B-24 and heard it calling "Peter" without any results. Another crew flying on July 4 was the 36th Squadron crew of 2d Lt. John C. Broten, on their ninth mission.[6] The flight to the target was uneventful. The pinpoint was established and the proper reception signals were given. The airplane came in low over the target, made a very good drop, and headed back toward England. In the vicinity of Orleans, at 1,000 feet, a German night fighter suddenly appeared behind and below the B-24. It raked the Liberator with deadly accuracy, and hits were made in every vital part, making it impossible for the pilot to start any evasive action. When the whole airplane became a mass of flames, the bail-out alarm was sounded. Lieutenant Tappan made his way to the top escape hatch, but at that moment there was a tremendous explosion: he was propelled out of the escape hatch, while the rest of the crew went down with their doomed ship. Tappan landed safely and, with the help of the French underground, successfully evaded the Germans. On August 13, he was in a small village when he saw an American soldier in a jeep and learned that the Allied line of advance had caught up with him. He, along with other British and American fliers hiding in the woods, was taken to Ninth Air Force headquarters on the Cherbourg Peninsula, and then to a landing strip from which Ferry Command returned them to England.

Also on the night of July 4, a Liberator piloted by Lt. John J. Meade failed to return from an operational mission to France.[7] At 0030 hours they were attacked by an ME-110 when approximately thirty-five miles south of Paris at 7,000 feet. The tail-gunner was instantly killed in the attack. His twin .50-caliber tail-turret machine guns ran away and fired continuously. With No. 2 engine out and the bomb bay in flames, Lieutenant Meade gave the bail-out alarm. All crew members jumped except Sergeant Syra, and all of them landed safely except Lieutenant Lovelace, who apparently collapsed his chute when it opened under him.

Meade landed in a clump of cherry trees, got out of his chute and Mae West, and ran into a marsh. He then walked and ran for several hours. The next day he stopped a Frenchman, who brought him civilian clothes and found a cave to hide him. He moved to a house in town, then to a farm where he found Bonnin, Dubois, Jones, and a Lieutenant Lafferty, a B-17 pilot.

The underground arranged for Meade and Bonnin to travel by train to Paris, where they spent three weeks waiting for papers to be prepared for them. They shared a room with three others, eating two meals a day consisting of macaroni. When they heard that the Americans were advancing toward Chartres, they headed that way and were placed in a camp hidden in the woods, along with about 150 other airmen waiting in hiding for the Americans to arrive. Finally, while he was in Chartres to buy vegetables, Meade saw an American colonel in a jeep. He hitched a ride to Corps headquarters, and two trucks were sent to pick up the men hiding in the woods. Meade was interrogated and then flown out from a beach landing strip in a C-47 on August 19.

Meade remembers vividly the day of liberation in Chartres: Frenchmen roamed the streets with a hand grenade in one fist and a bottle of cognac in the other. He saw them shaving the heads of the collaborationists. The people went wild with joy at the sight of the Americans. Once, when a sniper opened up from a church, an American half-track going down the street turned its turret around with lightning precision and in a matter of seconds there was no sniper and very little left of the church.

Bonnin and Mitchell had jumped at the same time. Bonnin saw Mitchell land about a mile away, but nothing further was seen or heard of Mitchell. Bonnin was given civilian clothes by a farmer, and he stayed in one room for five days, as the Gestapo were searching the town. He hid in a hayloft for three days, then met Jones and Lafferty, the B-17 pilot. The three men were taken by car to the farmhouse where they met Meade.

Sergeant Hines landed in an alfalfa field surrounded by a hedgerow. The sergeant walked west, and after several days he made contact with the Maquis. He joined a village resistance group, which armed and clothed him and put him to work stealing automobiles for them. When American troops came into the village he was returned to England, on August 25.

Sergeant Dubois was helped by French farmers for about three weeks, passing from house to house, until he met Meade, Bonnin, and Jones. He lived for about two weeks in a flat in Paris with about ten other Americans. Finally contacting Colonel Stephens of the Signal Corps, who was taking pictures, he was steered to a POW camp south of Paris. He was then sent to Normandy and flown out to England on August 30.

Sergeant Jones hid in the woods, inside wheat shocks, and in French homes, where he was fed and clothed. He met Dubois, Meade, and Bonnin, but they were separated again. A humorous incident occurred one day when a Frenchman learned that Meade flew a B-24 that made drops of supplies to the French resistance. Being eager for a tank to use in fighting the Germans, the Frenchman took Meade to his farm to pick out a landing site so Meade could bring him a tank!

Jones took a train to Paris, where he lived in a fifth-floor flat for five weeks, looking down on the Battle of Paris from his window. When American troops came, he immediately contacted them and was sent by truck to a POW camp, then by airplane to England.

Lt. David A. Michelson and Lt. William A. Jaxtheimer each flew a mission on July 4 to the same drop grounds, "Beggar 9," without success. The field said the Gestapo were active in the area that night.

Lt. Bernard A. Sandberg dropped on "Gondolier 13" on the night of July 6. A message from the reception committee said the operation was a "magnificent performance." Lt. Charles C. Deano and at least one other crew flew a mission to "Hermit 13" on the same night. The field acknowledged receiving the load successfully.

Russian troops overran much of northeastern Poland by the middle of July. Soon thereafter, the Western Allies broke out from Normandy. German troops fell back as armored units swept across France into Belgium and headed toward the Rhine River.

# 8      C-47 "Dakota" and Continued Summer Missions

Extended experimentation had been carried out at Harrington airfield with the C-47 troop-carrier/cargo airplane. A plan was formed to fly it on special operations that anticipated landing in enemy-occupied territory at night on wheat fields and other open sites. The C-47 was the military version of the Douglas DC-3, considered by many to have been the best and most versatile twin-engine airplane built in its day. It has enjoyed a long and noble civilian career and has been used by most prewar — and many later — American domestic airlines as an airliner. Over 400 of the DC-3s were still in airline service at the end of 1982.

In May 1944 Colonel Heflin took off in a C-47 at night. He then returned to land on a short stretch of runway by flashlight, unloaded eighteen men, and quickly took off again. Seven men stationed on the ground with ordinary flashlights had made a crude flare path to guide the airplane in for the landing. In this way the minimum stretch of runway required for a fully loaded C-47 was established. As many as twenty landings in a day were also made by Captain Stapel, learning to exploit the capabilities of the aircraft.

While this was going on, the OSS instructed agents in the field to be on the lookout for suitable landing places for the C-47s in occupied France. When such a place was found, aerial reconnaissance took pictures of it, to be studied when the place was later used in the special operations.

A crew was picked for the first operational mission: Colonel Heflin was to be pilot; Captain Stapel, copilot; Major Tresemer, navigator; Major Teer, bombardier; and T.Sgt. Albert L. Krasevac, radio operator. The C-47 to be used was modified by adding a fuselage tank holding 100 gallons of fuel. This extra fuel was essential, as it would take nine hours of flying time to make the thousand-mile round trip; the modification increased the fuel load of the C-47 to 906 gallons.

Before takeoff, the crew was given a private briefing by Captain Sullivan and the group weather officers. A map of the field, the photograph taken by reconnaissance, and regular navigational maps were used at the briefing. It was decided that the final takeoff would be from Bolt Head Base, on the Devonshire coast, southeast of Plymouth. There the airplane would be refueled for the mission to France.

At 2030 hours on July 6 the C-47 was airborne, carrying a load of eleven passengers, the crew of five, and 3,000 pounds of baggage. Each of the eleven agents had been trained in the work of organizing effective resistance to the Germans, who were engaged in frantic efforts to move troops to Normandy. The C-47 landed at Bolt Head, was fueled to capacity, and was again airborne at 2300 hours. The most critical part of the mission began at 2350 hours, after the coast had been crossed at Penvenan. The C-47 would be easy prey for even the most unskilled German night fighter pilot. It had no armor, armament, or self-sealing fuel tanks, and this area was known as the night fighter belt. As there was no observer in the tail of the airplane, there was serious risk of an unexpected attack from the rear.

At 7,000 feet the C-47 flew between Penvenan and the Loire River, over a solid overcast which provided good cover from ground detection. Major Teer took over the copilot's duties so that Captain Stapel could move to the astrodome to keep a 360-degree lookout for fighters. Colonel Heflin then descended to 1,000 feet. Four miles from the landing site, the navigator's Rebecca scope registered a clear signal. A moment later, a row of four reception lights, set at intervals of 150 yards, was spotted. The code letter "N" was flashed from the ground, and the airplane's recognition lights replied with "R." The Rebecca signal had brought the airplane on the downwind leg into the lights, so that after the code letters had been exchanged the pilot had only to swing the airplane around and land. The reception lights had been on for a total of one minute. Colonel Heflin made a perfect three-point landing on the improvised field, near Izernore in Ain, which only a few days before had been a wheat field, and which was now only half-harvested.

As the C-47 rolled to a halt, Major Tresemer got out to direct the parking of the airplane. The first words he heard when he stepped out were, "Jesus Christ, Yanks, am I glad to see you!" Tresemer had the disturbing thought that somehow they had returned to England by mistake, but the man who shouted the greeting turned out to be a Canadian gunner, who was taken back to England in that C-47 on July 9.

The first person to greet the airplane officially was an American lieutenant who was known simply as "Paul," and who was an agent in the resistance. Paul took charge, and with his help Tresemer directed the parking of the airplane. The C-47 was taxied to the base of a thousand-foot mountain, where it was parked at the edge of a grove of trees. Immediately, two platoons of Maquis troops began camouflaging it by setting trees in holes around the C-47, completely enclosing it. By this time the eleven passengers had been taken in hand by Maquis officials. The crew was then driven in two huge French cars to Maquis headquarters for a good meal of barbecued beef and potatoes.

Colonel Heflin and his crew returned from this historic first Dakota mission on July 9, bringing with them a red and silver Nazi banner which had been displayed at the headquarters of the Maquis of Ain. It was now inscribed in black crayon in French: "To my American friends, this trophy of the Maquis of Ain. Taken from the Germans in the night of July 5 at Belley by the Maquis of Ain."

Upon his return, Colonel Heflin stated, "I recommend that every assistance be given Maquis troops, as I have never before seen such spirit as was displayed by these people. By giving them much-needed supplies, I think it will shorten the war and save thousands of Allied lives."

Approximately one month later, on the night of August 4, a second Dakota mission was carried out.[1] The crew was made up of Captain Stapel, pilot; John Kelly, copilot; Sergeant Krasevac, radio operator; and a navigator-bombardier whose name cannot be recalled. The crew could not locate the reception party at the target near Lyon. As it was getting close to daylight, they headed south into the Mediterranean. After sending out an SOS on 500 KC, they were met by an escort of USAAF fighters and taken into a base near Bastia, Corsica. After a couple of hours on the ground, an attempt was made to contact headquarters in England by taking off and climbing to 12,000 feet, then radioing them on the aircraft liaison radio set. Having no luck in this effort, they landed, got the Joes aboard, and took off for Borgo, Corsica, an RAF fighter base near Calvi. The Joes went into Calvi to help coordinate the return flight.

The Stapel crew spent the nights of August 5 and 6 under the wing of the aircraft. They ate goat's milk cheese and hardtack, and washed them down with wine, compliments of the Joes. The RAF station had no quarters or rations for them. On the seventh, after receiving a telegram telling them to try the target that night, they flew back to an AAF base, refueled, and took off for the target. There they landed, picked up some personnel, left sacks of supplies, and proceeded back to England. They stopped en route at an emergency strip near Dover, as they were running low on fuel. Total flight time for this mission was 10:50 hours going out, and 11:10 hours on the return trip.

The last of the initial special missions was flown on the night of August 8, when Lt. Col. Robert Boone piloted a C-47 carrying 1,800 pounds of explosives to the target, along with eight Joes. This was the first cargo mission; the others had primarily been to carry agents.

By the middle of August two more C-47s had arrived for assignment to the group. With the two already on hand this made a total of four, so that one C-47 was assigned to each squadron. From that time on, two to four C-47s were dispatched nightly, transporting arms, ammunition, and other equipment to fields and captured airfields in France. Equipment carried included 2- and 3-inch mortars and ammunition, Vickers machine guns with spare parts and belted ammunition, Bren guns and ammunition, bazookas and ammunition, grenades, rifles, rockets, and two jeeps. Accompanying all these missions were from one to nine Joes, both going in and coming out. In nearly every instance, pilots and crews reported that field lights and receptions were excellent. A request was made for petrol at nearly every field. At one place the reception committee requested petrol because the Germans were only fifty miles away and the fuel was needed to go after them.

Capt. Paxton Coleman and Lt. Volney Peavyhouse, with crews of the 850th Squadron, flew a mission to the same target, "Spiritualist 6," on the night of July 10. Coleman reported that they found the pinpoint but the bombardier accidentally hit the switch, and the containers were dropped about a half-mile from the target. Peavyhouse identified the pinpoint but saw no sign of a reception committee. The field said that they kept large bonfires lit for over an hour but never heard the second airplane.

Lt. Richard L. Wright and crew dropped on "Smith 1" on the night of July 11. A message was received that the committee had received the load and four agents successfully. On the same night, Captain Coleman and crew dropped on "Murray 49." A message was later received that agents and containers had arrived safely.

The field acknowledged the successful drop on the night of July 15 made by Lt. John J. Oling on "Fireman A." On the next night, Charles C. Deano and two other crews were to drop on "Diplomat 8." All three crews found their pinpoint but saw no lights. They reported that the prison camp turned lights off and on as they passed overhead. A message was later received saying that the committee was on the drop site all night. At 2245 hours an airplane flew right over them but went on its way. Then at 2345 they heard airplanes and lit a fire. Much later, at 0230, three airplanes were heard.

A message from the field acknowledged receiving one agent and all material dropped on the night of July 17 by the crews of Lt. James A. Darby and Lt. David A. Michelson of the 850th Squadron.

On the next night, July 18, the crew of Lieutenant Michelson was dispatched on an operational mission to central France, "Dick 28A." The airplane and crew did not return. Through underground sources it was learned that the B-24 had collided with an airplane of the RAF engaged on a similar mission in the same target area. No chutes were seen, and it was believed that all men perished.[2]

One of the real dangers, and one most feared by crews engaged in the nighttime Carpetbagger operation, took its toll in this incident. Flying at night at low altitudes, with no lights and with other aircraft in the vicinity, placed the lives and destinies of all flying men with God and Fate.

A message from the field stated that nothing was dropped on the ground on the night in question. The missing American airplane apparently collided with one from Tempsford on an operation to "Dick 89." The two aircraft flew over the ground without replying to the signals, heading toward the Eureka situated three kilometers from the drop zone. The first turned over a nearby village, probably in order to drop its load on "Dick 28A." The other turned towards the Eureka, crossing the length of "Dick 89," and the accident occurred over the village. Eight bodies were found, and it was not thought that any of the crews could have escaped.

Lt. Rudolph B. Melinat, along with one other 850th Squadron crew, dropped on "Historian 37" that night. One pilot said he saw a dim reception, and the other pilot said he found the pinpoint and saw the code letter flash but saw no reception lights. The field acknowledged receiving one load.

On the night of July 20, Lt. James A. Darby, along with three other 850th Squadron crews, was to drop on "Permit 1." The first, second, and fourth crews made contact by S-phone but because of low cloud were unable to drop. The third crew dropped after successful contact. The field acknowledged the one load. On the same night, Lt. Richard L. Wright, with two other crews, dropped successfully on "Fireman 12."

Three aircraft and crews of the 850th Squadron, Lieutenant Darby's and two others, were to drop on "Diplomat 8" on the night of July 25. The field acknowledged the load dropped by the first airplane. The other two returned to base with their loads after being unable to drop. The same night, Lt. Charles C. Deano was to drop on "Permit 1B" but was unable to complete the operation because of no reception. The Maquis had been arrested. Lt. John J. Oling, along with at least two other crews, successfully dropped loads on "Permit 4" on the night of July 27.

Cpl. Eugene Michalek was lost on the night of August 4. Lt. Henry E. Gilpin, of the 788th Squadron, had flown a successful operational mission, "Salesman 15B," to France. Corporal Michalek dispatched the six packages in the load, and after the drop the Joe-hole was closed and the static lines were inside the airplane. The radio operator reported that at this time Corporal Michalek was wearing a backpack parachute and Mae West, and his safety belt was attached.

On the return trip, just as the B-24 passed the Loire at 8,500-feet altitude, Corporal Michalek carried some juice to the tail-gunner. About three minutes after crossing the coast the airplane made a violent maneuver, and the tail-gunner saw the casualty bag fly out the window, but nothing else. About thirty minutes later, the crew discovered that Michalek was missing. The Joe-hole was half-open, with the safety belt and the interphone lines dangling out of it; the camera hatch was closed. The airplane was immediately turned around, and a search was made of the area for two or three hours. Air-Sea Rescue was called by radio, but nothing further was learned.

While on their thirty-third mission on the night of August 6, Lt. Robert C. McLaughlin and crew of the 788th Squadron failed to return from Belgium.[3] They found their target but then were surprised when German flak guns opened up on them close to the target area. Their airplane was hit, and the order was given to bail out after the gasoline lines to engines 1 and 2 were severed, setting the whole airplane on fire. Lieutenant McLaughlin was the last to bail out, landing in a wooded area. There he hid his chute and Mae West and spent the night in a shed filled with straw. The next morning, when an old woman came out to feed her rabbits, he explained to her that he was an American airman and needed help; she willingly complied. He was given an old overcoat, fed, and put to bed. He stayed in the area from August 8 until September 2, and when the Allied armies arrived he went north with the 3d Armored spearhead to Mons, then returned to England.

Knapp and Arlin met in the same underground network after successfully bailing out, hiding their chutes, and walking away. Knapp injured his knee and ankle, but at a nearby farmhouse he was given coffee and food, civilian clothes, and medical attention. About thirty minutes later, Arlin came in.

Arlin had landed in a tree and hung in his parachute harness there all night. He managed to get down the next morning and was soon discovered by a woman and a child. When he took out his wallet, some Dutch money fell out of it, and the woman and child quickly walked away. He went to sleep, and upon awakening saw two men approaching: the woman had sent the Maquis to kill the "Boche" with Dutch money. Knapp had told them of the crashed airplane, however, and after satisfying the Maquis that he was an American he was taken to the house where Knapp was hiding.

They were moved to a house where a Maquis chief who had been wounded was hiding, and they stayed there for twenty-five days, hiding in the hayloft when a German patrol was out. Finally, they were taken by a British army captain to the American lines, then sent to Paris and on to England.

Sergeant Bear had bailed out of the front of the bomb bay and landed safely near the French-Belgian border. At dawn he found a small canal which was heavily weeded; he hid there and slept all that day. On August 8 he approached a sheepherder who took him to a village and helped him get a passport. He was given directions to the French border, and he went to Mauberge, Le Cateau-Cambresis, and Guise. His papers identifed him as a deaf-mute, and he was not bothered with questions. The FFI transported him by automobile to a camp near La Vallée-Mulâtre, and when the American lines caught up with him on September 5, he was taken to Paris and sent back to England.

Sergeant Lee had been fighting the fire in the bomb bay when he heard the alarm. He jumped, landing about five miles from the airplane and injuring his ankle. He later learned that the B-24 had crashed near Le Cheval Blanc, France, about twenty miles from the Belgian border. He could hear the baying of hounds, so he quickly hid his chute and started running. At a farmhouse he was fed and then hidden in a hayloft, as German troops were searching the area. He stayed at the farm for six days, joining the American forces near Dampierre on September 1. From Paris he was returned to England.

Sergeant Heath hid his chute after landing and kept out of sight for three days, walking only at night. He approached a farmer and asked for help, but the farmer either could not or would not help him. A small boy hid him and arranged for him to receive clothes, and another farmer took him into his home. There he learned that three Gestapo officers were in the village and his presence was extremely dangerous for everyone. A Maquis chief took him to Chateau Percia, where he stayed four days; but a woman who had helped him was taken prisoner, and the Gestapo began a search of the entire village. Warned by a fourteen-year-old boy, Heath hid in the woods for two weeks before learning that the Americans had advanced to within eleven miles of the village; he met them on August 30.

Sergeant Adamson had bailed out successfully, and at noon the next day he was approached by a farmer who gave him civilian clothes and told him that he would be guided to the border. Several days later, a false passport was delivered for him, but the local Maquis chief advised him to stay where he was. From that time on, he was in contact with the navigator and the bombardier of his crew, who were only four kilometers away. They exchanged notes with the help of a nurse who was caring for Lieutenant Arlin. Through his crewmates, Adamson learned that Lieutenant Olenych and Lieutenant Reagan had been captured, taken into France, and arrested by the Gestapo. Adamson made his way to the American forces on September 4 and was sent back to England.

On the night of August 8, Capt. William L. Bales and crew of the 850th Squadron were flying at an altitude of 7,500 feet about twenty minutes inside the Belgian coast when they were attacked by several fighters. On the first pass, cannon shells entered the tail turret, wounding S.Sgt. Silas S. Stamper, the tail-gunner, and starting a fire in the turret. Captain Bales began evasive action, which forced the B-24 into a flak area. Heavy flak scored direct hits on the bomb bay, starting a fire and knocking out the interphone. T.Sgt. Leo J. Ensminger, radio operator, was wounded in the buttocks and leg. Lt. Milton Silverstein, navigator, administered first aid to the wounded men while Lt. James J. Doyle, copilot, worked at putting out the fires. Then Doyle manually lowered the bomb bay doors, cut the shroud lines on the containers, and dropped them in the channel, knocking off the rear door of the bomb bay as they went out.

Captain Bales landed the airplane at Castlecamp, England, on three engines. There the wounded men were taken to the hospital for emergency treatment. Bales recalls:

> The German planes were JU-88s, armed with cannon. One shell went completely through the B-24, entering at the bottom and going out the top, tearing out a hole the size of a washtub. We lost one engine which was hit during the attack and had to be feathered. Just before landing at the Limey base at Castlecamp we unfeathered it. After landing, the British ground crews put in about a barrel of oil . . . and said that we would not be able to take off again.
>
> Ensminger, whose leg was laid open from his hip to his knee, was laughing and suffering no pain. In addition to the morphine given him by Silverstein, he had been given shots of morphine by at least three medics as he passed by on the way to the ambulance. He was out of it.
>
> The next day, I decided we would return to Harrington. An MP said we could not leave on three engines and pulled out his pistol to back up his authority. I thought about that a minute, pulled out my .45 and said we were, too, going to leave. He backed down, we taxied out to the runway, revved up our engines, and took off for home.[4]

# 9 Obtaining — And Concealing — Information

The *Stars and Stripes* of World War II was the soldier's newspaper — it was read and believed as were few other publications, civilian or military. The editors considered reporting the war as serious business, but humor was welcome. Many a homesick, war-weary soldier was helped through trying situations by the levity printed in the *Stars and Stripes*. Some of America's favorite cartoonists and comic-strip artists enlivened the tabloid and lightened the burden of war. "Mail Call," the letters-to-the-editor section, was another favorite of many an unhappy soldier. The newspaper's correspondents were sometimes found in the thick of battle, and their coverage was supplemented by reports from AP, UP, Reuters, and International News Service, as well as from individual American newspapers.

An article in *Stars and Stripes* in July 1944 was careful to disclose nothing vital about the secret night operations being carried out by the Carpetbaggers:

> Eighth Air Force planes have dropped by parachute thousands of tons of arms, ammunition and other supplies to the French Forces of the Interior, who now are engaged in widespread operations against the Nazis, it was disclosed yesterday. Although the work of supplying the French resistance troops has been carried out by air for

months, it was not announced previously because of the danger of helping the Germans determine the scope and character of French preparations.

On several occasions, hundreds of Eighth heavies dropped thousands of supply containers in daylight to Maquis forces deep in France. Bastille Day, July 14, was marked by a large-scale mission. The flights, which are continuing, demand extraordinary skill and courage. Flying under the most difficult navigational conditions, often meeting flak and fighters, the pilots must find the exact pinpoints at which the French are waiting. Then the supplies must be dropped with such accuracy that they may be collected quickly. . . .

In the middle of July, the Carpetbaggers were visited by a muscular, soft-spoken British major who had been one of the passengers on Colonel Heflin's C-47 when he returned from France. As agent in the field and one of the chief Maquis organizers, the major operated under the code name of "Marksman" in the Department of Ain, northwest of the city of Lyon.

The officer congratulated the crews for their good work in getting the material to the French patriots, reporting that the resistance groups welcomed all the material they could get and needed more if they were to continue on the same scale as before. He said that in the past ten months they had killed 1,000 Germans. A series of questions were then asked of the Englishman:[1]

Q. What type of arms can the Maquis make the best use of?
A. Light weapons, with a few heavies, and they would like more mortars and heavy machine guns. They are not quite ready for anything heavier, as Jerry sometimes appears suddenly while the Maquis are carrying out operations and they have to disappear very quickly. . . .
Q. How many members make up the Maquis of Ain?
A. Between 4,000 and 5,000. Numbers are limited only by quantity of arms available. Attacks are constantly being pressed against the Maquis by the Germans. At the present time a major battle is going on against 40,000 Nazis, and is going rather well. However, ammunition is urgently needed. An established practice by the Germans is to make reprisals against the civilian population. Most attacks are abetted by Vichy-led French forces, . . . as dangerous as Jerry himself, since they form a French Gestapo. Most wear military uniforms, but there is also a force of plainclothes Milice, who are the most ruthless. . . . The only way the Maquis can compensate for their inferior numbers is in guerrilla-type fighting — lightning raids

or quick lethal forays from ambush. The Maquis of Ain have been going strong now for 12 months. . . . All troops are volunteers and go through a rigorous training program and a strict military discipline. . . .

Q. Is there any authenticated instance of torture by the Germans?
A. There have been many instances. . . . The Maquis wounded are invariably beaten to death when Jerry finds them. Formerly the Maquis made it a practice not to keep German prisoners very long — although they never beat prisoners. Recently, however, they have adopted a new policy: they keep prisoners alive and have formally notified the Germans that a ratio of three to one is in effect — for every Maquis soldier killed or tortured by the Germans, three prisoners will be killed. In line with that policy, the Maquis have in recent weeks killed off 57 German prisoners in one batch and 34 in another.

In answer to a question about the Maquis food problems, the major said that the situation was satisfactory, but in times of major battles serious shortages developed. The Maquis were very grateful for the American K-rations dropped to them.

Q. How do the Maquis establish the trustworthiness of a recruit?
A. A new man is placed for three weeks in a camp where he is under constant observation, while his papers and stories are investigated.
Q. Of what composition are the Maquis of Ain?
A. Mostly French, but with many Czechs, Spaniards, and Jugoslavs.

When asked to elaborate on his reference to strict military discipline among the Maquis, the major said that for the least infraction of regulations the penalty was death. He told of a man who had stolen a pair of socks from a comrade and was put to death for the offense.

Q. Do the Maquis of Ain have a policy of cooperation with other resistance groups?
A. Yes. In the event of an attack a diversion will be created by a neighboring group in order to give Jerry the idea that his rear is always vulnerable to attack, and the plan has worked very well.
Q. What constitutes a good drop?
A. Material dropped within 400 yards of the reception lights.
Q. Do the Maquis have their own doctors?
A. In the last six months they have managed to acquire four doctors. Many doctors and hospitals in German-held towns cooperate with the Maquis. They take in wounded Maquis soldiers,

camouflage their battle wounds as one illness or another, and
give them the best treatment possible. If a wounded man is captured by the Germans and brought to the hospital, they help
the Maquis to get the man out. . . . If an Allied flyer is in a
hospital he has an excellent chance of being taken out. . . .

Q.  Has evasion become more difficult since D-Day?
A.  Not necessarily. The French people are more than ever willing
    to help out, and evasion is still possible.

The personnel at Harrington were very much impressed by
"Marksman" and the matter-of-fact manner in which he had conducted
the session.

An organizer of the resistance movement in Denmark spoke to
the personnel of Harrington airfield on August 2. The tall, pleasant-
looking Dane in civilian clothes spoke in a clear voice and immediately
won the attention of the Carpetbaggers.

He began by explaining the difference between resistance in Denmark and resistance in other occupied countries. In France, for example, he said, the Maquis had large bodies of organized troops centered
in mountain strongholds, and they had successfully liberated substan-
tial portions of their country. In Denmark, however, there are not
many mountains or forests from which guerrilla fighters could operate,
and resistance consisted of individual acts of sabotage and terrorism.
Nevertheless, such acts made an impressive total: the Nazis admitted
that more troops per capita were used in the occupation of Denmark
than in any other country in Europe.

The speaker reported that the Danish underground required large
quantities of high explosives and pistols. They did not need machine
guns or Sten guns at that time, as they did not fight pitched battles.
He talked about the difficulties of making drops in Denmark from the
point of view of both the Carpetbaggers and the reception committees.
It was difficult for the committees to meet secretly at an indicated
ground, as a square mile was hardly to be found that did not have
houses within it. There were no mountains to screen the flight of an
airplane, and the land was studded with German fighter airfields. The
goal was to reduce to a minimum the time spent over the country by
Carpetbagger aircraft, and for that reason the northern extremity was
best for Carpetbagger operations; whatever good grounds there were in
Denmark were located in the north.

It was better to have six airplanes in one night than one airplane on six consecutive nights, as multiple operations helped to confuse German observers and made it difficult for them to plot the course of a single aircraft. Very few reception committees have been surprised at their work, as the German soldiers patrolled in groups and showed very little inclination to walk about at night. About two-thirds of the material delivered by aircraft to the Danes had been put to use; the other third had been taken by the Germans.

The Danish patriots had a few Eureka sets, but they needed more. As for S-phones, the organizer had little faith in them, and he saw little use in the code letters flashed by the reception lights. An incorrect letter should not deter the pilot from making a drop.

In concluding his talk, the organizer gave the Carpetbaggers some valuable tips on how to get along in Denmark in the event any of them went down. Most of the population were anti-Nazi, but many of them were afraid to perform any anti-Nazi act, such as helping a downed Allied airman. Over one-half of the people, however, could be expected to take risks and help out. Not more than half of one percent of the Danish police were pro-Nazi. If a policeman should arrest an Allied airman, the chances were good that he would assist in his escape. There was plenty of food available. Peasants, who could not speak English, were to be avoided. The people most prepared to help were doctors and parsons.

A new underground rescue organization was being developed for the purpose of rescuing Allied airmen, but the airmen were advised to prepare themselves for a very strong interrogation by this organization as a safeguard against the Nazi trick of dressing their own agents up as Allied fliers in an attempt to gain information. A downed airman could make it on his own, if necessary, by making his way north to the Jutland coast, stealing a boat there, and traveling eastward to Sweden. The Danish coast there was still patrolled by Danish police, who would only wish him good luck. Stealing a boat was not cause for a stricken conscience: if the owner of the boat spotted the airman, he, too, would wish him a successful voyage. The same was true of bicycles. In one way or another, hundreds of Allied airmen had reached Sweden from the Jutland coast of Denmark, and not one accident had occurred.

Earlier in the year, Harrington airfield had been visited by a Maquis chief, a French patriot and organizer of resistance groups in the Haute-Savoie department of south-central France. Accompanying him were an American captain from the London office of OSS and a French officer. The American was to act as interpreter, but in fact the Maquis chief managed to express himself in English most of the time. He was of slight build, wore horn-rimmed glasses, and resembled a schoolteacher.

A session was held in which the Carpetbagger personnel were able to question the Maquis chief about the success of their operations into France. Some of the exchanges were as follows:[2]

Q. Has trouble from the Germans increased or decreased lately?

A. Substantially increased. Trucks traveling on the highways and roads are being stopped and searched. It is important for drops to be made precisely on the reception.

Q. How much material gets into German hands?

A. About 40 percent. However, the remaining 60 percent is put to good use.

Q. How far from the reception does the material usually drop?

A. Depends on aircraft altitude and wind. It is best to drop from 400 feet with no wind. From higher up the packages may go astray.

Q. Why are lights sometimes not lined up into the wind as they are supposed to be?

A. The wind in the air often differs from the wind on the ground. Also, some drops have been made across the lights instead of directly on the lights.

Q. How close to a particular drop ground can Jerry be depended on to be located?

A. He is sometimes on the spot before the parachutes descend to the ground. In one instance, a large-scale battle was fought by a body of patriots and a force of Germans, abetted by French militia. The patriots used weapons and grenades which had been delivered to them in large part by the Carpetbaggers. Eight hundred patriots were seized and summarily shot. For their help, some of the French militia received Croix de Guerre awards from Vichy. But that was only their first cross — other crosses are due them.

Q. Why are pinpoints sometimes moved without notice?

A. Because of unexpected German activity. [Colonel Heflin mentioned that a plan was to be put into effect soon for the airplane crew to signal to the reception when the drop was completed. This would eliminate the chance of the reception lights being turned off prematurely, as had occasionally happened.]

Q. What happens when the Germans discover material in or near a village?

A.  Usually nothing. However, if material is discovered in a person's possession, that person is shot.

Q.  How many people are required as a reception committee for one aircraft?

A.  Usually 25 men to each 15 containers.

Q.  Do many containers and packages drop without chutes opening?

A.  A very small proportion. When it does happen it is impossible to salvage such material, as the fall breaks it to bits.

Q.  From how far away does the reception recognize our aircraft?

A.  The sound of the aircraft is heard and recognized two or three minutes before it appears overhead.

Q.  When are the reception lights turned on?

A.  When the aircraft is first heard.

Q.  Does the underground know our outfit?

A.  No, they do not.

Q.  What steps does a committee take to safeguard a ground on the night of operations?

A.  Guards are posted, boards with nails sticking out are placed around the area. If the committee is detected, the German patrol calls up reinforcements, and if the committee is surprised at its work the two groups fight it out. If a member of a committee is caught, he is immediately shot. However, the Germans. . . send out their patrols at the same time each day. A patrol consists of four or five men, either German or French militia, one as bad as the other. When a road is blocked off, the patrol is strengthened to 15 or 20 men. In the event of detection, the particular ground becomes unusable for a time.

Q.  If a single Allied airplane is heard, is a city alerted?

A.  Even with one airplane overhead, the Germans beat the French into the shelters.

Q.  What is the degree of German aerial activity at night?

A.  Very slight. Rarely are German aircraft seen after dark.

Q.  Are some districts in France entirely collaborationist?

A.  Yes; but if you need help, approach working people and peasants rather than well-to-do people. Priests, too, have proven helpful. Approach a person when he is alone, not in a group.

Q.  Is it best to remain hidden a couple of days or to move immediately away?

A.  Get away from the scene at once. The Germans always make an immediate search of an area in which there has been an incident.

Q.  Would it be possible to put up a fight against German captors?

A.  Not likely, as arrests are usually made by two members of a patrol while others remain hidden behind bushes.

Q. How is the morale of the German troops?
A. Not so good, but they still fight. German SS troops are of high caliber, both as to intelligence and morale. The ordinary German soldier is quite unimaginative and does only what he is told to do.

The Maquis chief said that the reception committees waited every night with impatience for Carpetbagger aircraft, arriving at the ground at least one hour before the specified reception time and remaining until the last possible minute.

# 10 The Ill-Starred Original 492d; Nearing French Liberation

During the height of the air war in early August 1944, several organizational changes were made in the Eighth Air Force. The move to convert to an all B-17 Eighth Air Force progressed on schedule, and the necessary orders were issued to bring the force to authorized configuration.

The First Bomb Division was basically all B-17 and was not affected. The other two divisions, however, the Second Bomb Division with its all B-24 force and the Third Bomb Division equipped with both B-17s and B-24s, were deeply involved. All groups in the Third Bomb Division flying B-24s completed their conversion to B-17s during August. Their B-24s went to depots for overhaul, then were stored as replacement aircraft for the Second Bomb Division, which was to keep its all B-24 force. But the Second Bomb Division was to lose two heavy bombardment groups from its ranks.

Before the invasion of the Continent on June 6, two provisional groups and one provisional squadron had become operational as special units. With the provisional units the Eighth Air Force had outgrown its authorized size and something had to be done to reduce it to authorized strength. The 801st Bomb Group (Prov.) at Harrington airfield, the 802d Reconnaissance Group (Prov.) at Watton, and the

803d Bomb Squadron (Prov.) doing radio countermeasures work at Oulton had to be regularized. This was accomplished by removing the 492d Bombardment Group (H) based at North Pickenham, from the order of battle on August 7.[1] Its group and squadron designations moved to Harrington airfield, absorbing the Carpetbagger special operations of the 801st Bombardment Group (Prov.). This move also released the four squadron designations formerly attached to the 801st Bomb Group — the 36th, the 406th, the 788th, and the 850th.[2]

The 25th Group designation, which had been disbanded in the States, then was given to the 802d Reconnaissance Group (Prov.) at Watton to become the 25th Bomb Group (Reconnaissance).

In April 1944 the 492d Bombardment Group (H), under the command of Col. Eugene H. Snavely, with the 856th, 857th, 858th, and 859th squadrons attached, had joined the Second Bombardment Division, Fourteenth Combat Wing, as the thirty-eighth heavy bombardment group to join the Eighth Air Force. Their operations were to be high-altitude daylight strategic bombardment of Adolf Hitler's European Fortress. However, the group, stationed at North Pickenham, Norfolk, immediately began to encounter more than their share of adversity and quickly earned the dubious distinction of sustaining the greatest losses for a three-month period of any American B-24 group in the European theater during the war. Allan G. Blue, in his book *The Fortunes of War*, probably sums up their troubled record best: "They seemed to excel at being caught in the wrong place at the wrong time."

On June 19, the personnel and airplanes of the 858th Squadron were transferred to the other three squadrons. The 858th designation was sent to Cheddington and given to the night leaflet squadron there. The 492d Bomb Group carried on as a three-squadron group.

General Order No. 473 from Headquarters, Eighth Air Force, Office of the Commanding General (dated August 5, 1944) broke up the old 492d Bomb Group. The group and squadron commanding officers, staff personnel, combat crews, and ground personnel were game to the end and cannot be faulted for the group's violent history.

Forty-six combat crews transferred to other heavy bombardment groups in the Eighth Air Force. Most went to the 467th Bomb Group (H) at Rackheath, Norfolk, to make up a new 788th Squadron. Colonel Snavely, with most of his staff and several lead crews, went to the 44th Bomb Group (H) at Shipdham, Norfolk. Six combat crews had finished tours of thirty missions and been relieved. Forty-six of the original airplanes and fourteen replacement airplanes had been lost or salvaged. After flying their final mission, No. 67, on August 7, the 492d had on hand fifty airplanes: eighteen in flying order, thirty out of commission, and two nonoperational.

Twelve combat crews went to Cheddington, then on August 16 moved on to Harrington, most to the new 856th Squadron.[3] Capt. Armando C. Velarde's was the only 856th Squadron crew to return on June 20 from mission No. 34 to Politz.[4] They came home alone from three-quarters of the way to the target, having aborted because of a blown cylinder in No. 1 engine and the loss of the No. 2 supercharger. The 492d lost fourteen aircraft and crews that day.

On May 3, before the 492d began operations from North Pickenham, Lt. James G. Kuntz[5] had made a short approach and landed off the runway; the nosewheel collapsed and the aircraft skidded on its nose. Major damage was suffered, but there were no crew injuries. Upon returning to North Pickenham after mission No. 8 on May 24, Kuntz fell from the wing of his aircraft when examining flak damage. It was his final mission from North Pick.

When returning from mission No. 66 to Hamburg on August 6, the aircraft of Lt. Elmer D. Pitsenbarger was approaching the strip at North Pickenham for landing when a B-24 of the 859th Squadron pulled up in a steep climb directly in the path of the aircraft. In the collision and subsequent crash of the two airplanes, Pitsenbarger and one other of his crew were seriously injured, and one crew member was killed. Nine men in the 859th Squadron airplane were killed.

Returning from mission No. 46 on July 6 to Kiel, Lt. Curtis A. Abernathy had ditched his B-24 in the North Sea, losing two crew members. On mission No. 53 to Troarn, France, Lt. Stanley A. Seger and crew had abandoned their B-24 over the beachhead; one crew member was killed. On the same day, July 18, Lt. Ross D. White, on his first and only 492d mission from North Pickenham, had landed his B-24 at Thorny Island with major flak damage to both crew and aircraft. Thompson and crew flew eight missions from North Pickenham. On their eighth mission, on August 6, they came home alone from Hamburg on two and a half engines, with major flak damage to their B-24.

On August 13, at 0900 hours, Lt. Brendan Q. O'Brien and Sgt. John I. Kirychuk left North Pickenham via motor truck with organizational records of the 492d Bombardment Group (H) for a permanent change of station. At approximately 1500 hours, the 492d Bombardment Group (H) designation had officially arrived at Harrington airfield. The 801st Bomb Group (Prov.), the 802d Reconnaissance Group (Prov.), the 803d Bomb Squadron (Prov.), and the old 492d Bomb Group (H) all ceased to exist, and reorganization of squadron and group designations began.[6]

While all of this shuffling was going on, from twelve to thirty-seven operational missions were being flown nightly from Harrington. Carpetbagger combat crews routinely flew to France parachuting agents and supplies into territory still under enemy control. While agents, arms, and supplies were being dropped to the resistance forces, other missions were being flown for other purposes. Wilmer Stapel recalls one such mission:

> My most gratifying C-47 mission was flown on August 9, 1944. The target was Lake Annecy, France. The purpose was to pick up evadees and escapees and bring them back to England. Total flight time was 8:30 hours. Weather, cloudy and rain. Flew in clouds when nearing Lyon. Climbed over Lake Geneva, Switzerland. Found landing site after quick exit from Switzerland. Raining like mad. Muddy and cut-up dirt landing strip. After touch-down, just barely stopped before running into a tree attempting to groundloop aircraft as the end of the field was near. I was greeted by one of our own evadees, Johnny Mead, a bombardier from our squadron who had been shot down early in the year.
>
> Loaded up the aircraft with 36 people, plus crew. (Violated all safety regs as there were seats for only 32 plus crew.) It was still raining, field had areas of open ground. Lined up using the hypotenuse of field layout for maximum length, held brakes on, wide open throttles, dropped flaps on takeoff roll. Each time the aircraft hit a strip of plain ground it would slow up. Broke ground at very end of the field and a great big roar of elation was heard from the men who were sweating out the takeoff as much as I. I chose to bring them all out rather than leave a half-dozen or so behind. Made it back to England by adjusting return flight route to keep out of range of our troops and their guns, as the invasion front was somewhat fluid to say the least.[7]

The war went on. Night leaflet operations continued from Cheddington. On the night of August 10, a B-24 of the night leaflet squadron crashed near Madley, in Hertfordshire, while on a cross-country training flight. Eight members of the crew of ten were instantly killed, and the pilot died a few hours later. The tail-gunner, Corporal

White, the only survivor, was seriously injured. Crew members killed were 2d Lt. Chester Cherrington, Jr., Lieutenant Kingery, Lieutenant Preston, Lieutenant Wilson, Corporal Prieder, Corporal Patterson, Corporal Reseigh, Corporal Rushing, and Corporal Specht.

The airplane of Lt. James R. Bailey of the night leaflet squadron was attacked by two enemy fighters on August 14. As one of them made a pass at the tail of the Bailey crew's B-17, the tail-gunner got in a long burst from his turret. The top-turret-gunner then got in a short burst as the fighter went over the top of the B-17. The fighter blew up in the air, and the second fighter left. S.Sgt. Charles Williams, the tail-gunner, received credit for one enemy fighter destroyed. The B-17 received no damage and returned to base with no injuries.

A Jedburgh team of agents was parachuted behind the German lines by a Carpetbagger crew on the night of August 14 at approximately 0045 hours. Jedburgh teams, dropped by Carpetbagger aircraft to join resistance groups in enemy-occupied territory, consisted of three highly trained men: two officers and one enlisted man. At least one of the officers was supposed to be a native of the occupied country involved in the operation, and the enlisted man was a qualified radio operator. Their duties were to equip and train groups for guerrilla activity, to communicate special orders and conduct other radio communication, and to lead groups in operations against the Germans. On the night of August 14 the team consisted of two Frenchmen and an American major, William E. Colby (later to become director of the Central Intelligence Agency). This team was to help establish a flank guard for General Patton's rapidly advancing Third Army to prevent a counterattack on the army's exposed flanks.

The 856th Squadron crew of 2d Lt. Richard L. Norton, Jr., also left Harrington on the night of August 14 for a mission to France.[8] Nothing was heard of the B-24 or its crew until a letter arrived from the 93d Evacuation Hospital, dated September 8 and addressed to the Commanding Officer, 36th Bomb Squadron, 801st Bomb Group. The letter stated that Sergeant Gillikin had come to the hospital as a patient the night before. His bomber had crashed on the night of August 14 and he was the only survivor. He had been found and cared for by French peasants, along with another member of the crew who could not be saved. It was likely that Sergeant Gillikin would lose several fingers, but otherwise he would recover.

More articles about the resistance forces supplied by the Carpetbaggers appeared in the newspapers of London. Readers were given vivid pictures of the war raging behind the front lines between the men of the FFI and the Nazis, but such articles never disclosed that the operations to arm the resistance forces were being carried out by a secret force of black-painted B-24 Liberators flying at night from Harrington airfield. In August 1944 this report by BUP and Reuters appeared:

> The men of the Maquis — the French Forces of the Interior, estimated to total between 500,000 and 1,000,000 — are causing confusion and panic everywhere behind the German Armies in France. The Maquis are now well-equipped, for it was revealed yesterday that thousands of tons of arms and other supplies have for months past been dropped for them by the RAF and United States Air Force. . . . These supplies enabled the Maquis to bring unsuspected weapons to bear against the Germans. . . .
>
> The pilots have to find the exact pinpoints at which the resisters are waiting. . . . The big bombers have had to come down lower than they have ever flown before in operations, to be sure of getting the containers on the targets and to prevent any of them scattering outside the target area, where they might have been found by the Germans, and cost dozens of innocent French lives.
>
> Sometimes the bombers went out in huge formations of hundreds. More frequently they dared the Luftwaffe by flying out by squadrons. Their activity now explains for the first time the frequent coastal reports from southeast England of masses of heavy bombers flying towards the Continent — reports which were never followed up by announcements of bombing operations.

On the night of September 8, the 856th Squadron crew of 2d Lt. Lawrence Berkoff left Harrington for a mission to France.[9] Immediately after takeoff, Sergeant Rinz, the engineer, noticed that No. 2 engine was trailing an unusually long tongue of flame from its exhaust. Berkoff made several circles of the field while keeping the engine under observation until just a small bit of flame could be seen coming from the flame arrester. Berkoff decided to head for their target, but Rinz kept watch on the No. 2 engine. At 2325 hours, as they neared the southern coast to England, the decision was made to turn back, as the red-hot glow of the exhaust would make a perfect target for night fighters. As the airplane was on its return course, No. 1 engine began to act up and finally quit cold. Berkoff immediately began to adjust controls and feather the prop on No. 1 engine. Then No. 2 began to run roughly. With both engines ineffective, the airplane began to lose altitude rapidly, and it became impossible to maintain a straight and level flight. It soon became evident that the airplane could not be controlled, and Berkoff gave the order to bail out.

At 3,300 feet the crew bailed out until only Berkoff and Rinz were left. Rinz yelled for Berkoff to get out and at about 1,000 feet dropped from the bomb bay. The airplane then went into a spin and dove straight down, crashing just below Rinz. Berkoff, fighting the controls of the B-24 to allow the others to get out, was killed. All other crew members made safe jumps, suffering only minor injuries.

The crew and airplane of Lt. James M. McLaughlin of the 858th Squadron went down on the night of September 16, which was supposed to be the last night of Carpetbagger special operations. The weather was extremely bad as the B-24 took off from Harrington airfield. It was the crew's thirty-fifth mission and the final one to finish their tour.[10] Flying by instruments, they crossed the channel and continued on into France. The pilot climbed to 4,500 feet ten minutes from the initial point, which was over the town of Charmes. At that instant they were hit by a flak barrage. No evasive action was taken, because the elevator was shot off and the pilot had no control of the aircraft. As it fell off to the right, McLaughlin sounded the bail-out alarm and attempted to stir the copilot. But Lee had apparently been hit by flak: a cockpit window was broken. McLaughlin then jumped, following the radio operator out. Landing in a tree, he freed himself from his chute and hid in the woods until morning.

At daybreak McLaughlin found empty K-ration boxes, indicating that he was behind the American lines. Soon he was met by American troops, who escorted him in to the 313th Regimental Headquarters of the 79th Infantry Division. He was later taken to the site of the crashed B-24, where four bodies were found and identified as Lieutenant Lee, Lieutenant Skwara, Sergeant DeVries, and Sergeant Brewer.

McLaughlin later met members of Battery A, 115th AA Gun Battalion, whose fire had brought the B-24 down. The battery had just moved into the area that morning and had orders to fire at any aircraft not responding with IFF (Identification — Friend or Foe) signals. Unfortunately, Carpetbagger crews had orders not to use IFF over the Continent. Nothing further is known of the fate of the other three crew members who bailed out of the doomed airplane.

One of the combat crews that had transferred from North Pickenham to Harrington with the 492d Bombardment Group designation on August 16 was that of Lt. Stanley A. Seger. In June 1944 the Seger crew, No. 3446, had left Bangor, Maine, flying a brand-new B-24J via the North Atlantic route to Ireland.[11] In mid-July the Seger crew was assigned to the 492d Bombardment Group (H), 856th Squadron, at North Pickenham.

On a bombing mission on July 18, damage from flak to three of the four engines required the crew to bail out at 3,000 feet over France. Sergeant Craig's chute failed to open, and Lieutenant Torado's chute ripped; he injured his spine and broke his leg in several places.

Seger later related how it felt to bail out of an airplane and to place his life in the hands of the Almighty and his trust in a small patch of silk called a parachute:

> When the moment came to leave the ship Marvel handed a chute pack to Carter, one to Craig, one to me, and took one himself. The chutes given each of us were not necessarily the same chutes each of us had brought on board back at North Pickenham. Any of us could have been given the chute little John Craig wore to his death. It could have been any one of us — we lived and he died and nobody knows why. Marvel says that each night he still includes little John Craig in his prayers.[12]

Seger's crew did not fly operational missions again until they got to Harrington. With a new bombardier, Lt. Richard S. Hayman, and a new radio operator, T.Sgt. Ralph P. Beaman, and after two gunners had been taken from their crew of ten men, they flew their next operational mission on the night of August 31.

Beaman's story is interesting. A private, he had been radio operator on the command ship piloted by Colonel Snavely, CO of the 492d Bombardment Group, when the 492d air echelon left Alamogordo, New Mexico, on April 1, 1944:

> I enlisted to become a pilot and was plagued with 20–30 eyesight which kept me out of the cadet program. Next I tried for liaison or glider pilot and got bounced for "flight inaptitude." I asked for air crew, and the eye test knocked me out of gunnery so off I went to ground crew radio mechanic's school at Truax Field in Madison, Wisconsin, after a short stint at Scott Field, Illinois, where I did get in R.O. training. After a few more schools . . . I was assigned to the 492d when it was formed up in New Mexico. I got to know the communications officer while on C.Q. and ended up as his way out and my way in to combat flying. Snavely got the idea that he would crew his plane with all the staff officers heading up the function — i.e.,

the engineering officer for flight engineer, communications officer for R.O., group navigator, etc. Apparently both my guy and the engineering type didn't know their basics, so Sergeant Rose and I, both I believe listed as passengers, were their stand-ins. . . .

My first mission was to Kiel in early July, followed by Bernberg, two to Munich, one to the St. Lô area, and Hamburg. When Ham [Lieutenant Hamilton] and all his crew except the R.O. whom I had replaced, and the F.E. (who went "Flak Happy" after Bernberg) finished, I went with Stan Seger because it was his R.O. who was killed in their bailout. We got all the way to the planes for a daylight raid and it was scrubbed once, but I never got off the ground with Stan on daylight — all my missions with him were the Carpetbaggers and leaflet jobs plus some gas runs to Belgium. . . .

I volunteered for a ground R.O. job working with a rather hush-hush outfit in Annecy, France. We were part of the "underground railroad" bringing out and back to England the boys who went down.[13]

The Seger crew's first eight missions from Harrington went as follows:

[To "Bruce 6A," LaRoche, France, August 31]: Our own artillery shot a few bursts of flak at us over Cherbourg, but when we set off the colors of the day they stopped and also turned the searchlights off. No reception over the target. The weather was bad in spots but at 8,000 feet we missed most of it. We went through one bad thundershower.

[To "Bob 281," north of Belfort, France, September 1]: Bad weather was encountered over southern England. . . . We saw fires of houses, etc., close to the defunct Maginot Line. Pill boxes and gun installations were visible close to the target. Reception was there and the drop was good. Same weather coming back and we flew the Channel at 11,000 feet, above thundershowers. . . . We were diverted to Docking. It had a grass field and it was raining, the combination made it impossible to stop, and we went off the runway into a field, which collapsed the landing gears and twisted the fuselage. No one was injured.

["Jacob 1," Briare, France, September 5]: Flew at 9,000 feet, above the weather. . . . We hit the weather front at Loire River, which was our IP, [and] we saw the target lights through the lower patches of clouds. We let down to 200 feet and completed our drop. Flew at 11,000 feet on the way to our base. . . .

["Mark 19," Chattelerault, France, September 7]: Flew under the weather over England and when we hit the Channel we flew through the storm until we were above the clouds. . . . We dropped under a 400-foot ceiling.

["Messenger 35," Besançon, France, September 8]: We flew above all weather to the French coast, then we let down under it to 4,000 feet. It was clear at the target area and good reception was waiting for us. Some ground troops shot small arms fire at us but missed. We saw many small towns on fire and the outlines of burning buildings. There was also a lot of fighting on the ground and explosions. An easy ride home.

["Bob 200," Besançon, France, September 11]: Good weather in and out of the target, for a change. We met no opposition, found the target and dropped the 3 Joes (2 Americans and a Frenchman; it was the third jump as a team for the Americans). All went out except 4 small bundles. We were unable to locate the lights again so came home uneventfully with the 4 bundles.

["Dick 35," Quarra, France, September 12]: Again we had fair weather all the way to and from the target. The reception was there but the target was poor, we were still able to drop on it though.

["Salesman 35," Limoges, France, September 15]: We had fair weather to the target but there was a cold front at the target. We went down to 300 feet and saw it, and made a successful drop. The target was a French air field and had a good beacon, otherwise we would never have been able to find it. . . .[14]

The final liberation of France in September brought about the end of the C-47 Dakota operation. By September 18 the operation had completed thirty-five missions, transporting approximately 104,000 pounds of arms and ammunition. They had also carried seventy-six Joes in and 213 Joes out, and operated from twelve different bases and fields in newly liberated territory.

Near the end of operations an incident occurred when a C-47 piloted by Captain Stapel nosed over while landing, damaging the propellers and the nose section. The reception committee had set up flare path and landing signals differently than briefed, and the airplane landed on soft ground instead of the runway. After rolling a short way, it hit a ditch. No injuries were suffered by the crew or the Joes, and a repair crew was immediately dispatched from Harrington airfield with repair equipment. The C-47 was repaired on the spot and returned to Harrington only five days later. The efforts of the officer and the three enlisted men responsible for making repairs to the Dakota earned them a commendation from Colonel Fish, CO of the group:

. . . Working under highly adverse conditions, the subject officer and enlisted men [Capt. Tommy King, T.Sgt. Joseph Green, Sgt. John Miller] displayed pre-eminent devotion to duty, accomplishing their task considerably before the time allotted, improvising brackets and fittings and performing sound repairs with few tools and makeshift equipment. Their accomplishment reflects the highest credit upon themselves and the Army Air Force.

Captain King, engineering officer of the 857th Squadron, was billeted with his men in the area and worked under extremely hazardous conditions. King stayed at the home of Dr. Roberteau, a close relative of Claudette Colbert, of film fame. Throughout the period of German occupation it had been impossible for Miss Colbert and her mother to communicate with their people in this area. Upon his return to England, King posted a letter from Dr. Roberteau to Miss Colbert which explained to her the situation of her family; this was the first report she had received in four years. A grateful letter of appreciation was received by King from her in return.

Captain Stapel, who had flown the C-47 that nosed over on landing, summarized what followed:

> I believe it was McManus that was second to the target that night. We pulled out all secret equipment and papers. When McManus landed we hitched a ride home with him. It was several days later that Captain Tommy King and his help went back to the field and repaired the aircraft for a return flight. . . .
>
> I spent the later part of September and October in group operations . . . while the crews flew gas into Belgium to aid General Patton's invasion forces. [15]

11    Fuel for Patton —
And Other Special Missions

Most of France had been liberated by the middle of September 1944, and full-scale Carpetbagger special operations ceased. The 492d Bombardment Group's airplanes were quickly modified, and the units joined in a wholesale delivery of gasoline to fuel the tanks of the Armored Corps, which had advanced in many places to the German border. Many of the ports, including the port of Antwerp in Belgium, were not yet under Allied control. It was clear that the only way to get the urgently needed gasoline was by air transport. On September 19, staff personnel left Harrington for a base in Belgium. Included were weather personnel, the radio section, the medical section, and the flying control officer.

The Eighth Air Force ordered the B-24s modified for hauling tank fuel to designated airfields in the newly liberated territory. Unneeded auxiliary fuel systems in the airplane were disconnected and blocked off, then marked with a white patch on each auxiliary wing-tank filler cap to indicate that the gasoline was 80-octane tank fuel. Two 400-gallon bomb bay tanks were installed in front, and six 100-gallon P-51 belly tanks were installed in the rear, with three more 100-gallon belly tanks installed over the Joe-hole door, all vented to the outside.

The 492d Group was to deliver 115,000 gallons of 80-octane gasoline daily, allotted at a rate of 2,000 gallons per airplane. Gasoline motor transports hauled the fuel to Harrington, and fuel storage facilities on the base were converted for the operation, as the railroad siding could not load the transports at night. With this facility the airplanes were loaded twenty-four hours of each day.

On September 21, the first twenty-five airplanes were dispatched to the advance base, on which the longest runway was only 4,500 feet. All of the airplanes and crews remained overnight and returned the next morning. At first the unloading facilities were inadequate, but within three days additional unloading pumps had been installed. By this time sixty airplanes were being dispatched each day, requiring only five hours for the trip.

Many obstacles were overcome to accomplish this operation; limited facilities and shortages of personnel and equipment all added to the difficulty of the task, but it was carried out with the utmost success. The captured enemy airfields had been built on grass and dirt, and the surfaces were not constructed of sufficient strength to support the weight of a fully loaded heavy bomber. A U.S. Engineers detachment was often on the field to fill in bomb craters and potholes with its heavy equipment, causing soft spots and making a very rough landing surface. Brakes were applied on the B-24s when touching down, and if a braked wheel hit a filled-in crater, that wheel would slide, causing the airplane to swing around at a right angle to the runway. Also, many of the airplanes had blowouts when landing, and in some cases they broke through the hard-surfaced taxi strips and had to be pulled out with the Engineers' "cat" tractors. In some cases, additional lengths of hose were connected to the fuel pumps and strung out across the field in order to unload a stuck airplane.

When the fuel-hauling operation ended on September 30, the group had delivered 822,791 gallons of gasoline to three different airfields in France and Belgium. A total of 326 airplane loads had reached their destinations.

At a formal ceremony at Harrington on September 22, attended by General Doolittle, General Partridge, and General Sanford, General Koenig of the FFI made awards of the French Croix de Guerre to members of the original Carpetbagger special project. Among those receiving the awards were:[1]

*Ordre de l'Armée*: Lt.Col. Robert Fish, Lt.Col. Robert Boone, Lt.Col.
   Rodman St. Clair, Maj. Edward Tresemer, Maj. Charles Teer
*Ordre de Division*: Capt. Charles Shull, Capt. James Baker, Capt.
   Frederick Burk, 1st Lt. Charles Matt, 1st Lt. Robert Martin
*Ordre de Corps d'Armée*: Maj. Bestow Rudolph, Maj. Benjamin Mead,
   Maj. Lyman Sanders, Maj. Claude Cummings, Capt. Walter Gar-
   nett, Capt. Fred Edwards (deceased 2 September 1944), Capt.
   Wilmer Stapel
*Ordre de Brigade*: T.Sgt. James Mays, T.Sgt. Armen Hartzie, T.Sgt.
   Frank Scigliano, T.Sgt. George Larson, S.Sgt. Leo Babik, S.Sgt.
   Horace Ragland

   Lt. Robert Callahan and Lt. Oliver C. Carscaddon, Jr., were
awarded Silver Star medals at the the formal ceremony as well:

   Robert Callahan . . . For gallantry in action, while serving as navigator of a B-24 aircraft on June 27, 1944. . . . Just as Lieutenant
   Callahan; was preparing to jump, he noticed that the bombardier's parachute was out of his reach and afire. Acting with coolness
   and courage, he instructed the bombardier to lock his arms about
   him and they would jump together, using one parachute. Although at a fairly low altitude, Lieutenant Callahan delayed pulling the ripcord in order to lessen the shock, which might have
   broken the bombardier's grip on him. Lieutenant Callahan sustained a broken ankle on landing. His gallant actions on this occasion saved the life of the bombardier.

   Oliver C. Carscaddon, Jr. . . . For gallantry in action against the
   enemy on July 4, 1944. . . . With the fire reaching what appeared to be uncontrollable proportions, he gave the order for the
   crew to abandon plane. The entire crew, with the exception of the
   engineer, whose parachute had been damaged, bailed out. Determined to save the life of the engineer, if possible, Lieutenant Carscaddon remained at the controls of the burning aircraft and
   headed for England. . . . Lieutenant Carscaddon's gallantry, skill
   and disregard for personal safety saved the life of his comrade, to
   uphold the highest traditions of the Armed Forces of the United
   States.

   After the liberation of the Haute-Savoie department of France in
September, the Mediterranean Air Force sent in personnel to the area
adjacent to the Swiss border to pick up air force men who were beginning to escape into France from internment in Switzerland.
These efforts, however, did not represent an organized repatriation

movement. As most of the internees in Switzerland were from units of the Eighth Air Force, and since the need for such a movement clearly existed, the work was delegated to the Eighth Air Force, who then designated the 492d Bomb Group to handle the repatriation mission. Colonel Fish, CO of the group, named the 856th Squadron as the operating unit.

The operation was established at Annecy, France, in October. Captain Shapiro was administrative and intelligence officer, and Captain Dresser, medical officer. Later both were replaced by other officers. Enlisted men at various times included sergeants Beaman, Townsend, Tipton, Carter, and Abelow. The Hotel Beau-Rivage on Lake Annecy was taken over for a base, where the United States Strategic Air Force in Europe (USSTAF) kept one of its officers, Captain Wortmann, as advisory CO. The USSTAF controlled the operational end of the mission with the responsibility of getting the escapees safely to the Hotel Beau-Rivage. Personnel of the 492d Bomb Group operated the hotel and took charge of processing the escapees — clothing, feeding, billeting, and interrogating them and providing necessary transportation, first by motor vehicle to Lyon-Bron airport and then by C-47 to England.

Arrangements were made to airlift Fifteenth Air Force combat airmen to Naples by ATC airplanes. A small staff was kept at Lyon to coordinate information on weather conditions and the availability of airplanes. Weather information was provided by a USSTAF weather office at Bron airport. To house the staff and provide billets for aircrews and escapees in the event of stopovers, the Chateau Marieux at Collonges au Mont d'Or was acquired, and personnel were sent to act as drivers and mechanics.

When word was received that escapees had crossed the border into France, a driver and a staff officer set out to the point where the crossing had been made. After their dogtags were checked, the escapees were driven to Annecy, sometimes under the worst possible conditions: huge drifts of snow made mountain roads dangerous, especially the hairpin turns. At the Beau-Rivage; the men were fed a hot meal, assigned to rooms in the hotel, given clothing, toilet articles, cigarettes, and hot baths. Their stay at Annecy lasted anywhere from overnight to ten days, and during that time they were restricted to the hotel. As soon as possible, they were interrogated and a complete account of each escape was recorded.

Communication was maintained with Harrington and Lyon. Annecy was kept informed of weather conditions and the possibility of flights each day to England or Italy. When word was received that flights were to be made, the men were moved by motor vehicle to Lyon. From October 5 to October 14, eighty-one Eighth Air Force crewmen, eleven Fifteenth Air Force crewmen, and twelve American ground forces personnel had been repatriated by this operation. B-24 pilot Abe M. Thompson remembers Lyon:

> In the fall of '44 we had some kind of special operation out of Lyon. I remember spending several weeks over there, but flew no missions at that time. I recall that Ernie Holzworth handed me the C-47 flight manual one day and said, "Study it." In a day or two I made *one* transitional flight with somebody, and maybe two or three landings. The day after that I took a load of something to Lyon. I think St. Martin was along, and maybe Clarke or Groff, with an engineer who knew the airplane. Holzworth was there also, but may have come on another flight. (Or was it Bill McKee?) Anyway we found rotten weather at Lyon, and I flew two VFR traffic patterns in the soup. Missed the first one but broke out pretty well lined up on final the second try. Don't think they had an instrument approach, in working order.
>
> We off-loaded right near the runway, where they had a few dozen bedraggled German soldiers standing out in the drizzle, cooped up behind a wire fence. One of the Maquis saw me staring at these sad sacks, took me over to the fence, and said, "Pick one out, and we'll shoot him for you!" I know I put the quietus on that idea, as best I could.
>
> We stayed at an old hotel, faded elegance, where they had very little food but excellent service. There was a trio of ancient violinists to play classical music while we dined. We always had vin rouge, or vin blanc. We saw a few females with their hair shorn off — something of a culture shock to a simple farm boy.
>
> The French were glad to see us, having just been "liberated," as we called it. We got a few free hugs and kisses, from both males and females. We had a Thanksgiving feast I'll never forget. . . . Group sent us a big turkey. Or maybe we got it from the Army. Bill McKee rounded up three rather mature females to roast it, and I think we ate all afternoon. The menu was (a) turkey, (b) bread, and (c) wine. Nothing else! But I think the three of us, with help from the three women, ate that whole turkey.[2]

Forrest S. Clark, formerly radio operator on a 44th Bomb Group B-24, remembers Annecy all too well:

I was shot down on a mission to Lechfeld, Germany, on April 13, 1944, and interned later in Switzerland at Adelboden and Wengen. In December about 15 or 20 of us left from Geneva and made our way to the mountains with a French guide. We did most of the walking at night and hid out during daylight. We stayed at a variety of places; one I distinctly remember was an abandoned sanitarium or hospital for the mentally ill, so we were told. It was cold and there were many mountains, and we had to swim to get across a very cold river at one point. It was also apparent that there were dogs coming after us. At one point we walked through a small village one at a time, hoping we would not be discovered and caught. (Some were.)

We walked three days over the mountains . . . to reach the border of France and then sought refuge in a farmhouse. I don't know where the farmhouse was, but the next day as we were walking toward a small village a couple of jeeps picked me and my buddy up and took us far into Annecy to a hotel on the lake. It must have been the Beau-Rivage. I do remember there were some Germans still holding out nearby and a lot of free French underground people. I was at Annecy for four days in December 1944 . . . according to my war log.

We went on by convoy to Lyon after making it to Annecy. I remember we were put into a hotel in Lyon which had been a Nazi SS headquarters a few weeks before, and were fed at a large prison on a hill by young German prisoners — looked like 16–17 years old. I later rejoined the 44th Bomb Group and came back to the States in January 1945.[3]

Ralph Beaman has also recorded his memories of Annecy:

I was assigned to Annecy as one of two radio operators in the unit. We used very sophisticated codes, encoded on a geared, wheel-type gismo, with only the British Bomber Code as a fallback. Everything was very hush-hush and you were only told what you needed to know. For example, I knew we were part of an "underground railroad" running escaped flying personnel (all USAAF) but I assumed they were out of German camps and had gone into Switzerland as part of the way out.

We had German prisoners in Beau-Rivage and a contingent of uniformed French troops, who apparently were there to guard them and us. (They did guard duty outside around the area, we did not.) The Jerry were combat troops (I remember a tanker who spoke English), and we were told that they had been taken when Annecy was liberated. They (Jerry) used Beau-Rivage as a rest center, according to the G.I. scuttlebut, and these guys stayed too long. We also had a German nurse who took parole and worked with our medical officer. . . . [In 1983] I talked to two people who lived there — one for over 25 years — and they *did not know* Americans were there during the war.

One of the high points of my career was sending a message we relayed (quite common), which originated in a prisoner-of-war camp in Germany, warning the fighter groups not to strafe certain roads because Jerry was moving American prisoners away from the Russians. I also remember that Maurie Rose, the Indianapolis race driver, who was a USAAF officer in Transportation, was a "guest" at one time. Also, I have a memory of quite a fuss after we had a bunch of escapees pass through and the word was passed around that we had passed along a Jerry.

There was another OSS outfit on the lake but we minded our business and they theirs. I don't know what they were up to.

As I recall, Sergeant Tipton was a mechanic and "woodsman" type, a crack shot. We used to hunt ducks with .30 caliber carbines. He was in on going into the "woods" to bring out the escapees, but never talked about it. None of us talked shop, even to each other. I also recall Captain Wortmann. I recall that we always went armed because it was a period of relative unrest among the French factions and a time when Jerry was infiltrating killers into radio stations, command posts, etc., in remote areas. We had the arms loaded and cocked now and then, but had no real problems. However, all in all, my memories of Annecy are quite pleasant, which explains why I went back.[4]

Near the end of the fuel-hauling operation in September, Headquarters, Eighth Air Force, decided that it would keep one squadron for Carpetbagger operations and find other duties for the other three squadrons of the 492d Bomb Group. On October 20, Colonel Fish, Colonel Boone, and Major Akers (engineering officer) were called to Pinetree near London. They met there with colonels Todd, Byrnes, and Stewart of the Operations Section of the Eighth Air Force and received orders on future operations of the group.

The plan outlined was for the 857th, 858th, and 859th squadrons to operate at medium level, 10,000 to 12,000 feet, in heavy bombardment at night and to put out a maximum effort of fifty aircraft per mission. They were to become operational within thirty days, and a target date of November 20 was tentatively agreed upon, if the necessary training facilities and aircraft were available for training the combat crews for night bombing.

A few days later, Headquarters wrote the commanding general of the First Bomb Division that authority had been requested for the conversion of the 492d Bomb Group to B-17 aircraft. Three squadrons were to prepare for a limited number of night bombing missions, and orders were being issued assigning the group to the First Bomb Division, 40th Combat Bomb Wing, for administration; operational control was to remain with Headquarters, Eighth Air Force.

Because the resistance forces needed less assistance, only the 856th Squadron was to continue to carry out OSS commitments. Direct liaison between the 492d Group and OSS was authorized in connection with all operations for OSS.

On October 9, B-24H No. 42–94841 crashed after hitting the moorland of Twizlehead Moss about five miles from the village of Holme in Yorkshire at 1600 hours.[5] After skidding along the ground, the aircraft burst into flames. F. O. Frank Cser, bombardier, and S.Sgt. Curtis Anderson, gunner, managed to get clear of the wreckage and were taken to a nearby hospital for treatment of burns and other injuries. Cser later died of his injuries.[6]

An airplane of the 406th Night Leaflet Squadron ran out of gasoline while on a mission on the night of October 12. Unable to locate a suitable place to land, Lt. Edward J. Shannon, pilot, and his crew bailed out. All made safe landings except Lieutenant Wiley, the bombardier, who broke his leg when he hit the ground. On the same night, another airplane of the 406th Squadron developed engine trouble over France. Lt. Harvey L. Comin, Jr., pilot, successfully landed at Le Bourget, France, with two engines out.

On October 22, Colonel Heflin was assigned to the War Department in Washington D.C., and Lt. Col. Robert W. Fish assumed command of the 492d Bomb Group. In late October the 857th, 858th, and 859th squadrons began to prepare for bombing operations at night in conjunction with the RAF, while the 856th Squadron carried out special missions for the OSS and the Annecy operation continued to ferry air force personnel back to England.

Lieutenant Burton, an agent who had been dropped on the night of June 12, 1944, by Colonel Fish and his crew at a target called "Hugh 1" near Chateau Rouge, France, returned to Harrington airfield on November 2 to talk to the combat crews of the 856th

Squadron. Accompanying Burton into France on that night had been two others, all of them members of a Jedburgh team. All three were paratroopers, being dropped for the purpose of organizing harassing units.

The airplane came in a bit low, and the containers, packages, and Joes were dropped. Tragically, the noncommissioned officer was killed, as his chute failed to open. Lieutenant Burton landed safely, but the other officer broke both legs in landing.

Burton said that he had few complaints about the procedures used by the 856th Squadron. He pointed out, however, that it was not unusual for material and personnel dropped to go far beyond the lights.

The main objectives of his group in France were to blow up bridges and rails and to disrupt transportation and communication lines. Two line repairmen for the district had volunteered to help, and they suggested a very successful method of cutting the telephone and telegraph lines; one of them cut lines one day, and both worked at repairing them the next. Invariably, they "forgot" to repair some of their own cuts.

Before the Western Allied armies began their large-scale offensive on the west wall of Germany, the Allied propaganda headquarters, as ordered by SHAEF, started a program to prepare the people of Nazi Germany for the events to come. The German people involved were those living and working in the 50- to 100-mile-wide belt immediately behind the front lines, from the sea in occupied Holland to the Swiss border. This area covered the Great Ruhr and Saar valleys, with such industrial areas as Cologne, Saarbrucken, Strassburg, Dusseldorf, Essen, Dortmund, Munster, Frankfurt, and others. The people in this area were to be told by leaflets what to expect, how to act, and what to do when Allied armies advanced into their cities, towns, and villages. Soldiers of the German armies were told that the fight was hopeless and they should give up in order to spare their lives and prevent the complete destruction of their homeland. As a further incentive, surrender tickets were dropped with detailed instructions on how to use them, and information was given on what to expect in an Allied POW camp.

On November 5, seven crews of the 856th Squadron were sent on temporary detached service to the 406th Night Leaflet Squadron at Cheddington. They were to supplement the crews there in a massive leaflet-dropping effort beyond the front lines. The crews were those of Lt. James G. Kuntz, Lt. Frederick Lemke, Lt. Robert W. Bronar, Lt. William L. Borden, Lt. Stanley A. Seger, Lt. Arden B. Walling, and Lt. Curtis A. Abernathy. They arrived at Cheddington on November 6, ready to fly their first mission that night, but it was scrubbed because of weather conditions.

The crews from the 856th Squadron handled mostly the targets over what was known to the RAF as "Flak Alley," all up and down the industrial valley of the Ruhr. The target area was entered at high altitude and at top speed. After making the drops, the pilot headed for home, descending all the way, trying to outspeed flak and enemy night fighters. Weather was their most nagging problem, but if they could get off the ground they were dispatched on their missions and were often diverted to other airfields upon their return. These crews and airplanes flew in weather that kept all other operations at a standstill.

The 406th Night Leaflet Squadron was temporarily raised in strength to twenty-one aircraft and twenty-four combat crews, with the result that the 406th's tonnage-dropped figure during November set a record that was not surpassed until March 1945.

Lt. Stanley A. Seger and his crew were among the seven crews sent to Cheddington. Here is part of his mission log of the night leaflet operation:

> Moulden, Germany. November 8, 1944. . . . Had rockets fired at us over Chanes at 25,000 feet and flak at intervals over Belgium and Germany. Had trouble with bundles getting out and three were wedged in rear bomb bay, and front right bomb bay door was flying loose. Good weather at field, only ice formed on the windshield in traffic pattern and runway was icy. All went well.
>
> Bonn, Germany. November 9, 1944. . . . Went to 23,000 feet and 15 minutes from the target we went to the top of a thunderstorm. Did 180 degree turn and went to Dunkerque, our alternate. The controls started to freeze and the ship was hard to fly. Made it back o.k.
>
> Cologne, Germany. November 10, 1944. . . . Flew in at 22,000 feet, saw searchlights and flak at Brussels and Aachen. They shot down one ship below us. Came back at 23,000 feet and let down over the English Coast. Had to fly traffic pattern with the windows open to see out. All went well.[7]

On November 15, Lt. Frederick Lemke and crew had departed on their eighth leaflet-dropping mission from Cheddington. Weather closed in at home base while the mission was being carried out, and they were diverted to the RAF station at Oulton, Norfolk. All aircraft leaving Cheddington airfield on that night, consisting of six B-17s and nine B-24s, were diverted to other bases in England upon their return. Of the eight aircraft and crews landing at Oulton, three took off on November 18 between 1500 and 1530 hours. B-24 No. 42–94775, flown by Lieutenant Lemke, crashed at 1540 hours after hitting a tree with a low wing when attempting to return to land, instantly killing six of the crew.[8] Lieutenant Lemke and his crew had bombed targets at Kall, Zingsheim, Nettersheim, and Dahlem, Germany, as briefed. In the fatal accident at Oulton the aircraft was demolished and the log destroyed. Bradley, Albright, and Koliada were in the waist section of the Liberator when the crash occurred and were the only survivors. Frederick Lemke, Frederick Bofink, Henry Salmons, Gordon Elmore, Garrett C. Parnell, Jr., and Leslie Cazzell were buried in formal ceremonies and with full military honors at the Cambridge American Cemetery on November 22, 1944.

Garth Bowen, at the time copilot on Lt. Robert W. Bronar's crew, recalls: "We flew up to the Military Cemetery at Cambridge to attend their services. I recall a miserable rainy day. All of us were somewhat irritated by a grave crew of German POW's shoveling. I suppose we were a little sensitive at that time." [9]

Lemke had grown up in Cedarburg, Wisconsin, and he spoke excellent German. On occasion he is said to have called the control tower in fluent German just to shake them up a bit. James Albright has recorded some of the events of those days in 1944:[10]

> Lieutenant Lemke was an outstanding pilot and very cautious with our airplane. Lieutenant Bofink was trained as a fighter pilot and was not happy at first being put on a big lumbering heavy bomber as copilot. We worked hard at convincing him how lucky he was to be flying with such an intelligent and dedicated crew!
> . . . Our crew trained together for about five months at Casper, Wyoming. I was married there with my whole crew in attendance.
> When Olsen and Johnson were taken out of our crew I was kept because I was both a radio operator and gunner and could fill in when needed. I flew with another crew on one mission when their

radio operator was ill. We had no ball-turret and no waist guns. . . . We really did not have much "fire-power" at all.

Most of our missions were flown at night; night fighters, flak, and searchlights drove us crazy. We did haul 80-octane fuel for General Patton's tanks three or four times during the day when he ran out of gas near Belgium. . . . We were called "flying service stations" at the time.

Albright survived the Lemke crash, along with Bradley and Koliada:

One thing was very evident about this situation [immediately returning to land at Oulton after taking off to return to Cheddington] which I will never forget. We definitely had a premonition about this particular flight which I can't really explain. For instance, Gordy [Elmore] wired his flying boots on because he felt that he would have to bail out and he wanted to protect his feet.

The one reason for our returning to land that fatal day has been overlooked time and again. As you know it was a British base we were diverted to from our own. They gassed-up our airplane and Les Cazzell started up the engines, which he had never done before. Lemke and Bofink came out and got on board for takeoff as we all took our positions. Immediately after becoming airborne I noticed gasoline was pouring down over the wing past the hot superchargers. I called "Fritz" to let him know, but he was already aware of the situation. The very last thing he said was, "Do you guys want me to take it on up so you can bail out or do you want me to land it?" We all agreed that he should land it.

Please be sure that the fellows who died did not suffer at all. I recall talking to the people who were attending us right after the crash and they said that everyone was out but that six died on impact.

Don Prutton of Norwich, England, who was a sergeant flight engineer with the RAF stationed at Oulton airfield, described the accident in a letter to the author:

I certainly remember the crash. . . . I still have the small pocket diaries I kept at that time — very brief, and liberally sprinkled with the RAF slang of those days; aircraft were always "kites," the ground was the "deck," and most things were either "wizard" or "dicey." Vocabulary seems to have been very limited! The entry in my diary for Saturday, November 18, 1944, reads as follows: "Again uneventful as far as flying was concerned. The

weather keeping most kites on the deck. An American B-24
crashed in the wood here. 6 killed (burn out)."

I certainly remember the crew being with us for two or three
days. . . . I was at that time a sergeant flight engineer flying
with 223 Squadron at Oulton, in RAF B-24s. The American non-
commissioned officers used our mess, and as many of my friends,
but not I, had spent some time training in U.S.A. they had something in common, and we saw quite a lot of [the author's brother's] crew during their short stay. It is clear from my diary and my
flying log book that we did very little flying for about a week
around that time, so we were all sitting around the mess waiting
for the weather to improve.

Several of us were at the airfield when the American B-24 took
off on November 18. I remember it circling or flying across the
airfield quite low. According to [other sources], there was trouble
with a fuel cap, and they wanted to land. We of course did not
know this, and thought they were just making one or two passes
over us before heading for base. We waved to them I remember,
then there was a very steep left bank, too steep, and too low; the
aircraft slipped down behind the trees, there was the sound of a
crash, and a cloud of smoke. This is still quite clear in my memory — it is the only crash I have actually seen happen.[11]

# 12   Night Bombing Operations

The transition from Carpetbagger work to night bombardment operations by the 857th, 858th, and 859th squadrons proved difficult to accomplish in the allotted time. In late October a conference was held with officers of Headquarters, Eighth Air Force, to discuss the problems encountered, the most important being details of the operation and the equipment to be used.

Airplanes used in Carpetbagger work had no oxygen systems (they had been removed as unneeded equipment), and it was not considered practical to install a complete new system in the B-24s. Targets were to be oil refineries and airfields free of heavy flak defenses, and the small-caliber ground batteries protecting these targets would give little opposition at an altitude of 10,000 to 12,000 feet. The B-24s would fly at 8,000 feet to the target along routes plotted to avoid heavy flak and areas where German night fighters were concentrated. Just prior to reaching the target, they would climb to 10,000 or 12,000 feet for the bombing run. The combat crews would go on oxygen at that altitude, supplied by large emergency oxygen bottles. After the bomb run, the airplanes would return to base at 8,000 feet, and oxygen would not be needed. Oxygen would then be used again on landing, to give the extra stimulus that improved efficiency by thirty percent.

Aircraft would fly on the basis of individual takeoffs and navigation, and the group would do its own target-marking for better efficiency and success of the missions.

Plans called for the extensive use of 500-pound bombs; target selection would be done by Eighth Air Force headquarters, and bombing would be done during the dark periods of the moon. Each squadron was to have twenty-four combat crews and eighteen airplanes, including the Pathfinder squadron, whose airplanes would be B-24Ls equipped with H2X sets. Bombing aircraft would be B-24Hs equipped with Sperry bombsights. Targets submitted from headquarters were to be received before noon for the night's operation; briefing would be conducted during the afternoon and early evening. All aircraft would arrive over the target in bomber stream within a three-minute time period to enable the attack to flood enemy defenses. The H2X aircraft were to precede the main force to the target by about one minute and release target indicators and incendiaries for the main force to drop on. Navigation equipment to be used would include 73 LORAN sets and the Gee units already being used in Carpetbagger operations.

Six men were brought in from Alconbury to supplement bombsight maintenance personnel. Bomb shackles were available for only twenty-six B-24s. Headquarters was contacted about the shortage, but the necessary shackles were slow in being delivered. Each airplane was to carry a K-19 camera and radar-jamming equipment. Nine-member combat crews manned the aircraft, including the top-turret, tail-turret, and waist guns. Group equipment control was established to conform with the First Bomb Division's standards and practices, and arrangements were made to secure electrically heated suits, oxygen masks, oxygen bottles, and flak vests.

Instructors from the First Bomb Division guided key personnel in bombardment procedures and the maintenance of equipment. A few personnel were sent to various First Bomb Division stations to receive instructions and training, and key men from the First Bomb Division were placed on detached service to Harrington airfield to assist the maintenance section on the use of the new equipment. Three RAF officers were assigned to the First Bomb Division and placed on duty with the group to act as liaison between the Black Liberators and the RAF. Squadron Leader Slade, DSO, DFC, handled the operations end;

Squadron Leader Trilsbach, DFC, instructed the Pathfinding unit; and Flight Lieutenant Booth, DFC, instructed the navigator-bombardier teams on the use of the H2X instruments.

The group was not able to meet the target date of November 20. Delay in modification and installation of critical equipment and a shortage of bombsights and mounts caused a two-week hold-up in the program. Obtaining modified aircraft further held back the start of operations. Then, more time was lost in locating suitable bombing ranges and obtaining training devices.

Headquarters, Eighth Air Force, decided in mid-November that if the project was to be carried out it might as well include targets such as Kiel, Bremerhaven, Wilhelmshaven, and other seaports that were relatively lightly defended. These targets were protected, however, by large-caliber flak installations, and a minimum bombing altitude of 18,000 feet was required. It was immediately determined that the Carpetbagger aircraft, with no oxygen, would not be satisfactory for this plan. Reluctantly, the Eighth Air Force finally allocated oxygen-equipped B-24s, allowing the squadrons to operate in a normal, nighttime, high-altitude manner.

Meanwhile, a request was made by group headquarters for permission to allow personnel of the group to fly on operational missions with the British RAF 156 Squadron for training purposes. Because the British night bombing operations were similar to the operations to be carried out by the three squadrons of the 492d Group, the experience would be valuable to the American combat crews. The request was immediately approved by Headquarters, First Bomb Division.

During late November, a review was made of the 856th Squadron crews and airplanes available to be reorganized to fit into new plans for Carpetbagger special operations. The engineering and maintenance sections of the squadron had kept their airplanes in such good condition that they were the best Carpetbagger aircraft in the group. Most were the old-model B-24Ds, while the other squadrons had the newer Hs and Js. The condition of the 856th Squadron's airplanes was so good that they were kept, although many were the same ones that had started the Carpetbagger special mission. One B-24D had been in the squadron for over a year and had logged more than 800 combat hours.

Many of the original combat crews in the squadron finished their tours and returned to the States. Capt. William G. McKee and Capt. Emanuel Choper returned to the squadron late in November after a period of leave, as did Lt. Col. Rodman A. St. Clair, squadron CO. These three officers, along with Capt Ernest S. Holzworth, operations officer, Capt. Walter L. Garnett, Jr., and Capt. Charles G. Shull, Jr., squadron navigator and bombardier, respectively, were the only staff personnel remaining of the 36th/856th Squadron of early Carpetbagger days. Holzworth had been named operations officer when Maj. B. A. Mead returned to the States. McKee was designated assistant ops officer, and Lt. Ross D. White designated squadron gunnery officer. White also assumed the duties of assistant ops officer in the absence of McKee, who was placed in charge of the operation at Annecy, France.

The 856th Squadron combat crews were formed into four flights: Captain Choper was flight leader for A Flight; Capt. Robert W. Bronar was flight leader for B Flight; and Lieutenant White was flight leader for C Flight. The squadron was short a flight leader and crew for D Flight.

Lt. Curtis A. Abernathy and his crew were among the seven crews of the 856th Squadron that had been sent to Cheddington on November 5 to help out the 406th Night Leaflet Squadron. Abernathy and his original crew had arrived in the ETO in early June 1944 and were assigned to the old 856th Squadron at North Pickenham. On July 6, when returning from a mission to Kiel, they were forced to ditch their battle-damaged B-24 in the North Sea. Two members of the crew, Lt. Richard S. Krear and Sgt. Ralph F. Del Prese, were not recovered, and the others were badly injured or shaken up. They did not fly again from North Pickenham. Abernathy was sent to Harrington airfield when the old 492d Bomb Group was broken up. His crew completed sixteen missions with the night leaflet squadron successfully, and they looked forward to their seventeenth mission, which would be the final one to finish their tour. They had flown every night that weather permitted, and sometimes when weather was unfavorable.

On December 11, they left Cheddington on their final mission, to Holland, at 1645 hours. After they found their target without incident, and while they were on their dropping run, an oil pressure problem on No. 1 engine required its shutdown; the drop was made with the remaining three engines. They then turned over the North Sea and headed for home. Upon reaching the coast of England, they were diverted to Woodbridge because of the dead engine and also because the weather was not good anywhere else. Lieutenant Abernathy brought the airplane over the Woodbridge field at 2,500-feet altitude. He had to circle the field for thirty minutes to free the windshields of ice, but he then turned into the base leg and descended to 1,800 feet. On the last turn of the pattern, from the base leg to the final approach and while the airplane was in a ninety-degree bank to the left, No. 2 engine suddenly revved up and ran away. With one engine dead and one running away at high speed on the pivoting left wing, it was impossible to raise the wing up to level.

The airplane slowly began to stall and lose altitude. Struggling with the controls, the pilot and copilot somehow managed to lift the wing of the lumbering B-24 and found that they were just off course for the runway and skimming the treetops. They decided to try to bring the crippled aircraft up into level flight and go around again for another try but found it was impossible to regain complete control. Continuing to lose altitude, and after clipping the tops of some trees, they decided it was time to put the plane down for a crash landing. The B-24 crashed in the approach zone just short of and to the left of the runway; the plane was completely demolished, but, miraculously, all crew members escaped uninjured.

The Allied armies had advanced to the western border of Germany by mid-December 1944. Then, on December 16, the Germans began one last effort to win the war in Europe. A slight penetration was made of the Allied lines in front of the American VIII Corps and to the right of the V Corps in the Ardennes region. This was the beginning of the Battle of the Bulge. It was through this region that the Germans had made their great attack of 1940, which drove the British army from the Continent and forced France out of the war. Von Rundstedt, the German commander who had directed that attack, was now leading this new effort.

The German armies advanced rapidly through the center of the breakthrough. The cities of Brussels and Antwerp, in Belgium, were their primary objectives. To succeed, they first had to take Liège, in Belgium, where the Allies had large stores of supplies that were critically needed by the German army. Liège was not taken, however, and the German advance was stopped far short of its objectives. The Battle of the Bulge lasted one month, from December 16, 1944, to January 16, 1945, a period when extremely bad weather interfered with Allied air support for the ground troops. Losses on both sides were high.

After the Germans broke through and until they had been finally driven back across the Siegfried Line, all requests for leaflet drops were withheld by the U.S. Third Army headquarters. The weather was consistently bad throughout this period. When the fighters and bombers could operate, it was felt that their strength should be used in support of the ground forces. But since the Germans were throwing in new troops, until then held in reserve some distance from the front, it seemed advisable to start up a large-scale leaflet dropping operation again. German troops in the line in combat with Allied forces could be reached by artillery-borne leaflets, but the only way that the large enemy forces being shuttled back and forth in the interior of the salient could be reached was by high-altitude bombers operating from England.

The Psychological Warfare Branch of the Third Army decided that every effort should be made to use high-altitude bombers. Aerial photographs were studied each day, and other sources of information searched for suitable targets and reported them to Pinetree. A close check was kept on the results of the leaflet-dropping flights. All operations reported from Pinetree were entered on the daily work reports, and these accounts were impressive. Day after day it was possible to list many towns and villages in the salient that had been reached during the previous night.

As the Germans fell back and Allied forces advanced, other reports began to come in of the results of the high-altitude, leaflet-dropping operations. Personnel working closely behind the advancing front lines were able to see exactly where the leaflet bombs had been dropped. Leaflets still to be found were picked up and returned to headquarters with notations indicating where they had been found. When possible, an indication was made of the date on which they had been dropped. These records were then carefully compared with the records of the requests, and with the records of the reported drops, with gratifying results. Again and again, confirmation that the original operation had been carried out as planned and on schedule was obtained in this way.

All prisoners taken during the operation against the Ardennes salient claimed to have been deeply impressed by the leaflets. Even toward the end of the operation, many German soldiers believed that they were defending a flank under difficult circumstances but that the spearhead of the German attack had passed on to Liège, Brussels, and even Paris. When they found copies of the leaflets and read about the true state of affairs, they were often ready to capitulate. It was estimated that more than half of the prisoners taken in the last week of December and during the month of January had seen the leaflets; a great many still had leaflets with them, and in most cases they proved to be those that had been dropped by high-altitude bombers.

The First French Army, Fifth Armored Division, reported that several German soldiers carried on their persons leaflets dropped by the Allies — in particular, "safe-conducts," on red paper. A number of the German soldiers held this leaflet in their hands when surrendering. Lieutenant Hesse, a German officer, said that the leaflet gave his men food for thought; politically speaking, as well as from the standpoint of treatment of prisoners, he considered it well written, accurate, and with no exaggerated statements. Lieutenant Wiesser, a convinced Nazi, would not speak during interrogation, but he later said that the leaflets had influenced his men a great deal and were a serious threat to their morale. The paragraph dealing with the treatment of prisoners tempted many of the German troops to surrender. They were convinced that they were encircled and that it was futile to fight tanks with rifles, but they were afraid to surrender because they believed that they would be shot by "de Gaulle's troops." The leaflets gave them the confidence to surrender.

The month of December proved to be the coldest month on record in forty years of English history. With the cold came an unaccustomed snowfall which covered the ground most of the time until February. The combination of freezing temperatures and heavy humidity created a layer of hoarfrost from one-half to three-quarters of an inch thick, making runways icy and slick. A snow-removal plan was instigated by Capt. Clyde V. Ellis, station snow-removal officer, in order to keep Harrington airfield open to traffic. The plan called for using three snowplows, six trucks with sand and salt, and 400 men with shovels. However, that many men proved to be too many on the runways and perimeter track; they were reassigned to clear dispersal areas, hangar areas, and access to other buildings and roads. A mixture of sand and salt sprinkled on the runways and the curves in the taxi strips worked well, and ten trucks and fifty men could clear and sand three runways in two and a half hours. All runways and taxi strips could be cleared and sanded in five hours.

During this period of bad weather, the group's night bombing force continued to have problems in becoming operational. Bombardier training was held up because there was a shortage of bombing range, navigation equipment, and operators for the H2X sets. To complicate matters further, two types of H2X sets were being used, resulting in separate maintenance problems. Then the 859th Squadron, under the command of Lt. Col. Leonard M. McManus, was taken from the group's night bombing force and sent on detached service to Brindisi airfield, Italy — way down on the heel of Italy's boot — to join the 885th Squadron, which was engaged in supplying the resistance forces in northern Italy, southern France, and the Balkans.[1]

With the departure of the 859th Squadron, only the 857th and 858th were left on the night bombing force. Eighteen new crews arrived from the States and were immediately placed into the training program, which continued to be limited by bad weather and equipment shortages. During December, the units received some new B-24L airplanes equipped with the Norden bombsight and complete oxygen systems. The group was now flying B-24Ls and some old B-24Hs, although many of the latter were not suitable for high-altitude operations because of operational fatigue.

A change in group command was made on December 17, 1944, when Col. Hudson H. Upham was appointed CO of the 492d Bombardment Group.[2] Upon the appointment of Colonel Upham, Colonel Fish reassumed his former duties as deputy group commander. At the same time, Maj. Lyman A. Sanders, Jr., was promoted to group operations officer; Maj. Edward Tresemer to group navigator; Capt. James Baker to group bombardier; Maj. Albert G. Schaefer, Jr., to assistant operations officer; and Lt. Edwin E. Mays to group H2X operator. All other staff officers continued their duties as before.

During late December, the 492d Group's night bombing force went out twice on missions to France to attack enemy-occupied coastal defenses. These missions mostly provided combat-crew experience rather than inflicting damaging blows on enemy defenses. The first high-altitude heavy bombardment night mission of the group was dispatched from Harrington on December 24, 1944, at 1100 hours. The mission was to bomb the target of Pointe de la Coubre, France. Eighteen airplanes were scheduled, but only twelve got off: one aborted before reaching Initial Point; eleven made the bombing run, and nine of those attacked. One of the two planes that did not attack had mechanical trouble, and the other failed to locate the target marker.

The force went in at 18,000 feet in bomber stream. The airplanes were over the target for four minutes, dropping eighty-eight 500-pound RDX bombs. The Pathfinding aircraft totaled three, one of which dropped target indicators on the target; the others overshot the target by half a mile. Bombing results were reported as being fair, with several sticks bracketing the target indicators.

On the day before Christmas of 1944, the Eighth Air Force dispatched the largest armada of warplanes in history, with over 21,000 combat airmen flying in 2,031 heavy bombers and 936 fighters on missions over enemy territory. Other thousands were involved in the dispatching of those airplanes.

During the first five months of 1944, American air forces and the RAF had so decimated the Luftwaffe that it was virtually helpless during the first stages of the invasion of the Continent on June 6. Prior to the invasion, thousands of tons of munitions, agents, and supplies were dropped to resistance forces, and emergency cargoes of food, medical supplies, and other vital materials were flown to ground forces during the critical month of August. Some 900 million leaflets were dropped on enemy-controlled areas by night. Of the five highest and most cherished awards that the United States could bestow for valorous conduct, 594 were awarded to members of the Eighth Air Force during 1944.

# 13     Renewed Carpetbagger Operations

Late in December of 1944, Headquarters, First Bomb Division, wrote to Headquarters, Eighth Air Force, expressing concern: some difficulty in the administration of the 492d Bombardment Group (H) was being experienced because tactical control of the group was retained by the Eighth Air Force. Insufficient information about the operations and future plans of the group was reaching First Bomb Division headquarters, and the information was getting there in a roundabout way. It was suggested that all matters pertaining to the group be routed through the First Bomb Division, and that a directive be issued by the Eighth Air Force clarifying the status of the group.

In a few days the requested directive was issued. The 492d would remain under operational control of the Eighth Air Force until such time as the group converted from B-24s to B-17s, and Eighth Air Force headquarters would determine the time for the conversion. All training of B-24 personnel was to be the responsibility of the Eighth Air Force, and all training of B-17 personnel would be done by the First Bomb Division. In all other matters the group was to be handled in the same way as the twelve other heavy bombardment groups attached to the First Bomb Division. It was very clear, then, that until the group converted to B-17s the planning and ordering of operational missions was to be done by

Headquarters, Eighth Air Force, with information passed to the group through First Bomb Division headquarters.

As 1944 neared its end, five pilots and three crews were among the Carpetbagger combat crews of the 856th Squadron who had been with the old 492d Bomb Group when it was flying high-altitude daylight bombing missions from North Pickenham, prior to August 7. Seger, Thompson, and White, along with their crews, were among these; Abernathy and Kuntz had accquired new crews on their move to Harrington. Other combat crews who had arrived during the special operations were those of Lt. Arden B. Walling, Lt. Elmer M. Heaberlin, Capt. Robert W. Bronar, Lt. Robert J. Swarts, Jr., and Lt. William L. Borden. Four new crews just arriving from the States were those of Lt. Melvin A. Friberg, Lt. William H. Hudson, Lt. Donald F. Heran, and Lt. Roger B. McCormick.

The 856th Squadron began renewed operations on the night of December 31. Lieutenant Thompson and crew, accompanied by Lieutenant White, squadron assistant operations officer, took off from Harrington for a mission to Norway, which was completed successfully. On their return they reported they had "intercepted the only train in Norway — wasn't appreciated; and also came over a convoy on the way out and they didn't like that either." They said that the target, lights, and reception were very poor, but five days later confirmation was received from the field that "the party" had arrived safely.

Thompson and his crew, No. 2911, had left Bangor, Maine, on June 8, 1944, flying via the North Atlantic route to Ireland.[1] On July 12 they were assigned to the 856th Squadron at North Pickenham. The Thompson crew flew eight high-altitude daylight missions with the old 492d Bomb Group before the group was broken up. On August 3, 1944, all members of the crew were awarded the Air Medal "for meritorious achievement in accomplishing with distinction numerous aerial operational missions over enemy occupied Europe. The courage, coolness and skill displayed by each of these individuals . . . materially aided in the successful completion of these missions. Their actions reflect great credit upon themselves and the Armed Forces of the United States."

A mission to Hamburg on August 6 was the last high-altitude daylight strategic bombing mission for the Thompson crew, as the old 492d Bomb Group flew their sixty-seventh and final mission on the following day, before being disbanded. One of the crew recalls:

I think we were well known for a couple of missions we flew. (The

Adjutant was writing us up for medals, he said.) But the situation was so unsettled in July-August 1944, and the senior people so demoralized, that administration was poor also.

The records verify his memory. Very few combat crews in the old 492d Bomb Group managed to fly as many as eight daylight high-altitude bombing missions without serious mishap of some kind. The Thompson crew had been thoroughly tested and considered themselves very lucky.

On August 16, the Thompson crew was sent to Harrington via Cheddington to the Carpetbagger special operation. Sergeants Rohde and Page were transferred out of the crew and sent to Italy. After a short period of on-the-job training, the crew flew their first low-level night mission on August 31. Lieutenant Clarke, the navigator, had kept a detailed log of their daylight bombing missions, but when they began flying for OSS hardly anything was recorded. After the first mission he wrote, "Mission #9 (Black), Date: Aug. 31, Target: France." This style continued for a while, and then came this one: "Mission #18 Bobby." No date was given, but the records show that they dispatched one agent on the night of November 10, 1944. No other Carpetbagger airplanes were out that night.

Excerpts from the story of the agent "Bobby," published in *The Secret War Report of the OSS*, follow:

> BOBBY. "Bobby" was the first J-E [code name "Joan-Eleanor," a small radio set which an agent on the ground used to transmit information to an airplane circling above him and recording the information on a wire tape] equipped agent dispatched. Parachuted from London into Ulrum, Holland, on November 10, 1944, his job was to lay the foundation for an underground railroad along which subsequent OSS agents would be infiltrated from Holland into Germany. "Bobby" was also instructed to report such intelligence as he might incidentally gather in the course of his mission.
>
> The J-E plane made first contact with "Bobby" on November 21, and regular communication continued until March 30. "Bobby's" early contacts yielded such items as information on German preparations to flood the Polder River, enemy troop movements at Arnheim, erection of water barriers between Ens and Winschoter Diep and results of Allied air raids on the Gaarkeuken docks.

Bill Clarke recalls that three or four unsuccessful attempts were made before "Bobby" was finally dropped:

> "Bobby" had grown up in the area of Ulrum, Holland, then

moved to the United States with his family sometime before the war. The drop zone was approximately four or five miles inland from the coast so we really were not over enemy territory as much as on most of our missions. It was a four- or five-acre field with which "Bobby" was well acquainted so there should be no hitches. Because of our several unsuccessful dry runs to dispatch "Bobby" (I still clearly recall the route) it became known as "Abe Thompson's Milk Run," or something like that.

The mission on the night of November 10 went as planned. "Bobby" was dropped and we returned to Harrington. A few days went by and nothing had been heard from him. We were then called in, and we went over the whole mission, pointing out exactly where he had been dropped. After several more days went by and still no word had been received from him, we were called to London to go over the whole thing again.

"Bobby" finally made contact and explained the delay. During his absence from Holland, an irrigation ditch had been dug across the small field onto which he had been dropped, and he had landed in the water in the ditch. It took several days to dry out his radio and get it in working order again.

I wish I could find a detail map of the area where the drop was made. It may have been more than four or five miles inland. I remember that we came out between two small islands. We had a new group commander on board, and as we exited the coastline we had antiaircraft fire from both islands and the mainland, at which time we were probably between 50 and 100 feet altitude. Following the mission, the commander told Abe and me that we would have had no chance if we had lost an engine at that altitude, and that we had the wrong aircraft for the job. Later . . . they brought in A-26s and Abe started another tour in it.

The dry runs mentioned were not intended as "dry" but the clouds hung so low along the coast, and with our weather forecasting they were unable to predict that cloud coverage, so if they estimated a 50 percent chance we took off. We could drop supplies at 400 feet but had to be at 600 feet to drop the "Joes." I remember that on more than one occasion we found the field but were down in the 300 to 400 feet area. When we climbed up we were in the soup and couldn't drop unless it was visual.

The London trip is a bit foggy — I remember going over the charts again and getting the paper work ready to go but for the life of me I can't remember any of the details of the trip. Maybe Abe and Ernie Holzworth, the ops officer, went with whatever wheels made the trip.[2]

On January 4, 1945, Capt. Robert W. Bronar and crew of the 856th Squadron, on temporary detached service with the 406th night leaflet squadron at Cheddington, took off on their "paper route" mission which was in the Ardennes salient. At 22,000 feet, just prior to reaching the target area, No. 4 engine suddenly went out. Captain Bronar made the necessary adjustments and decided to complete the mission. He then headed for Brussels in order to reach the safety of friendly territory as soon as possible.

As the airplane struggled toward the Belgian capital, a British antiaircraft battery at Namur, Belgium, opened up at the unidentified aircraft. The crack-shooting British hit the left wing and No. 2 engine on the first salvo. With flak bursting all around them, Bronar ordered that the colors of the day be shown, but a malfunction of the flare gun prevented the firing of the colors. The airplane was then hit with two more salvos that damaged No. 1 engine.

They were now losing altitude fast, and the pilot gave the order to bail out. Everyone went out but the pilot and the copilot. Radio contact with the ground was attempted without success, and at 8,000 feet the copilot was ordered out. The flying speed of the airplane gradually became slower and slower, and suddenly it began to stall out. Deciding that the safe return of the airplane was not possible, Captain Bronar put it into a glide and jumped out at 4,000 feet. He landed in a small clearing and followed a lane to a house, where an elderly woman, mistaking him for a German in the darkness, slammed the door in his face.[3] Calling out to her in broken French, he managed to convince her that he was an American flyer, and he was taken into the house and fed. Walking on, he was soon approached by an American convoy and taken to the 39th Field Hospital at Charleroi, Belgium. There he established contact with the personal pilot of General Hodges, who flew him to England in the general's C-47 on January 8. The rest of the Bronar crew landed close together. After grouping up, they went to Namur and were soon returned to England.[4]

Lt. Abe M. Thompson and his crew flew the first mission flown for the purpose of parachuting agents into Germany. From the *History of the 856th Squadron,* on microfilm at Maxwell AFB, Alabama, the mission is summarized here:

On January 21, 1945, Lt. Abe M. Thompson and his crack Carpetbagger crew took off from the 856th Squadron's advanced base at Lyon, France, carrying personnel to be blind-dropped at their targets in Germany. As this was the first mission to be performed in this new territory the Thompson crew had to pioneer the technique and routes, flying over the very active area directly behind and ahead of the Western Front, feeling out the dangers which might lie there.

The crew left Harrington several days before the mission was laid on and made final preparations while waiting for favorable weather. On January 21 they proceeded on course across the Western Front near Belfort and along the Swiss-German border to Lake Constance before turning northward to the target area. A heavy overcast and icing conditions were encountered above 1,400 feet. Thompson had to climb to 6,200 feet to cross over the defenses of the front lines and through patches in the overcast, observing intense artillery action all along the battle lines.

Proceeding along course, the plane reached the turning point and let down through the overcast, breaking out just after I.P. at 1,500 feet. At the general area of the first target, the exact pinpoint could not be located, so Thompson turned back to I.P. and went back over the route again. This time the target was located and a search was made in the immediate area from the 600-foot dropping level to determine a satisfactory spot for the blind-drop. After a pattern run, the Joes were safely dispatched.

The aircraft then proceeded north and northwest to the second target and made a pattern approach to effect the drop. The Joes were made ready and positioned over the Joe-hole. At the precise moment that the first one was to drop, his leg bag slipped, the top strap around his thigh came unfastened, and the leg bag fell through the Joe-hole, dangling outside the aircraft but still fastened to the Joe's ankle. Sergeant Osborne, the dispatcher, and the other agents came to his rescue, holding him and cutting away the leg bag. Because of the loss of equipment, this drop was now impossible, and Thompson turned the aircraft to the third target. The overcast was continuing to develop and the ceiling was now under 1,000 feet, but the target was located and the personnel dropped without incident.

The operation went off more smoothly than expected; Thompson and his crew had now pioneered a new kind of mission. Carpetbagger operations to Germany opened a new chapter in the history and achievements of the 856th Bomb Squadron.

Thompson remembers flying down the middle of a big lake, even though Clarke was telling him that he was violating the Swiss border: "I knew that, but did it anyway, as I really needed a few minutes of safety, to relax a bit." [5]

Osborne recalls the incident with the leg bag this way:

When the Joe was pulled out of the airplane I held him until Meyer came back and helped me pull him up out of the Joe hole. The other four Joes had already been dispatched. I think that Thompson and possibly I was put in for the DFC but Group turned it down. [Thompson was awarded the Distinguished Flying Cross, as were Clarke and Groff, in April.] [6]

Osborne also recalls: "Clarke was rated the best navigator in the Group. Our crew flew most of the missions to Norway and Denmark and we were always right on when arriving at the location of the drop."

On the night of January 29, the 856th Squadron crews of Lieutenant Kuntz and Lieutenant Walling took off at 1817 hours for a Carpetbagger mission to Norway. Immediately thereafter, a blinding snowstorm set in, preventing flying all over England. Another three missions scheduled to Norway had to be scrubbed. Radio contact was attempted in an effort to call them back to land at a diversionary airfield before everything was completely socked in, but contact was never made and the two crews proceeded to their targets without knowing what faced them upon their return.

The pinpoints were found, the reception lights identified, and the drops made, then the airplanes turned homeward. At 0300 hours as they approached the Scottish coast they picked up their call signals and learned that England was completely closed. A break in weather soon occurred at Leuchars, Scottland, however, and the two crews were able to land there without incident after all. A total of 121 sorties had been scrubbed from the 38th Group and Tempsford operations because of the weather, and the completion of their missions by these two crews came as a surprise to OSS and the other Carpetbagger units.

At the end of January, Lt. Col. Rodman A. St. Clair, Capt. Emanuel Choper, Capt. Joseph A. Bodenhamer, sergeants Leinninger and Scozzavava, and Corporal Johnson — all of the 856th Squadron — left on detached service to reorganize the Annecy operation. Accompanying them were Colonel Upham, Major Tresemer, Major Messner, and Major Fletcher, all of group headquarters.

About the middle of February, arrangements were completed through diplomatic and military channels for an official exchange of American and German internees remaining in Switzerland. The Annecy operation had by this time repatriated 465 Eighth Air Force crewmen, 132 Fifteenth Air Force Crewmen, six Twelfth Air Force crewmen, four Ninth Air Force crewmen, thirty-five RAF crewmen, twenty American ground forces personnel, and one Pole, for a total of

633; with the 120 sent back by the Mediterranean force, a grand total of 783 men were repatriated. The official exchange was to be made at the rate of two Germans to one American, but the Allies got the best end of the deal: the Germans were mostly middle-aged ground forces personnel, while most of the Americans were highly trained combat air crewmen.

Personnel of the Annecy operation were assigned the job of taking the repatriation train from Geneva to Marseilles. The 856th Squadron was represented by Capt. Joseph. A. Bodenhamer, Capt. Ralph V. Everly, T.Sgt. Roland P. Blazon, and S.Sgt. Samuel Abelow. A total of 512 men were repatriated in this manner on February 17, bringing to an end the Annecy operation.

The Carpetbagger crews of Lt. William H. Hudson and Lt. Roger B. McCormick, both of the 856th Squadron, dropped on the same target in Norway on the night of February 23. Although both reported that the site was too small for an effective dropping area, field confirmation followed a few days later: "A message from the field sends congratulations to both pilots for an excellent drop."

On the night of March 5, Lieutenant White and his Carpetbagger crew, of the 856th Squadron, flew a mission to Denmark. After arrival at the pinpoint, White reported that he was in the target area for twelve minutes, made three runs over the target, but saw no signs of a reception. Eight days later, OSS headquarters reported that they had received a message from the field stating that the reception group was present but was surrounded by the enemy. They had to forfeit the opportunity to receive the badly needed material and supplies.

Lt. Robert H. Fesmire and crew of the 856th Squadron flew a mission to Denmark on the night of March 6. A few days later, a message was received reporting that the supplies had been found by three men who tampered with them. One container exploded, killing the three men. The rest of the supplies were taken by the Germans.

During this time, a humorous incident was reported in one message. A report was received that "a plane dropped a load after a man on the ground struck a match to light a cigarette, and packages rained down on the village. . . . But the load was recovered safely. . . ." The targets acknowledged the receipt of another five loads, and because of the number of crews in the area and the general mixture of the loads dropped, it was not possible to determine who had done this masterful job of "light and signal identification."

Lt. Col. Earle J. Aber, Jr., CO of the 406th Squadron (Night Leaflet), was killed in action by Allied flak on the night of March 4. Returning from a successful mission to Amsterdam, Rotterdam, and Utrecht, the airplane, B-17 No. 43-37516, was hit by friendly flak, not American. German night fighters had made an unexpected raid over England's east coast, and two of the enemy aircraft were below and heading east at the same time that Aber's B-17 was heading west, into England.[7] The waist of the B-17 filled with flak holes, the control cables were hit, the airplane was on fire, and Lieutenant Morton, the bombardier, was seriously wounded in the right leg and right eye.

The order to bail out was given when the aircraft was at 8,000 feet and heading for Woodbridge, in Suffolk, near the eastern coast. By this time Staff Sergeant Ramsey, the tail-gunner, had also been wounded. Colonel Aber and Lieutenant Harper, the copilot, had on their parachute harnesses and Mae Wests, but not their parachutes, as the others bailed out. Captain Stonerock was one of the last out. As he jumped at 5,000 feet he heard a sputter like a V-1 rocket, followed by a big explosion below him. The airplane broke up on impact with the water at 2120 hours. Divers went down two days later, but all that could be found was the wreckage, which was by that time buried in silt.

Colonel Aber, a graduate of Purdue University and a prewar radio announcer from Racine, Wisconsin, was twenty-five years old. He had been with the squadron from the time of its entry into night leaflet operations. Harper came to the squadron through the Royal Canadian Air Force, where he flew Spitfire fighters.

Maj. Robert H. Gaddy, formerly operations officer of the squadron, assumed command of the 406th Squadron on March 7.

During the first part of 1945, the activity of the 492d Bomb Group's night bombing force, the "Black Liberators," had been confined both by weather and because Headquarters, Eighth Air Force, withheld operational orders. Three "Bullseye" and several "Roundrobin" missions were conducted over England for crew training. The "Bullseye" missions were practice night raids in conjunction with night air defenses. Aircraft and combat crews were briefed and dispatched in regular procedure, with Pathfinder airplanes preceding the main force using H2X "Mickey" sets. They made standard rendezvous, turning points, initial points, bombing runs, and finishing

points, then practiced evasive action whenever encountered by searchlights.

Lt. Edward G. Blume, with full crew and Mickey operator Lt.
William L. Paul, went down on February 1 while on a training flight.
It was believed that the airplane went down after an explosion during
gasoline transfer. Group headquarters ordered that in the future all
electrical equipment was to be turned off during gasoline transfers.

The Black Liberators' target for the night of February 20 was
Neustadt, Germany. The mission was in conjunction with RAF 100
Group. Thirty-two aircraft were to be dispatched, nine of which were
to be Pathfinder aircraft. Thirty B-24s left Harrington at 2215 hours
with the PFF aircraft two minutes in the lead, arriving in bomber
stream over the target at 0103½ hours. The target was hit from
18,000 feet; the target flares were not visible because of 10/10 clouds.
Meager to moderate and inaccurate flak was encountered, and all aircraft returned to Harrington.

Thirty-two aircraft were prepared for the night mission of February 21 to bomb factories and a marshaling yard at Duisburg. The main
force arrived over the target at 2011 hours, and twenty-five aircraft hit
the target, with results thought to be good. Searchlights and some flak
were encountered in the target area. The B-24 of Lt. Richard R. Ladue
sustained serious battle damage, and another B-24 landed at Manston
with one wounded crew member. Two minutes after dropping bombs,
the tail-gunner on Ladue's crew, Sergeant Novak, observed an enemy
fighter approaching at 5:30 o'clock at 300 yards. The ME-210 came in
to 175 yards and broke away. Another ME-210 attacked, opening fire
at 300 yards and completely knocking out the tail turret. Attacks continued for another ten minutes, and hits were made on the Liberator.
The crew observed that four red flares were fired before the attacks
began. These flares seemed to stop the flak.

Two minutes after the B-24 flown by Lt. Col. Robert L. Boone
bombed the target, it was attacked by a fighter, and a second fighter
was sighted at 350 yards by Sergeant Dugan, tail-gunner, who opened
fire. A third attack was made from below the B-24, which had to take
violent evasive action throughout the attacks.

Missing was the crew of Lt. Gordon F. Wiebe. Their Pathfinder
B-24 had crossed the Rhine and was on its bomb run when it was suddenly coned by several searchlights. It dropped markers and bombs
successfully, with several hits in the target area; but, still in the searchlights, it was attacked by fighters. No. 1 and No. 2 engines were hit,

making evasive action impossible. The bomb bay became a mass of flames, and both the tail-gunner and the left waist-gunner were wounded. The tail-gunner was hit again on subsequent attacks. The left waist-gunner, wounded in the arm by a 20mm shell, stood by his gun as the fighter made second and third attacks, hitting the No. 2 engine again. An attempt was made to put out the fire in the bomb bay without success, and as nothing was heard from the tail-gunner it was thought that he was dead. The left waist-gunner had by now been hit in the leg. The interphone was shot out and the B-24 was out of control. As the plane began to lose altitude, S.Sgt. Karl E. Fasick, the right waist-gunner, and S.Sgt. Gilbert Smith, the left waist-gunner, decided to bail out. Fasick opened the escape hatch, helped Smith out, and jumped.

As Fasick descended he saw two chutes above him, and Smith saw three below him. It is known that seven of the crew managed to jump successfully. Fasick and Smith were both captured by Wehrmacht troops, along with Lt. Thomas G. Fraser, copilot, Lt. H. R. Smith, Mickey operator, S.Sgt. William D. English, radio operator, and S.Sgt. Steve Ferman, engineer. The seventh man to jump was not among those taken prisoner by the German troops. It is believed that the tail-gunner, Staff Sergeant Riedell, did not bail out and went down with the airplane. Three members of the crew were unaccounted for: Lt. Gordon Wiebe, pilot, Lt. John M. Stolberg, navitator, and Lieutenant Glover, bombardier. Fasick and Smith were held as POWs in a German hospital in Steenwijk, Holland, until April 12, when they were liberated by the Canadian First Army.

The target for the Black Liberators on the night of February 23 was the marshaling yards at Neuss. Twenty-four aircraft successfully bombed the target in bomber stream, with unobserved results because of cloud. Two B-24s reported attacks by fighters, but all aircraft returned to Harrington. Twenty-three B-24s bombed the yards at Wilhelmshaven on the night of February 27. The RAF sent twelve Mosquitos as fighter cover from the initial point to the target. Light, ineffective flak was encountered over the target area. One B-24 reported flak being fired from a boat; another received major damage from flak and was forced to land at Woodbridge with three crew members slightly injured.

The target for the night of February 28 was the goods depot at Freiburg. The RAF sent twenty-four Mosquitos as fighter cover. Flak was light, and no fighters were seen. After twenty-two B-24s dropped bombs from 19,000 feet, several fires were reported in the target area and results were believed good. The Black Liberators bombed the railway docks at Emden on the night of March 3 with very good results. Flak was meager, no fighters were sighted, and there was no battle damage. The RAF sent twelve Mosquitos for cover.

A night bombing mission was flown on March 5 to the railway station at Wiesbaden. Thirty-one B-24s bombed in bomber stream on markers laid down by PFF aircraft from 19,000 feet through 10/10 undercast. Twelve RAF Mosquitos went along as fighter cover. Targets were hit on the night of March 7 by nineteen B-24s. One airplane was damaged, and the Liberator flown by Lt. Joseph A. Imperato was reported missing. A few more night bombing missions were flown during March and April, all without aircraft losses.

On March 12, the 857th Squadron was relieved. A majority of the combat personnel joined the 856th and 858th squadrons, with Maj. Charles G. Daby, Capt. Tommy King, Capt. Roscoe E. Klinger, and Lt. Roy O. Shackel joining group headquarters. On the thirteenth, Lt. Col. Jack M. Dickerson, CO of the 857th Squadron, also transferred to group headquarters. The designation of the 857th Squadron, with Capt. Ivon Ressler, adjutant, Capt. Paul O. Messner, surgeon, and Capt. Elmo Grove, communications officer, moved to Bassingbourn to become the designation of the First Scouting Force and Weather and Bomber Relay Flight of the First Air Division. (After January 1, 1945, the three bombardment divisions in the Eighth Air Force became air divisions.) Ivon Ressler has described the weather-scouting function of the new force, which flew fighter aircraft ahead of the bombers to find clear routes to the targets, but could find no record of exactly how the decision was made to use the 857th Squadron in this new operation. He has worked out an explanation that he believes is plausible:

> Somebody at a high enough level noticed, or was informed, that the 492d Bomb Group, having run out of Carpetbagger missions, gasoline-hauling missions, night-bombing missions, and day-bombing missions, was not very busy. Soon came the decision to remove most of the 857th Bomb Squadron personnel, including all flying people, and send the rest along with the squadron designation . . . to Bassingbourn, simultaneously transforming the scouting force into the 857th Bomb Squadron. Jackpot! An interesting twist at the end of a variegated career for a heavy bombardment squadron: flying fighters exclusively.[8]

On March 14, the 406th Squadron (Night Leaflet) joined the 492d Bomb Group, moving to Harrington airfield with their more than twenty B-24s and B-17s. On moving day, B-24 No. 41–28871, piloted by Lt. Edwin M. Canner, crashed on landing at Harrington, killing the navigator, F. O. Gerben A. Cochoorn. On the same day, the 856th Squadron, which had been operating independently since October 1944, lost its independent status and came under control of the group.

The radar section of the 406th Squadron was incorporated into the group radar section, which introduced the British "Boozer" system to the group. The "Boozer" was a warning system that enabled combat crews to monitor enemy radar tracking, antiaircraft fire control, and enemy fighter radar from their airplanes. Also at this time, a new and vital aid to Carpetbagger operations — the H2X — was first used. For navigational purposes it proved invaluable in coastal approaches, avoiding flak positions, and locating pinpoints.

# 14    To Berlin and the Alps

In early March the 492d Bomb Group was told by Headquarters, Eighth Air Force, that emphasis henceforth would be on Carpetbagger operations. Because these operations would be carried out in exceptionally dangerous territory, twin-engine A-26 aircraft were brought in. Initially, the A-26s were to be used to drop agents into the city of Berlin. Each agent was equipped with a small transmitter that emitted a conical signal pattern very small in diameter at the point of transmission but some sixty miles in diameter at 40,000 feet.

The A-26s had to be modified for night work, and combat crews trained with the airplane. At this time, missions with the B-24s averaged ten to fifteen each night, but missions with the new A-26s were flown at a much slower pace at first. The armament on the A-26s was removed and a new plexiglass nose was added. The airplane, built by Douglas, could fly at well over 350 miles per hour, with a crew of three or four, and had a range of 1,400 miles. When the armament and armor plate were removed, both the speed and the range were increased dramatically.

The 492d Bomb Group navigator, Maj. Edward C. Tresemer, Jr., was lost on the first A-26 mission, dispatched on March 19 to the Dummer Lake area in Germany to deliver an agent.[1] The aircraft, A-

26 No. 43-22524, was later found on a moor near Bramsche, Germany. All members of the crew were killed.[2] The loss of this aircraft left the group with only four A-26s and one trained combat crew. A few days later another A-26 was lost as the result of a nosewheel failure on landing. Five of the first nine missions were successfully completed with the A-26s.

Ross D. White remembers with admiration the modified A-26:

I had a mission to go and drop two agents in northern Germany, near Kiel, but had to pick them up at a U.S. night fighter base in Germany. Some of the fighter pilots there saw this black-painted A-26 parked on the ramp and became curious. They waited around operations until I came to take off. They asked me where I was going but I could not tell them where I was going or what I was doing. They said they were going on a night mission and would escort me. I then told them "No." They said that since they were flying the radar-equipped P-61 "Black Widow" night fighter I didn't have a choice. That airplane was fast but the A-26 I was using, all stripped down, was faster. I said they would never be able to keep up. They all thought that was nonsense.

I took off, turned on course, finished my mission and returned to land at the fighter base for fuel, where I met some of the same pilots. They said that they had lost me after my first turn out of traffic and were amazed at the speed of the A-26. Because they took off with some of them ahead of me and some behind me they were sure they could keep in touch, with their radar. A couple of them said that they saw me once on their radar but could not keep up.

Incidentally, the two agents were Germans who had surrendered in North Africa. I saw one after the war in Paris, and he said that when I pulled that trap door on him he thought he had bought the farm. They lost their baggage in the drop.[3]

White had a chance to fly the British Mosquito but chose the A-26. The Mosquito was built of plywood by De Havilland, with two 1,636-HP Rolls Royce Merlin twelve-cylinder "V" type engines. Capable of flights of over 40,000 feet, the Mosquito was manned by a crew of three or four and was used for high-altitude work, circling over the agents on the ground and recording, on a small wire, messages transmitted from the ground.

Both the A-26 and the P-61 were powered by two 2,000-HP, 18-cylinder Pratt and Whitney "Double Wasp" radial engines, driving three-blade props on the A-26 and four-blade props on the P-61. An electrically operated trap door was installed in a plywood false floor in the forward part of the A-26 bomb bay. Just prior to dispatching an agent, a green light mounted forward of the trap door was activated by the pilot; this alerted the agent to kneel down on the door and prepare to be dropped. The trap door was then activated from the cockpit.

On March 18, Lt. Randolph J. Sheppard and crew took off from Harrington at 2000 hours for a night cross-country training flight as part of the Carpetbagger OTU program. The crew had shortly before arrived from the States and was assigned to the 857th Squadron and then reassigned to the 856th Squadron. At 2115 hours, while on the Cinderford-Shrewsbury leg at 2,100 feet, their B-24 struck the side of the Berywen mountain range in the vicinity of Llangying, North Wales. At that point the range reached the altitude of 2,150 feet and was estimated at a fifteen-degree incline.

The aircraft had been flying up the valley, and it struck the ground while in level flight, coming to rest 500 yards from the point of impact. The nose and waist sections were smashed and large portions of the fuselage in these sections torn from the aircraft, carrying with them the bodies of the bombardier, the navigator, and both waist-gunners, all of whom were killed instantly. The tail-gunner was thrown out of his turret and landed in the midsection of the airplane, uninjured. He immediately crawled out through the waist window, into a downpour of rain, and climbed up on the wing to help the co-pilot get the rest of the crew out. The copilot was badly shaken up; he had a broken leg, and bruises and lacerations on his face, hands, and legs. Nevertheless, he was able to climb out the window and make a hurried examination of the exterior of the airplane to determine that there was no danger of fire or explosion. The two men freed the engineer from the upper turret, then helped the injured radio operator and the pilot to get out through the escape hatch. The pilot had leg and skull fractures and serious cuts. The radio operator had a broken pelvis. Parachutes were used for bandages and to shelter the injured men from the rain.

The copilot and the tail-gunner then set out in different directions to seek help. The tail-gunner made his way along the mountainside in the darkness and rain, but, unable to see, he soon decided to return to the wrecked airplane before he became lost. He later learned that had he gone any further he would have walked into a quicksand bog, and beyond that was a 500-foot cliff. The copilot moved down the mountain and just before dawn found a shepherd, who rode him on the handlebars of his bicycle to the headquarters of the Home Guard.

There a search and rescue party was formed. They had a hard time finding the wreck in the rain and fog, but suddenly out of the mists a flare burning in a slow arch gave the rescue party the location of the crash site. The radio operator had managed to crawl back into the wrecked airplane, where he found a flare and the flare gun; he was able to get only halfway out before he became exhausted, fired the flare, and collapsed.

The injured were taken down the mountain and were evacuated by RAF and civilian ambulances to a hospital nearby. John A. Rogers, Val D. Shaefer, Willie Kouser, and Whitney Holata were buried with full military honors at the Cambridge American Military Cemetery on March 23, 1945.[4]

Early in the month, OSS headquarters had informed Eighth Air Force headquarters that the full and exclusive use of the 856th Squadron would be required for upcoming supply and intelligence missions. All Carpetbagger operations were to continue under the 492d Bomb Group, with operational control of the 406th, 856th, and 858th squadrons retained by Eighth Air Force headquarters. If the OSS requirements exceeded the capability of the 856th Squadron, then the 858th was to be used as needed. The First Air Division was told several times during the month that the 492d Bomb Group's status was still "secret" as far as publicity was concerned, and no date had been set for the removal of the classification.

On March 19, detachments of the 856th and 858th squadrons were sent to Dijon, France, to begin operations from there. Agents and transmitters were to be dropped into the mountainous and dangerous "National Redoubt" area in southern Germany and the Austrian Alps. Intelligence was badly needed by the Allied armies, which had by that time advanced deep into Germany. The airplanes used were mostly B-24s, but some A-26s and Mosquitos were used on a total of fifty-four missions, with intelligence acquired from eighty-five agents, all of it invaluable to the Allied armies. These missions also enabled the group to check for the first time the efficiency of LORAN instruments inside Germany.

The Dijon detachment was made up of personnel of both the 856th and 858th squadrons, with Capt. Milton Shapiro, 856th Squadron S-2, as intelligence officer. Capt. Joseph W. Hartley was the first commanding officer and operations officer, followed by Capt. George Bledsoe, Jr., then by Capt. Clifton G. Clark. Staff and combat personnel lived in tents on the field with no floors and no running water. The airfield had not been used for night operations, and special arrangements had to be made for the Carpetbagger airplanes. A major problem was the lack of special heavy equipment for maintaining the aircraft, with a lesser problem being a shortage of personnel.

The operational cycle at Dijon began at 1200 hours daily, when the OSS telephoned a list of missions to Captain Shapiro. A weather and bombline check determined which missions could be undertaken that night, and the CO then assigned missions to the crews. An effort was made to combine as many targets as possible for each crew, as there was a maximum of four crews available at Dijon. The number of targets assigned depended on the distribution of enemy airfields and antiaircraft guns, and the aircraft load for each target, with the maximum being three targets for each crew. A teletype message was then dispatched to the advanced movement liaison officer, giving data on the missions and serving as clearance through Seventh Army and First French Army lines and Allied night fighter patrols. However, when time was short and the situation called for a change of pinpoint, Dijon assumed the initiative of making any needed changes.

During the afternoon, current flak information was obtained. At 1630 hours Captain Shapiro briefed the crews flying that night's missions, and a final weather briefing was given before takeoff. Upon their return, the crews were interrogated by intelligence, and weather information obtained during the mission was immediately forwarded to the station weather officer. This was most valuable for the medium bombers scheduled for takeoff soon after the Carpetbagger aircraft returned. Complete information from interrogations was sent to Harrington, along with reports on the night's missions.

Strictest security was successfully maintained throughout the operations at Dijon. An indication of the effectiveness of security control was the extreme curiosity shown by First Tactical Air Force personnel stationed at Dijon. Their speculations about the black-painted Liberators ranged from radar-jamming or leaflet operations to reconnaissance, but no unauthorized person was known to have guessed the truth.

The DOCTOR team, consisting of a radio operator and an observer, was the first team to work with the guerrillas in Austria. The two men were recruited in Belgium in November 1944. Secret intelligence staffs in London trained and equipped them, supplied documents, and arranged to have them dispatched from Dijon by the 492d

Group. The radio operator was a Belgian from the Belgian Air Ministry, where he had worked as a telegraph operator; he had also worked as a carpenter. The observer, a Belgian from Boitsfort, was the son of a government official. He was of independent means and had been a student all of his adult life.

A mission was accepted to send this team into the region of Kufstein, in the Austrian Alps, on the border between Bavaria and Austria. From this point they would be in a position to check on traffic to and from the Brenner Pass, and they could also see what was happening in the National Redoubt region of Salzburg-Rosenheim and Berchtesgaden. The observer had a safe address in Kufstein.

A pinpoint was chosen by the Belgian Desk and the Eighth Air Force, on top of a plateau — Coore, some twelve kilometers south of Kufstein. This plateau was an excellent spot for dropping agents, being protected by woods all around, but it was an extremely difficult pinpoint to find. The Carpetbagger airplane had to navigate first to a mountain named Kitzbuhlerhorn, then take a course straight to the west over very dangerous country.

Beginning on the night of March 2, three attempts were made to complete the mission. A successful drop was finally made on the target at 0038 hours on March 23 by the crew of Capt. George Bledsoe of the 858th Squadron. Weather conditions in the Bavarian Alps made the drop extremely difficult, but in clear moonlight the two agents were safely parachuted from the B-24 into five feet of snow. A message from them two days later reported that they had been rescued by three men who were by strange coincidence deserters from the Wehrmacht, hoping to start a mountain resistance movement. The three men had, only the night before, spread a large Austrian flag on top of a nearby mountain, hoping to attract the attention of Allied flyers and obtain assistance with their movement. The two agents said nothing to discourage the three deserters' admiration and astonishment at the speed of the Allied response.

On March 28, another message was received from the team, requesting food, supplies, weapons, radio, and clothing to be dropped on the night of April 2. After a security check sent to the team on March 31 proved that they were safe and the information being sent out was genuine, this second drop was made, again by Captain Bledsoe's crew.

From their mountain hut, the team joined the three Wehrmacht deserters in working to build up a network of sabotage and intelligence agents in the area. Fourteen containers were dropped with arms and supplies on April 2 and twelve more were dropped on April 24, along with two more agent teams consisting of two Dutchmen each. In all, sixty-six messages were received from the three teams. All contained extremely valuable information, such as the locations of a jet base near Munich, a trainload of gasoline, and an oil depot in the Halle area.

On April 26, 1945, a Distinguished Unit Citation was awarded the 492d Bombardment Group (H) for operations from Dijon. The citation read, in part, as follows:

> 1. Since March 18, 1945, the 492d Bomb Group has completed for this organization 54 successful operations from the Dijon base. This is an extraordinary record of achievement which has been accomplished in the face of innumerable difficulties. . . . The officers did everything in their power to be cooperative and helpful. We cannot commend too highly the work done by all officers and men involved, especially the Commanding Officer and the Intelligence Officer.
>
> 2. Although it is impossible at this time to evaluate fully the results of these operations . . . the information already obtained from the agents who were dropped has been of very great value to the Allied armies. . . . It is safe to say that no group of this size has made a greater contribution to the war effort.

# 15      Victory in Europe: Mission Completed

At the beginning of April 1945, Adolf Hitler and Nazi Germany were on the ropes, but Hitler's dream of dividing his enemies still appeared a remote possibility. Relations between the Western Allies and the Russians had never been good, and now that the common enemy was being pushed back the Soviet Union had become more difficult than ever because the British and the Americans had become less essential to its safety. The Russian belief that the Western world would overthrow Stalin's regime if possible surfaced all too plainly as the war in the west reached its climax. The Soviet Union feared that the Western Allies might come to terms with the Germans on the western front, leaving the Russian forces on their own in the east.

In order to prevent the possibility of an accidental clash, Gen. Dwight D. Eisenhower insisted on a clearly marked line of demarcation between the advancing Western Allied armies and the Russian forces. The American Ninth Army reached the Elbe River on April 11, 1945.

Top priority was given to Carpetbagger operations throughout April, for stiff resistance was still being put up by the enemy. Three Carpetbagger Liberators and crews went MIA while on missions to Norway. Lt. Eugene Polanski and his crew, of the 856th Squadron, with four or six men of the Norwegian operations group of OSS, were lost on the night of March 31 when they crashed in the Orkney Islands off the north coast of Scotland.[1] Nothing is known of the cause of the crash. On the night of April 6, while on a mission to Norway, the 856th Squadron crew of Lt. William H. Hudson went MIA. Word was received on April 30 that the B-24 had crashed into the slope of a mountain and all crew members were killed.

A couple of weeks earlier, on the night of March 24, several 856th Squadron crews, including the crews of Lt. Donald F. Heran and Lieutenant Hudson, had flown a mission to Jaevsjo, Norway, to drop ski troops.[2] After takeoff from Harrington airfield, they flew to Lossiemouth, Scotland (an RAF station), where their B-24s were re-fueled. The drop area was a frozen lake, completely surrounded by mountains, straddling the Norway-Sweden border northeast of Trondheim. All went well with the drop despite the fact that all of Norway looked the same at night in the winter: nothing but snow and mountains. On their way home, they refueled at Lossiemouth again, then returned to Harrington.

A few days later, it was learned that the troops that Lieutenant Heran had dropped were on target and landed safely, but Lieutenant Hudson's crew had had one minor "glitch" in their drop: they had dumped the troops out on the wrong lake quite a distance from the target, and in Sweden! After "capturing" a native and determining their location, they proceeded to the nearest town and boarded a train for Stockholm, where they managed to procure a flight back to England.

Early in the month of April, the copilot on Hudson's crew, while fooling around in the bar at the officers' mess, fell off a bar stool and broke his arm. When the time came for another mission to drop the troops who had previously missed the target, Hudson's crew was selected again for the trip, only this time with a different copilot. The mission on the night of April 6 was flown in the same manner as that of March 24. This time they found the right lake, but for reasons unknown, crashed into the surrounding mountains with the loss of all crew members and four OSS men.[3] An American OSS detachment of para-ski-troops headed by Maj. William E. Colby heard the crash of the airplane on April 7, but it was April 29 before the site was located. The bodies of the Hudson crew and four members of the Norwegian operations group of OSS killed in the crash were removed from the wreck and wrapped in parachutes.[4] The OSS men were Lt. Blaine E. Jones, SC; Cpl. Knut J. Falck; T-5 Bernard N. Iverson; and T-3 Robert N. Anderson. All were buried under a rock cairn on Pluk-ketjernfjeld Mountain, overlooking Lang Lake. After a short cere-mony, three volleys were fired over the common grave, and an American flag was placed to mark the location.

Lt. Donald F. Heran and crew flew twenty-four missions: four-teen to Norway and Denmark from Harrington, and ten to Germany and Austria from Dijon. Heran has written the following account:

> The missions were interesting because we never knew what we were carrying until we arrived at the aircraft. On some missions we had the whole bomb bay filled with canisters of automatic weapons and ammo. On others we carried all sorts of supplies from bicycle tires to medicines. On all missions from Dijon, except one, we carried per-sonnel. An Alsatian girl (17 years) was dropped at Munich. On an-other mission a Wehrmacht corporal in full uniform was also dropped near Munich. A group of French "organizers" were dropped close to a French prison camp near Regensburg. An entire mobile hospital was dropped on a mountain near Kitzbuhel, Austria. Com-munications men were dropped at Hof, Plauen, and Chemnitz, Ger-many. It was not what we were trained to do in the United States but it was different and exciting.[5]

Lt. Ralph W. Keeney and crew, of the 858th Squadron, went MIA while on a mission to Norway on the night of April 20.[6] At ap-proximately fifteen miles inside the coast, Lieutenant Divine suddenly felt the B-24 shudder. He thought that they had been hit by flak, but when he looked down he saw a German ME-110 night fighter below them. The pilot tried to escape the attack, but the enemy fighter suc-cessfully knocked a large hole in the main gasoline tank, and the flaps and aileron on the left side were shot out. The pilot tried to reach Swe-den, but after encountering intense antiaircraft fire he sounded the bail-out alarm. Everyone reached the ground safely except Marangus, who was unable to find his parachute; he jumped piggy-back with Bra-bec, but he either slipped or jumped when some distance from the ground and was killed.

The men were taken to several different civilian hospitals, where some were arrested by German troops while undergoing treatment. Those who were taken prisoner were released on May 7, when the Ger-mans acknowledged their capitulation by moving all Allied POWs into rooms without bars on the windows or guards in the halls.

At about this time Colonel Fish requested of the commanding

general, USSTAF, through the First Air Division, the destruction of airfields in northern Denmark and southern Norway, from which German night fighters were operating. The 492d Bomb Group was sending airplanes to these countries at low altitudes during the hours of darkness, and the sorties were being flown by individual aircraft that were extremely vulnerable to attack by fighters with radar. Losses of the group had increased materially during April. It was expected that still heavier fighter attacks would occur because of an anticipated increase of concentration of German fighters in Norway and Denmark. But a reply from Headquarters, Eighth Air Force, by command of General Doolittle, stated that, because of the tactical situation and political considerations involved, it was deemed inadvisable to attack any Norwegian airfields at that time.

On a hot and sunny day in mid-April, the personnel of Harrington airfield gathered to honor the late commander-in-chief and president of the United States, Franklin Delano Roosevelt. President Roosevelt had died at Warm Springs, Georgia, at 1635 hours on April 12. The American flag was flapping softly in the slow breeze at half staff; roaring warplanes passed over on their way to and from the day's operations. At the base of the flag, surrounded by a guard of honor, wreaths and flowers were laid as a final tribute.

During the last three weeks of April, Carpetbagger missions to Norway and Denmark were carried out to seventeen targets on 160 sorties with only twenty-seven failures. Very few A-26 missions were being flown, as the Western Allied armies were rapidly advancing and anticipated targets were now behind the lines. "Red Stocking" missions being flown by the Mosquito aircraft were averaging one each night with good success. Seven new crews joined the group and were immediately placed in training for Carpetbagger work. Several Carpetbagger airplanes and crews made emergency landings at fields on the Continent within territory now occupied by Allied armies. Had these landings been made two or three months earlier, both the airplanes and their crews would have been lost.

During the middle of April, a change in command of the 492d Bomb Group was made. Lt. Col. Robert W. Fish again became CO of the group, relieving Col. Hudson H. Upham, who was appointed CO of the 306th Bomb Group (H) at Thurleigh.

At 2033 hours on the night of April 26, Lt. Jean R. Anderson and his 406th Squadron crew departed on their seventh leaflet-dropping mission to northwestern Germany. After reaching 8,000 feet they ran into very foul weather, with four to five inches of ice forming on the cowling. The power was turned off, and after gliding to 6,000 feet the ailerons locked. The bail-out alarm was immediately sounded: Lieutenant Halle, the copilot, was the last one to jump. Anderson stayed with the airplane to allow the others to get out, but as the co-pilots' chute opened the airplane hit the ground and exploded. Lieutenant Anderson never had a chance to bail out.

During April 1945, two villages in France paid tribute to five American airmen who had died there in a crash one year before. The villagers of St. Cyr de Valorge and Tarare built a monument to honor these men, and when it was to be dedicated Lt. Col Robert Boone was invited to be present as a representative of the American Carpetbagger units. This was to be the first of a series of memorials to honor Allied airmen who had died delivering supplies and agents to the French resistance forces.

The public square at St. Cyr, near where the crash had occurred, was packed with people from the two villages. Flags of France, the United States, and Great Britain were flying, while bands played the national anthems of the three countries. There was much cheering, and hundreds were in tears as speakers told of the stirring days of the resistance. The official party and the villagers then gathered in the village church, where a priest spoke, eulogizing the fliers. After the mass, the villagers moved to the monument for dedication. Colonel Boone gave his address, which was translated into French by an interpreter. He said that he was happy to be on the ground in daytime to see the beauty of the country — something that was impossible to see at night — and to feel the warmth of the French people — impossible to feel in a Liberator airplane. He said that the men in his outfit remembered the dead men well, and to him the ceremony was evidence that the men fought not only for, but with, France in the War of Liberation. After the ceremony, the party moved to a banquet hall for dinner. Colonel Boone was given Lieutenant Ambrose's identification tags and part of his bracelet, which he promised to send to the lieutenant's relatives in the United States.

The five men in whose honor the monument was erected were Lt. George W. Ambrose, pilot; Lt. Robert H. Redhair, copilot; Lt. Arthur B. Pope, navigator; Lt. Peter Roccia, bombardier; and S.Sgt. Charles M. Wilson, engineer.

On April 25, 1945, patrols of the 69th Division of the V Corps, which had seen action in the thick of the battle of the beaches at Normandy, met elements of the Russian army's 58th Guards Division on the Elbe at Torgau, about seventy-five miles south of Berlin. The final severance of Nazi Germany was complete. During this time the Eighth Air Force thoroughly pounded Berchtesgaden, on the border between Bavaria and Austria, which was a symbol of Nazi invincibility. By the third of May, Berlin was in flames and the northern flak of the Russian army was sweeping across Germany. All German resistance collapsed, and German troops began giving themselves up to the Allied armies by the thousands. On May 7, at 0241 hours at Reims, France, the unconditional surrender of Germany was signed at General Eisenhower's headquarters. The next day was officially declared V-E Day.

Many of the personnel of the Carpetbagger units had started second tours of duty by V-E Day, and some had finished second tours. Capt. Abe M. Thompson and Lt. David C. Groff had started second tours, this time in the A-26 airplane. They flew five missions in A-26s; one was a drop within the city of Berlin. Then on May 10, two days after V-E Day, they flew ten members of the Norwegian exile government back to Oslo, the capital of Norway.

On June 5, Colonel Fish was relieved as CO of the 492d Bomb Group and transferred to the 41st Combat Wing in France to become CO of the 384th Bombardment Group at Istres. Lt. Col. Jack M. Dickerson replaced Colonel Fish but was on leave at the time of his appointment. Lt. Col. Robert Boone was relieved as CO of the 858th Squadron on the same day and transferred to group headquarters as temporary CO. On the sixth, Maj. Ernest S. Holzworth assumed command of the 858th Squadron. The next day Colonel Dickerson returned from leave and assumed the duties of group commanding officer; Colonel Boone then became group executive officer.

Group personnel's main preoccupation during June concerned the final disposition of the 492d Bomb Group and its 406th, 856th, and 858th squadrons. Combat crews were kept busy, coming and going daily to and from the Continent, flying for OSS with VIPs and material to such points as Oslo, Copenhagen, Wiesbaden, and Paris. On June 30, Capt. Roscoe E. Klinger assumed the duties of group assistant adjutant.

Crew training was being kept up, particularly of the navigators, in anticipation of movement to another theater of operations. However, because of the high state of efficiency required of the combat crews throughout operations in the Carpetbagger special project, the training was mostly routine. Morale was sky high when it was finally learned that the 492d Bomb Group would return to the States.

Early in July, Major Holzworth became CO of the group. Captain Klinger was appointed adjutant. In mid-July, Captain Thompson and Lieutenant Groff were assigned a B-24D to fly home across the Atlantic. On this, their flight home, they carried as passengers Lt. Col. Rodman St. Clair, CO of the 856th Squadron, and his staff. They all kissed the ground at Bradley Field, Connecticut. The date was July 16, 1945.

Former 856th Squadron Flight Leader Abe Thompson's keenest memories are of World War II and crew No. 2911: "That was a time of testing, and only good men passed the test." [7] Bestow Rudolph, former operations officer of the 858th Squadron, recalls, "The Carpetbagger work was most interesting and I have said many times that if I must fight another war I want to do the same thing — but then I stop and think that I was crazy to do all the different things I did and maybe I should re-think that statement." [8]

Robert W. Fish, a former group CO, has written:

> Most of the men actually engaged in the Carpetbagger mission never did know the whole story. For security reasons we attempted to give to any one individual only that information which he needed to conduct his portion of the total mission. I can understand why many of the people who participated give the impression of being confused. Our security program was successful. [9]

# Photographs

*(Top)* General William J. Donovan and aide at "Area H" with Robert L. Stroud (right). Photo-Stroud. *(Middle)* William E. Colby (right). Photo-Stroud. *(Bottom)* Prince Serge Obolensky (center) prepares for mission. Photo-Stroud.

*(Top)* Robert L. Boone above piano. Photo-Rudolph. *(Middle)* Left to right: Lyman A. Sanders, Robert L. Williams, unidentified ladies, Rodman A. St. Clair, and James E. Estes. Photo-Rudolph. *(Bottom)* Left to right: Heflin, Tresemer, Stapel, Teer, Krasevac, with Nazi banner given them by the Maquis of Ain. Photo-Ressler.

The King and Queen of England at Alconbury. Photo-Rudolph.

Bob Hope at Alconbury. Photo-Rudolph.

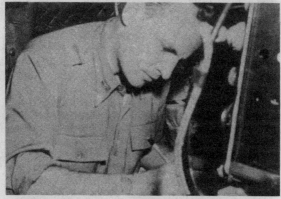

*(Top)* Left to right: Newcomb, Heiberg, Ressler, Bacon, Kuntz. Girls are employees of American Red Cross. Photo-Ressler. *(Middle)* Fred W. Edwards, killed in a fall, September 1944. Photo-Rudolph. *(Bottom)* Sanders and Callahan with badly burned crewmate, Sadler. Photo-Ressler.

(*Top*) Part of 20,000 1903 Springfield rifles to be packed for dropping. Background: Small arms ammunition packed for dropping. Photo-Stroud. (*Middle*) Agents receiving French francs. Photo-Stroud. (*Bottom*) Female Nazi collaborators with shaven heads. Annecy, France. Photo-Rudolph.

*(Top)* Hotel Beau Rivage at Lake Annecy in October 1983. Photo-Beaman.
*(Middle)* Memento from Hotel Beau Rivage. Photo-Stroud. *(Bottom)* Hotel in
Paris. Photo-Rudolph.

*(Top)* Grave of William W. Nicoll and four crewmates in France. Photo-Ressler. *(Middle)* Albright at Cambridge American Cemetery, June 1984. Photo-Albright. *(Bottom)* For many there was no flight home.

*(Top)* Containers loaded into B-24 at Harrington. Photo-Stroud. *(Middle)* B-24s on ground, C-47 takes off in background. Photo-Ressler. *(Bottom)* Carpetbagger B-24D at rest. Photo-Ressler.

*(Top)* General Koenig of France, Commander of the FFI, decorates the Carpetbaggers and General Doolittle. Photo-Ressler. *(Middle)* Rudolph crew with Maquis at Annecy. Johnny Mead is in front center. Photo-Rudolph. *(Bottom)* R. C. McLaughlin crew. Photo-Arlin.

*(Top)* 492d Bomb Group Staff and Squadron Commanders: Seated, left to right: Cummings, St. Clair, McManus, Fish, Heflin, Edenfield, Boone, Dickerson, Teer. Standing, left to right: Bell, Akers, Watkins, Kucer, Fletcher. Gans, Tresemer, Sanders, Bosworth, Cunningham, Barber, Silkenbaken, Sullivan, Messer. Photo–Ressler. *(Middle)* Ambrose crew prior to leaving USA. Photo-Heddleson. *(Bottom)* Beaman (center) and friends at Annecy in January 1945. Photo-Beaman.

*(Top)* Coleman crew with crew chief. Photo-Ressler. *(Middle)* Bales crew prior to leaving USA. Photo-Bales. *(Bottom)* Left to right: Bowen, Bronar, Dixon, and Kibbie at combat crew rest home O/A January 1945. Photo-J. Bronar.

*(Top)* Crance crew. Photo-Rudolph. *(Middle)* Fitzpatrick crew. Photo-Rudolph. *(Bottom)* Harrison crew. Photo-Rudolph.

*(Top)* Hartley crew. Photo-Rudolph. *(Middle)* Heran crew prior to leaving USA. Photo-Heran. *(Bottom)* Holzworth crew. Photo-Rudolph.

*(Top)* Jackson crew. Photo-Rudolph. *(Middle)* Kelly crew. Photo-Rudolph. *(Bottom)* Lee crew. Photo-Allan.

*(Top)* Mead crew. Photo-Rudolph. *(Middle)* McKenny crew. Photo-Rudolph.
*(Bottom)* Lemke crew. Photo-Bradley.

*(Top)* Melinat crew. Photo-Ressler. *(Middle)* Peavyhouse crew. Photo-Rudolph. *(Bottom)* Pipkin crew. Photo-Rudolph.

*(Top)* Pratt crew. Photo-Rudolph. *(Middle)* Rudolph crew with crew chief. Photo-Rudolph. *(Bottom)* Seger crew prior to leaving USA. Photo-Seger.

*(Top)* Simon crew. Photo-K. Simon. *(Middle)* Smith crew. Photo-Rudolph.
*(Bottom)* Stapel crew. Photo-Stapel.

*(Top)* Stinchcomb crew. Photo-Rudolph. *(Middle)* Van Zyl crew with ground crew. Photo-Rudolph. *(Bottom)* Thompson crew prior to leaving USA. Photo-Parnell.

*(Top)* Ward crew. Photo-Ebner. *(Middle)* Wiebe crew. Photo-Ressler.
*(Bottom)* Wolcott crew. Photo-Wolcott.

St. Clair, CO 856th
Squadron.
Photo-Ressler

Dickerson, CO 857th
Squadron.
Photo-Ressler

Boone, CO 858th
Squadron.
Photo-Ressle

Colonel Heflin, CO
492d Bomb Group.
Photo-Ressler

Lt. Colonel Fish, Dep-
uty CO 492d Bomb
Group.   Photo-Ressler

McManus, CO 859th
Squadron.
Photo-Ressler

*(Left)* Garrett C.
Parnell, Jr.

*(Right)* Schreiner at
Leuchars AFB,
Scotland.
Photo-Schreiner

Items packed into containers. Photo-Stroud.

Pass issued by FFI. Photo-Stapel.

Beaman at Lake Annecy in October 1983. Photo-Beaman.

Lake Annecy and the French Alps. Photo-Rudolph.

# Addenda to Revised Edition

Soon after *Carpetbaggers* was published, I received a letter from a French aviation historian who lives in Lyon. His name is Serge Blandin. He wrote, "The problem with that kind of book is that it can never be considered as definitive." And later, "Many corrections will have to be made (there is no such book without corrections!)."

He was right on both counts. This addenda section is an effort to correct at least a few of the errors and to bring it up to date in some areas.

I knew that *Carpetbaggers* was not conclusive, that many more stories and photographs would show up. And I think that even after the last Carpetbagger has passed on to greater things there will be stories untold and stories unpublished. It is not possible to record in a book like this all the history, all the good times, all the bad times, all the heartaches, headaches, and jubilation experienced by the men of the Carpetbaggers over a period of twenty long months in their young lives.

My conscience was soothed somewhat when Col. Robert W. Fish compiled his excellent book, *We Flew By Night*, which contains numerous first-person accounts of graphically described single-crew missions deep in enemy territory in the dark of night at treetop altitudes. Dedication, determination and personal sacrifice in times of downright terror and fear were almost standard operating procedure for combat crews with a single-minded purpose of getting the job done.

And back at the base, awaiting their return, were their friends and comrades, those who performed all the endless intricate and detailed work of maintenance on the airplanes, planning the missions, and all the thousands of other vital and essential duties that went with the flying of every single mission. These are things that do not show up in the records. These skilled people were fundamental to getting the job done. Without them, nothing would have been accomplished, nothing proved.

Among the airbase supporting units at Harrington were Headquarters and Headquarters Squadron, 39th Service Group, 1094th Quartermaster Company, 21st and 32nd Engineer Company with F and E Platoons, 352nd Service Squadron, 35th Station Complement Squadron, 1077th Signal Company, Group Radar Section, 1561st Ordnance with S&M Company, 18th Weather Detachment, 1020th Chemical Company, Base Medical Detachment, and 1139th MP Company.

In September 1988 I was honored to be invited to a Carpetbagger reunion in Las Vegas, where I met many of the men I had written about in the book. I was surprised to find so many interested in their old outfit — thanks to the movers and shakers of the 801st/492nd Bomb Group Association: Sebastian Corriere, president; Igor "Pete" Petrenko, secretary-treasurer; Richard "Si" Sizemore, vice-president and editor of the association newsletter, "The Carpetbagger"; and Ivon Ressler, director (now deceased).

It has been written that the Carpetbaggers were the only group assembled entirely from personnel already in the ETO. The original group was assembled from personnel who had arrived in England in August 1943 and had roots going back to the United States and prewar operations in California and later anti-submarine patrols off the East Coast, then anti-sub operations in the Bay of Biscay. In May 1944, two squadrons, the 788th and 850th, were brought in as complete units from heavy bomber groups flying high-altitude daylight bombing missions. Then in August 1944, twelve complete crews and four or five partial crews were brought in as filler crews from the disbanded 492nd Bomb Group based at North Pickenham. And, throughout operations, until the end of the war, a number of replacement crews and ground personnel were brought in from the States.

There were, then, five sources of personnel: the originals — Colonel Heflin's flyers, the 788th Squadron, the 850th

Squadron, crews from the disbanded 492nd BG, and replacement crews and ground personnel from the States.

Various individuals have had an opportunity to submit stories covering these five sources. Those contributions, prepared from memory, that appear here do much toward preserving the history of the Carpetbaggers. There are a number of men who performed magnificently and played a very important part in the Carpetbagger project but are not listed in the book. Sadly, their exploits are not reflected in the records that I have been able to obtain. I ask these men who are not listed to please accept this humble apology.

It should be noted here that there are numerous groups of avid and tenacious historians in France who, since World War II, have constantly researched old records and searched the French countryside for the crash sites of crews who went down while flying missions to help the French Resistance movement. The French people have not forgotten the Carpetbaggers and those who died in France. They have marked at least four of the Carpetbagger crash sites with impressive and well-kept memorials.

My thanks to all whose stories and photographs are included in this section. Also, a special thanks to Serge Blandin for his help with the spelling of French names and places and for numerous photographs. I apologize to those whose stories, for whatever reason, remain untold and unpublished.

—Ben Parnell

## From the Commanding Officers

The Carpetbagger mission during WWII in Europe was unique in the history of aerial warfare. The mission required long flights during the hours of darkness, at extremely low altitudes, deep into enemy territory. The missions were somewhat protected by the nap of the earth. In fact, the low altitudes at which most of the missions were flown provided their principal protective measure. The enemy's primitive radars could not readily detect them as they scurried across the landscape at treetop level.

Precise navigation was the prerequisite for success. Radio aids were non-existent. Pilotage and dead reckoning were our only reliable guides.

The group conducted a night vision school wherein crew members learned to greatly enhance their ability to see in the dark. Our surface maps of the continent of Europe were extremely accurate and in great detail. Trained crew members could discern those details, thereby confirming the location of their aircraft.

The original Carpetbagger crews were coerced into the mission. They had no choice. Subsequently, replacement crew members were offered some options. The mission and the procedures of Carpetbagger flights were explained to each new crew joining the group. They were offered an option. If they chose not to participate in the Carpetbagger mission, they would be assigned as replacement crew members in high-altitude daylight bombing units. I can recall only two crew members who took advantage of this option. Both were pilots.

By the concepts and procedures employed in our missions, we developed some of the best and most experienced instrument flying combat crews in the 8th Air Force. The Carpetbaggers flew when other mission crews stood down due to weather.

The Carpetbagger mission provided a most unique way for American airmen to strike telling blows against the German forces occupying the continent of Europe. This very uniqueness produced an esprit de corps among all members of the group.

— Robert W. Fish, Group Commander

## 36th/856th Squadron

Graduation and "wings" led several of us from San Antonio to March Field, California. In early 1942 I was reassigned to the 41st Bomb Group at Muroc Dry Lake in California and reported to a 1st Lt. Clifford Heflin, a big, robust, quiet officer — unless provoked.

We flew A-29s on anti-submarine patrol off the West Coast. Our planes were parked in small revetments spread out over the airfield. When an air alert sounded, we raced to our planes to await take-off orders, hoping they wouldn't come. If the orders came, we would gun the plane straight ahead and hope we were not on a collision course with another aircraft.

The 41st BG then transferred to Hammer Field, California,

and flew West Coast missions from there and TDY from Alameda Naval Air Station at Oakland, California. While at Hammer Field we were sent to Bakersfield, California, to check out in B-25s. Lieutenant Heflin was promoted to captain.

In August 1942, the 46th Squadron, led by now Major Heflin, transferred to Cherry Point Marine Air Station, North Carolina. We patrolled the East Coast for submarines. It was here that the 46th Squadron became the 22nd Anti-submarine Squadron. In April of 1943 the 22nd AS moved to Wilmington, North Carolina. We continued to fly anti-sub missions from Wilmington. However, excitement reigned as a few of us at a time were sent to Langley Field, Virginia, to receive training in the B-24 airplane.

Following a short temporary duty of anti-sub missions at Westover Field, Massachusetts, we were back at Wilmington getting ready to go somewhere. Then orders came and we were sent to England via Presque Isle, Maine, and Gander, Newfoundland. Landed at Prestwick, Scotland, after an overnight flight from Gander, then to Dunkeswell, England. When we left the States Heflin was a lieutenant colonel, my good friend Bob Boone a captain, and I was a first lieutenant.

When we started the Carpetbagger Project, I was a captain, the 22nd AS had become the 801st Bomb Group, Bob Boone had assumed command of the 406th Squadron, and I had assumed command of the 36th Squadron. The 801st BG had only two squadrons in the beginning. By the time the group settled down at Harrington Army Air Base near Kettering, both Boone and I were majors, Bob Fish was a lieutenant colonel, and Heflin a colonel. Boone and I were majors only thirty days when we were promoted to lieutenant colonel.

The chronological story of the 22nd Anti-submarine Squadron becoming the 36th and 406th Bomb Squadrons, then the 36th BS becoming the 856th BS and the 406th BS becoming the 858th BS, has already been told as well as I could tell it.

The work with the OSS was intriguing and interesting and without it the war would have been extended immeasurably.

I have never been associated with a finer group of men in Group Headquarters and especially the 856th Squadron before the war or since. In all cases they were dedicated, fearless in action, gentlemen off duty, more than committed as shown by the records attained. Losses were high, but the camaraderie excelled.

I add a personal note that the 856th, both officers and men, served in a gallant manner and can be as proud of themselves as I am of them.

Many interesting anecdotes and humorous instances, aside from the reality of war, could fill a book. Those involved quickly coming to mind are Pinky Williams, Sergeant Booth, Cliff Fulton, Sam Marshall, Ben Mead, Sebastian Corriere, Ernie Holzworth, Crickett Garrett, Ed Tresemer, Mac McClarren, and on and on and on.

I have the highest and warmest regard for each within the 856th.

—Rodman A. St. Clair

## 850th/857th Squadron

Jack M. Dickerson, squadron commander, is deceased.

## 406th/858th Squadron

I would like to pay tribute to Col. Clifford J. Heflin. He became my squadron commander when I reported to Hammer Field, Fresno, California in March of 1942. Cliff Heflin was a tough duck huntin', deer shootin', poker playin', cigar smokin', two fisted man's man. Saint (Rod St. Clair), Ed Tresemer and I spent this kind of quality time with him before we became too busy during the war, and these hours were enjoyed without any loss of his authority. From the very beginning at Fresno, the then Captain Heflin was truly in command. He expected his men to achieve superiority and we did. He was a superb pilot. His vigil over operations resulted in constant training which led to the high success rate of our missions overseas. Bob Fish was his second in command and right arm before he himself took over the group.

Mine was a fine squadron of young men. Most of us were in our early or middle twenties, a few in our teens, a few more thirty or a bit over. Charles McClarran, my executive officer, kept the administrative end running smoothly. Dr. Loren Martin and the other medics saw to our aches and pains and dispensed air crews their ~~whiskey~~ medication after each mis-

sion. Red Drasher was such an outstanding line chief that there
seemed to be no problem in maintenance that his men could
not solve. Rudy (Rudolph) and Archie (Archambault) took care
of operations when that duty called them. The rest of our team,
those talented and dedicated members of ground personnel
who accounted for 88% of the outfit, made sure that the other
12% had airplanes to fly and a product to deliver.

That 12% of fly-boys were the best in the business. Among
them, besides Archie and Rudy when they had crews, were the
crews of George Bledsoe, Ernie Fitzpatrick, Jack Munn, Abner
Pike, Denzil Prather, Harold Van Zyl, George Stinchcomb, Joe
Hartley, Willie Staple, Clinton Rabbitt, Bill Orban, Paul Karr,
Peyton Phillips, and John Lucey. My three good friends, Rod St.
Clair, Leonard McManus, and Jack Dickerson, would insist on
equal billing for talented personnel and I wouldn't argue with
them.

Finally, I say to all personnel, air and ground—Gentlemen,
I salute you. It was a privilege to have served with you. God
Bless.

— Robert L. Boone

## 788th/859th Squadron

Many members of the 788/859th "ground" echelon were
truly the unsung heroes of the organization. The numerous re-
locations, beginning at Wendover, Utah, in November 1943
and ending at Bari, Italy, in October 1945 placed extraordinary
burden on those members responsible for most of the planning, coordination, and execution of such movements. Also,
the daily activities of the various diverse functions of the squadron supporting the flying mission required the staff to work
closely together because of the interdependence between
them.

1st Sgt. Edwin P. McConnell, though relatively small in
stature, was very tall in leadership, diligence, and dedication.
His work assignments and after-work conduct of approximately 400 enlisted members permitted the commander to
devote his attention primarily to the flying end of the business.

Capt. Kenneth L. Bechtold, chief, Engineering Section,
and his flight line chief, M.Sgt. Curtis D. Rhoton, had the responsibility of maintaining the squadron's B-24 and C-47 air-

craft, approximately thirty in number. Bechtold and Rhoton superbly carried out their duties and responsibilities, often "around-the-clock" and under adverse weather conditions. Respect for their exceptional engineering knowledge, skill and devotion to "Perfect" aircraft maintenance objectives contributed immeasurably to the confidence of the aircrews in their aircraft.

The 788th/859th Bomb Squadron possessed many other unsung heroes among the non-flying members of the organization. These individuals, both officers and non-commissioned officers, performed above normal standards in shouldering responsibilities vital to the success of the flying mission. Such outstanding personnel served in the squadron's armament, transportation, engineering, intelligence, radar and medical functions. Unfortunately, their individual recognition must come from their own consciences and pride in knowing what a magnificent role they played during the "big war."

And to those numerous unsung heroes who did not return, God is their just reward. We remember them all with deep gratitude.

—Leonard M. McManus

## Carpetbaggers — How It All Began

In discussing the combat record of the Carpetbaggers with the author, Ben Parnell, we agreed that a look at the background of the organization and its operational agenda could be interesting. Ben asked me to write a few pages for inclusion in this edition of the book so readers would have some insight as to where the unit came from and why it had such a closeknit structure. Being a member of this organization from July 1942 to March of 1945, it became the only combat outfit that I knew during WWII. In order for the readers to appreciate its complete history, let us start from the beginning of not only the unit but some of the officers and men who were there from the start. I wish I could include all of those who started with this unit, but I cannot because of space and mainly because I have only been able trace a few of them. So let us begin.

The 19th Bomb Group at March Field, Riverside, California, was split into three units in May 1941. The three were: the

19th; the 30th and the 41st Bomb Groups. The 41st Group, consisting of the 46th, 47th and 48th Squadrons, was moved to Davis-Monthan Field at Tucson, Arizona. In this move were two men who would in time be two of the "main movers" in the Carpetbaggers, Clifford J. Heflin and Robert W. Fish. Also in this new group were William B. Cowart (known to me later as "Willie," who flew with me for many hours and through his engineering skills kept my aircraft flying and brought my crew home safely each time), Samuel (Sammy) Braudt (who maintained my aircraft as crew chief, and trained "Willie" what to do under many air emergencies), and Armond C. Hartzie, who later became the radio operator on Lyman Sanders' crew.

The 41st Group was under the command of Maj. A. Y. Smith. The 46th Squadron, which was to become the basis for the Carpetbaggers in months to come, was commanded by Capt. Charles B. Dougher. Dougher was later to become commander of the 41st Group.

Two other leaders-to-be came to the 41st when Lt. Robert L. Boone arrived from Hamilton Field, California, in June 1941, and Rodman A. St. Clair arrived from March Field, California, in early 1942. Little did Heflin, Fish, Boone, St. Clair, Cowart, Braudt, and Hartzie know that their lives would be closely related in the months to come.

Bob Fish met his baptism of command on December 7, 1941, when he was "Officer of the Day" at Davis-Monthan Field. He was leisurely having breakfast at the Officers Club when his waitress told him that the Japanese were bombing Pearl Harbor. It was hard for him to believe, but she proved it by bringing a radio to his table. Bob was a brand new first lieutenant. "Well," he said to himself, "what do I do in a case like this? Yes – contact my wing commander." But he was not at home. His group commander was on leave in Kansas. His squadron commander was out of town for the day. Lt. Bob Fish was "it," meaning, "head of the gang" – the squadron, the group, the wing, the base – all of it. So he calmly called the Tucson chief of police and requested that all military personnel seen be requested to return to the base. He called the local radio station and requested that they announce that all Air Corps personnel were to return to the base at once. Following these two great acts he went to the group commander's office, sat down, put his feet on the C.O.'s desk, and waited for some wiser and more experienced officers than he to arrive and take charge.

His actions were done properly because by midnight his 41st Group and squadrons were moving. The group moved on December 8 to Muroc Dry Lake in Central California (known today as Edwards Air Force Base). It seems that the 46th Squadron consisted of four B-18 aircraft. The B-18 was a twin-engine bomber powered with Wright R-1820-45 Cyclones 930 HP engines. It had a cruising speed of 167 mph, could climb at 1,355 feet per minute, could carry 4,400 pounds of bombs, had a top speed of 217 mph, and a service ceiling of 24,000 feet. The wingspan was 89 feet 6 inches and the length was 57 feet 10 inches. Later models had the Wright R-1820-53 engines, which boosted the horsepower to 1,000. Its range of 1,200 miles was increased to 2,225 miles when fuel and radar were added for anti-submarine work. There were 122 aircraft equipped for anti-submarine work out of a total of 217 produced.

Three of the B-18 aircraft from the 46th Squadron were flown to California during the night of December 7/8. Bob Fish flew the last B-18 out of Davis-Monthan Field shortly after daylight on December 8. Some of the 41st Group were based at Hamilton Field (just north of San Francisco) for about a week until the municipal airport at Sacramento, California, was made ready. The group flew B-18s on anti-submarine patrol off the Pacific Coast from the municipal airport at Sacramento, Muroc Dry Lake, Hamilton Field, and the Alameda Naval Air Station at Oakland, California. The pilots found it quite sporty to fly under the Golden Gate Bridge en route to and from patrols.

In March 1942, the 41st Group, all squadrons, men and material, moved to Hammer Field, Fresno, California. It was at this time that Capt. Clifford J. Heflin took command of the 46th Squadron. Heflin was born in Fresno in 1915. He became well known in the city because of his ability on the football field during his high school days. He became a "star" of the local community in this area and then went on to college at Fresno State. After three years, his eyes turned to the sky and the art of flying. He applied for and was approved for pilot school. Following this training he received his "wings" in the U.S. Army Air Corps. He married Patricia O'Neil, daughter of a

well-known Fresno rancher. At the time he became an Army
Air Corps colonel, it was reported that he was the youngest
colonel in the Corps. Colonel Heflin retired in 1968. He and
Pat established their home in Reno, Nevada, where he passed
away on January 20, 1980.

The 41st Group started to receive A-29 aircraft in January
1942, and by March of that year all squadrons were so
equipped. The A-29 was a two-engine bomber aircraft built for
the British, who called it the "Lockheed Hudson." It was a military version of the Lockheed Company's passenger aircraft. As
Bob Fish would say, "It was a poor excuse for a military aircraft, but it was better than nothing." It had a short range of
about seven hours, could carry four depth charges, and was
about the best we had in those days for the role of coastal anti-
sub work. Some of the 46th Squadron anti-sub flights were
being flown from Alameda Naval Air Station following the
group move to Hammer Field. It was at this time that I first
became acquainted with the A-29 and the 46th Squadron. I had
graduated from flight school in April 1942, and was assigned to
a fighter unit at Hamilton Field. The Group I was assigned to
was flying P-38 fighters. Being six foot four inches tall, I had a
problem getting into the P-38. It was possible with a "shoe-
horn," but my commander thought that maybe I would be better off in a bigger airplane. I didn't care for fighters anyway, so
I requested a transfer. While I was waiting I was assigned to the
Tracking and Intercept unit in downtown San Francisco. The
bomber liaison officer was from the 41st Group. He asked me
to go with him on one of his anti-sub flights out of Alameda
Naval Air Station. This flight was made on July 6, 1942. We
flew six hours and fifteen minutes. Ten days later, on July 16, I
was assigned to the 41st Bomb Group at Hammer Field, Fresno,
California.

Having later been assigned to the 46th Squadron, I soon
found that this unit was very closely knit. Captain (soon to be
Major) Heflin believed in an organization that worked hard,
played hard, and did it all together. It was at this time that I got
to know Cliff Heflin. I found him one to be trusted, admired,
and with great leadership ability. Throughout my military career I found that following his advice was extremely helpful.

On the 19th of August, 1942, the 46th Squadron departed

California. We flew our A-29s to Cherry Point Marine Air Station, North Carolina. This base was still being built; however, the base was very luxurious compared to what we had at Hammer Field. I compare this from a facility viewpoint. Some of our former airmen tell me that the food at Hammer Field was "out of this world" on the delicious side. At Cherry Point they classed the food as "in the pits," or, and not wanting to embarrass the Marine Corps, not so very good. It was here that I got to know Bob Fish. Although Bob had flown with me at Hammer Field, and helped with my checkout in the A-29, I knew him only as a very helpful instructor pilot trying his best to get this tall "drink of water" to be able to land the A-29 without "crashing" on each landing. Thanks to Lieutenant Fish, along with several other pilots, who spent many hours of patient instruction and put up with many bouncing landings, I finally got the idea that if you just relax, let the airplane do what it was made to do, it will land itself. Yes, I did get checked out in the A-29 airplane.

Bob Fish was born May 30, 1917, and was raised in the Michigan, Ohio area. He was studying for a degree in electrical engineering at Ohio State University when he entered the Army Air Corps Flying Training Program and received his "wings" on June 21, 1940 (Cadet Class of 40C). His first assignment was to the 19th Bomb Group, March Field, California. His military history continued (as outlined in this book), and through a regular commission he completed a full military career to retirement on February 1, 1970. He and his wife, Jean, were very important to me in those days when, as a second lieutenant, I needed encouragement to advance in pilot skills and make an effort to become just a little better than the general mold. I remember well one night at Westover Field, Massachusetts. A few of the pilots and crews had completed B-24 training and had been sent to Westover for thirty days of anti-sub duty at that base. For reasons unknown to me, other than the fact that my flying skills were not up to the others, I did not have a crew. I was given the job as night-duty officer in operations. One night at about 11:00 P.M. the telephone rang. It was anti-sub headquarters in New York. I was told that we were to select a crew for immediate reassignment. I called Bob and he asked me if I thought I was qualified to take a B-24 crew. I told him I would be glad to do so but didn't have much time in the airplane and had no crew. He said, "OK, your name will not go in the hat." Who drew the name from the hat I don't know, but I suspect it was Jean. Bob gave me the name and I called it in to headquarters.

Another man to come along as we settled in at Cherry Point was Robert D. Sullivan. Bob had completed Officers Training and Intelligence School and was assigned to the 41st Group at Hammer Field at Fresno. He was told to head for Cherry Point on the East Coast as the squadron there needed his services. Bob and his wife, Aurelia, arrived in December of 1942 to start a long and, as far as we combat crews were concerned, highly successful tour as our intelligence officer. In the future duty that we were destined to accomplish, intelligence was of prime importance and Sully, as we knew him, did an outstanding job. He was known as the guy with the longest, well-waxed handlebar mustache in England. Bob believes that the unit success was because of the leadership and personality of Colonel Heflin, and Bob Fish, who sat in the shadow of Heflin and saw to it that things got done right.

It was at Cherry Point that much "cementing" of the people in the organization took place. It was here that we really got to know each other and developed a lasting respect for each other. Now newly promoted Lieutenant Colonel Heflin and his wife, Pat, set the pace for the unity that soon became the expected norm for our squadron. Ground crews worked throughout the night to have our aircraft ready for a dawn take-off. The combat crews flew long hours over the Atlantic Ocean looking for submarines, which to my knowledge, we never found. But we, along with other squadrons at other locations, did succeed in keeping the subs down or away from shipping going up and down the U.S. East Coast. Here several were married, babies were born, and officers and men worked and played hard. It was in the nearby small town of New Bern where Bruce Cowart and his childhood sweetheart, Margaret, were married. As I have said, Bruce was later to become my flight engineer. To him I give credit, as I do others of my crew, for making all our combat, as well as other flights, very successful. William Bruce Cowart was raised in Fort Myers, Florida. Upon graduation from high school, he and a friend journeyed north to Montgomery, Alabama, to enlist in the U.S. Army Air Corps. His first assignment was to the 19th Bomb

Group. Bruce became a thirty-year Air Force man and had a very successful flying career.

Another to become a member of the organization a few days after Pearl Harbor was Keith E. Gott. Keith had just completed Photography School the weekend before Pearl Harbor. He arrived at Muroc Dry Lake and found that the 41st had no requirement for an aerial photographer. So he was told that he was now a gunner. He later went to Gunnery School, but from then on he was a gunner on Bob Boone's crew. Keith was born in Iowa and grew up in Iowa and Texas. He went to the University of Texas, where he met his wife, Lee, whom he later married at New Bern, North Carolina, while the squadron was based at Cherry Point. Keith was one of many members of the Carpetbaggers who, after flying one tour of combat, returned for another one. Keith tells a story of the Marine shavetail (that's a Marine second lieutenant) who complained to Colonel Heflin that our enlisted men were not saluting him. Heflin's reply was that they didn't salute him either. To this Keith adds, "We may not have saluted, but we sure as hell did respect him." And I think that was the sincere feeling of all officers and men. Another member of Bob Boone's crew to fly two tours was Roscoe Hardman. Bob also completed two, as did St. Clair.

While at Cherry Point we received three new crews that remained with us into the Carpetbagger project. These were piloted by Lieutenants Stapel, Van Zyl, and Wagstad. It was here, on March 8, that General Order Number 6 was issued by our headquarters changing the 46th Squadron name to the 22nd Anti-Submarine Squadron (H). In April 1943, the 22nd was moved to Bluethenthal Field, Wilmington, North Carolina. The Marines needed their base for full-time training, so we departed south to Wilmington. While based at Cherry Point and Wilmington and on temporary duty at other bases on the East Coast, we trained to fly and maintain the B-24. We flew hundreds of hours over water, most of them in A-29s. Three combat crews were lost. They disappeared while on patrol over the Atlantic Ocean. Nothing was ever found of these crews to my knowledge. The years have taken their toll in my memory department, but I remember four good friends who were on these crews: Lt. Charles H. Dingus, Lt. James W. Milliken, Lt. Fred M. Speake, and Lt. James G. Barr.

It was at Cherry Point that I got to know very well two other men who would play a major role in the Carpetbaggers in the months ahead. One was 1st Lt. (soon to be Capt.) Robert L. Boone. Bob Boone was born at Berkeley, California. He graduated from the University of California at Berkeley with a degree in economics. Because of his desire to fly, he entered the Army flying program and graduated from flying school in the class of 41-C at Barksdale Field, Louisiana. Bob obtained his wings from the first twin-engine school the Army had. So it stood to reason that, being a twin-engine pilot, he would be assigned to a single-engine fighter squadron. He checked out in the P-40, and after flying this plane for a while at Hamilton Field, California, he was transferred to Davis-Monthan Field at Tucson to become a part of the 41st Group's 47th Squadron commanded by 1st Lt. James C. Cochran. Bob Boone and his wife, Vickie, were part of the family supporting element who provided the encouragement for those of us who were not fortunate enough to be in the married category.

The other "prime mover" in this organization was Lt. Rodman A. St. Clair. Saint, as he was known by all, was a "Jolly-Charlie" type of individual with a great persuasive personality. He was born in the Philippine Islands to Civil Service parents in March 1917. Following his completion of college at Kansas State, with a degree in physical science, he applied for flying training and received his wings at Kelly Field, Texas, in Class 41-I. In early 1942 Saint was assigned to the 46th Squadron. He and his wife, Jane, became very favorite friends of mine, and I will never forget being concerned for Jane when Saint was on a mission.

Soon after our arrival at Wilmington, we were all flying the B-24D aircraft. The B-24 was a Consolidated Aircraft Co. airplane. The plane had a high-lift Davis wing located at shoulder height. The wing had a span of 110 feet, the aircraft length was 63 feet 8 inches and stood on a tricycle landing gear. It was powered by four Pratt & Whitney R-1830 engines, its cruising speed was around 190, top speed of 280, and landed at 85 to 90 mph. The empty weight, of most of the models, was 35,000 pounds and a gross of 50,000 to 55,000 pounds. Later R-1830 engines with supercharger developed 1,200 HP. The "Liberator" name came from the British, who bought hundreds from the U.S. Many models and different designs were produced. Because of this, it is impossible to give the correct specifications of this aircraft. The above should give the reader a general idea.

Above, you have the four men who, in my opinion, did the most to bring together the organization that was in the months ahead to become "The Carpetbaggers": Heflin, Fish, Boone, and St. Clair. This is not to imply in any way that many other officers and men of this unit did not have a tremendous part in the making of this squadron. I only wish that I had had more dealings with the enlisted men and could speak more of the part they played in the making of this tremendous organization. However, being in the officer category at the time and not knowing that I would be writing something like this fifty years later, I am sorry to say that all I can do is my best — and most of that pertains to the officers. As any military officer will say, without the large number of officers and men that back up the combat teams, not much would be accomplished. There are too many to put on these pages, but they were there, they did their part, and to them also goes the praise. One I would like to point out was our medical doctor, Paul J. Gans. He was always there when needed, and took care of us all — wives, babies, the works. He cared for all medical problems. I remember well when I was taking off in an A-29 early one morning to look for a submarine that had been reported in our area of responsibility. I had just broken ground at Cherry Point when my right engine cut out. I knew I could not make the tall pine trees at the end of the runway. So I landed back on the runway with my wheels up. As my crew and I crawled out of the aircraft, the fire department was arriving and right behind them was Doc Gans and his crew. How they got from the hospital to where I was in that length of time I will never know. At that time of the morning I would have still been in bed if not having to fly.

On August 14, 1943, orders came: "The Flight Echelon, designated Shipment No. 6496-B, assigned air priority No. APR 2-83723, consisting of twelve (12) combat crews of four (4) officers and seven (7) enlisted men, plus three (3) additional officers will proceed in twelve (12) B-24 VLR(E) combat aircraft from present station to Army Air Base Presque Isle, Maine, at a time to be designated by this Headquarters and thence to *** [blank in the orders for security reasons] ***." And so it was. We moved to Langley Field, where we were outfitted with all the overseas movement equipment that was required to be carried. I would be remiss if I did not mention an occurrence that happened at Langley Field. As we were readying our aircraft just before taking off, the wives of my crew members, who had followed us to Langley, were standing by the fence about fifty feet from the aircraft. I went over to tell them goodbye and they asked me to be sure and bring their husbands back to them. I promised them that I would. I am happy to report that with the exception of my co-pilot, who was transferred when we entered the Carpetbagger project and I do not know what happened to him, all the other crew members did return to the States safe and sound.

On August 17, we flew to Presque Isle, Maine. It was here that our plane was named *Playmate,* and the squadron received orders from Headquarters, North Atlantic Wing, Air Transport Command, to follow the North Atlantic route to the European Theater of Operations. In this case the route would be from Presque Isle, Maine, to Gander Field, Newfoundland, direct to Prestwick, Scotland. From Prestwick we were to fly our aircraft to our new base at Dunkeswell, England, or U.S. Army Air Force Station No. 102, as it was known in those days. (Another name for this base was Royal Air Force Station, Dunkeswell, Honiton, Devon.) On the nineteenth we flew to Gander, Newfoundland, and on the twentieth late in the afternoon we departed North America. As I looked down on the land slipping slowly eastward below *Playmate,* and watched the shadows grow long, I wondered if I would ever see this land again. Although I never heard any of my crew indicate this feeling, I expect that they were thinking much the same.

While writing the above my mind has gone over and over the questions: "What made this squadron such a closely knit and cohesive organization?" "What made it so well fitted for the Carpetbagger mission?" "Why did the men in these airplanes have such a great ability to organize and train others in the unique task of the Carpetbagger work?" And lastly, "Why did the esprit-de-corps of these few transfer to so many in the months ahead?"

Colonel Heflin once said that anti-submarine crews are ideally suited for Carpetbagger work. Each navigator is trained for precise navigation. He must take the aircraft to the exact spot at a water location. Each crew must operate as a complete entity because they have no one or nothing else to rely on. Each pilot is highly capable in the art of instrument flying and has flown many such hours. They fly very long hours over water. They must gauge their fuel supply to provide for any contingencies upon reaching land.

All these traits are found in anti-submarine crews and were present in the twelve crews going to England in August 1943. These crews had been flying combat missions over the coastal waters of the United States for hundreds of hours. Each crew was a complete entity within itself. The high spirit of desire had been drilled into each crew member. This feeling flowed down to all members of the squadron, whether it be an aircraft commander or the driver of a jeep. All members felt the same. I realize that bomber crews also had much of the same. However, it must be said that in the Carpetbaggers Group, it was up to each crew to do its own thing. The crew was given a target on one-half acre of ground to find at night in some occupied country of Europe. How they got there, delivered their material, and returned home was up to that crew. They had to arrive at that one-half-acre spot within the time period outlined. The timing was critical because the receiving party on the ground could only be put in danger for a short period of time. If the delivery aircraft was located by a night fighter while over Europe, they had only themselves, one crew, one airplane, to rely on to get out of the mess and accomplish their mission.

In my research for these pages, I received a letter from Bill Orban. Bill was one of our pilots who brought his crew to the Carpetbaggers a few months after we got into the business. I believe Bill provides the explanation in his letter. May I quote: ". . . and with outstanding leadership we were molded into a top notch outfit. We all felt responsible for our individual efforts and to me this is the key to our success. Each crew was competitive because it was up to them to perform and complete a mission. We were not flying somebody else's wing. We were proud of our accomplishments and those of the entire group. This built a camaraderie we still have to this day." And let me add that the Carpetbagger Association has just "that."

Listed below are the crews and aircraft that were flown to England on the 22nd Anti-Submarine Squadron deployment.

Operation Orders Number 146         18 August 1943
Par 1.         * * * * *

### Shipment No. 6496
#### B-24D (Aircraft No. 42-40933)

| | | | |
|---|---|---|---|
| 1st Lt. | Bestow R. Rudolph | O-659842 | (P) |
| 2nd Lt. | Gilbert J. Pohl | O-796433 | (CP) |
| 2nd Lt. | Charles W. Matt | O-660505 | (N) |
| 2nd Lt. | James W. Baker | O-733012 | (B) |
| T/Sgt. | Milton (NMI) Yates | 34083981 | (E) |
| S/Sgt. | William B. Cowart | 1405598 | (AE) |
| T/Sgt. | Edwin H. Hardesty | 15046628 | (RO) |
| Cpl. | Rodney W. Eaton | 10078054 | (AR) |
| Pvt. 1cl. | Ervin L. Smith | 34332146 | (ASV) |
| T/Sgt. | Emil J. Bayer | 38057888 | (CC) |
| Cpl. | William A. Perkins | 15069862 | (CC) |
| Sgt. | John M. Lawrence | 14056788 | (G) |

#### B-24D (Aircraft No. 42-40919)

| | | | |
|---|---|---|---|
| 1st Lt. | Benjamin A. Mead | O-724634 | (P) |
| 2nd Lt. | John A. Lucey | O-665063 | (CP) |
| 2nd Lt. | John A. Reitmeir | O-800667 | (N) |
| 2nd Lt. | John B. Mead | O-733075 | (B) |
| T/Sgt. | Elmer T. Anderson | 6291038 | (AE) |
| S/Sgt. | James P. Hall | 17013860 | (AE) |
| S/Sgt. | Phillips B. Latta | 7084841 | (RO) |
| Sgt. | Joel T. Williamson | 38068251 | (AR) |
| Cpl. | Deano H. Tatum | 37450617 | (ASV) |
| Pvt. 1cl. | Graham S. Hasty | 14050901 | (G) |
| M/Sgt. | Bryan K. Watts | 14029194 | (CC) |

#### B-24D (Aircraft No. 42-40859)

| | | | |
|---|---|---|---|
| 1st Lt. | Robert L. Williams | O-431584 | (P) |
| F/O | Joseph W. Hanley | T-120046 | (CP) |
| 2nd Lt. | Milton L. Remling | O-660520 | (N) |
| 1st Lt. | Charles R. Teer | O-434607 | (B) |
| T/Sgt. | Jesse A. Wallace | 38043713 | (E) |
| Sgt. | Major T. Callahan | 38032109 | (AE) |
| T/Sgt. | Glen O. Wichner | 6939905 | (RO) |
| Sgt. | James P. Boggs | 39255063 | (AR) |

| Sgt.      | Eddie P. Rush         | 34084010 | (G)   |
|-----------|-----------------------|----------|-------|
| Pvt. 1cl. | Vincent L. Stuart     | 19085137 | (ASV) |
| T/Sgt.    | Norbert J. Henrich    | 17025059 | (CC)  |

B-24D (Aircraft No. 42-40926)

| 1st Lt.   | Gerald S. Wagstad     | O-665744  | (P)   |
|-----------|-----------------------|-----------|-------|
| F/O       | Lorimer Peterson      | T-217     | (CP)  |
| 2nd Lt.   | Edward Martinez       | O-795278  | (N)   |
| 2nd Lt.   | Joseph P. Connor      | O-734428  | (B)   |
| T/Sgt.    | Earl W. Underwood     | 34201882  | (E)   |
| T/Sgt.    | Cornelius F. O'Leary  | 31160055  | (RO)  |
| S/Sgt.    | Jose A. Morales       | 38123436  | (AE)  |
| Cpl.      | John P. Garwood       | 19077717  | (AR)  |
| Cpl.      | Onnie George          | 35741477  | (ASV) |
| S/Sgt.    | Frederick N. Wagner   | 39007470  | (G)   |
| M/Sgt.    | John F. Griffin       | 18025259  | (CC)  |

B-24D (Aircraft No. 42-40921)

| 1st Lt.   | Claude H. Cummings    | O-431006  | (P)   |
|-----------|-----------------------|-----------|-------|
| 2nd Lt.   | Ernest S. Holzworth   | O-794407  | (CP)  |
| 2nd Lt.   | Albert G. Stout       | O-660529  | (N)   |
| 2nd Lt.   | Robert P. Nelson      | O-733085  | (B)   |
| T/Sgt.    | Leigh Van Hoose       | 34078672  | (E)   |
| Sgt.      | Earl H. Kilgore       | 13034085  | (AE)  |
| T/Sgt.    | Baker J. Guilbeau     | 14054060  | (RO)  |
| Sgt.      | Edmund C. Andrews     | 34357885  | (AR)  |
| S/Sgt.    | Fred Barrett          | 19020550  | (G)   |
| Cpl.      | Milton Bromberg       | 32305776  | (ASV) |
| Sgt.      | Lewis E. Hart         | 17019123  | (CC)  |

B-24D (Aircraft No. 42-40931)

| 1st Lt.   | Wilmer L. Stapel        | O-792649  | (P)   |
|-----------|-------------------------|-----------|-------|
| 2nd Lt.   | Hal M. Harrison         | O-737944  | (CP)  |
| 2nd Lt.   | Milton S. Popkin        | O-796591  | (N)   |
| 2nd Lt.   | Glen C. Nesbitt         | O-732647  | (B)   |
| T/Sgt.    | Edwin J. Meador         | 17003926  | (CC)  |
| T/Sgt.    | James B. Elliott        | 39307191  | (AE)  |
| T/Sgt.    | Wallace R. Goodman      | 36148716  | (RO)  |
| S/Sgt.    | Henry D. MacMillan, Jr. | 34315015  | (AE)  |
| S/Sgt.    | Leo E. Roettger         | 36226475  | (AR)  |
| S/Sgt.    | Eugene J. Wozniak       | 31128195  | (G)   |
| Pvt. 1cl. | Earl J. Propst          | 15070720  | (ASV) |

Par. 2                      * * * * *

### B-24D (Aircraft No. 42-40927)

| | | | |
|---|---|---|---|
| Capt. | Robert W. Fish | O-395147 | (P) |
| 1st Lt. | Milton A. Love | O-429666 | (X) |
| Capt. | Paul J. Gans | O-362813 | (M) |
| 2nd Lt. | James A. Cassedy | O-794634 | (CP) |
| 1st Lt. | Edward C. Tresemer | O-434010 | (N) |
| 2nd Lt. | John Kolkowski | O-668969 | (B) |
| T/Sgt. | William C. Jesperson | 19054277 | (E) |
| Sgt. | Harold E. Faulk | 330339156 | (AE) |
| S/Sgt | Albert L. Sage | 7000869 | (RO) |
| Sgt. | Minor J. Babin | 38198428 | (AR) |
| Pvt. 1cl. | Joseph L. Bennett | 34268666 | (ASV) |
| Sgt. | Samual L. Cooper | 38043025 | (G) |

### B-24D (Aircraft No. 42-40937)

| | | | |
|---|---|---|---|
| Capt. | Robert L. Boone | O-372863 | (P) |
| 2nd Lt. | Charles E. Archambault | O-795682 | (CP) |
| 1st Lt. | Fred W. Edwards | O-724298 | (N) |
| 1st Lt. | Charles G. Shull | O-725089 | (B) |
| T/Sgt. | Roscoe I. Hardman | 15013710 | (RO) |
| Sgt. | Lester W. Anderson | 31155441 | (AR) |
| T/Sgt. | Leo F. Dumesnil | 34078638 | (E) |
| Sgt. | Charles J. Roth | 18046376 | (AE) |
| Sgt. | Keith E. Gott | 18038065 | (G) |
| Sgt. | John H. Forciea | 16047068 | (ASV) |
| Lt. Col. | Clifford J. Heflin | O-22617 | (CO) |

### B-24D (Aircraft No. 42-40939)

| | | | |
|---|---|---|---|
| 1st Lt. | Harold R. Van Zyl | O-665743 | (P) |
| 2nd Lt. | Peyton F. Phillips | O-736560 | (CP) |
| 2nd Lt. | Lawrence Rivkin | O-796602 | (N) |
| 2nd Lt. | William E. Elkouri | O-733643 | (B) |
| T/Sgt. | Harold I. Qualls | 19079149 | (E) |
| S/Sgt. | Henry R. Hettinger | 18071440 | (AE) |
| T/Sgt. | Udell W. Olson | 18069815 | (RO) |
| T/Sgt. | Joseph C. Parker | 34290522 | (AR) |
| S/Sgt. | Charles S. Ralph | 36314204 | (ASV) |
| S/Sgt. | John F. Zsadany | 32436546 | (G) |
| M/Sgt. | Clyde N. Knezzle | 17016389 | (CC) |

Operations Order No. 147                              19 August 1943
Par. 2                             * * * * *

### B-24 Aircraft (No. 42-40925)

| | | | |
|---|---|---|---|
| 1st. Lt. | Rodman A. St. Clair | O-431531 | (P) |
| F/O | Paul B. Weaver | T-187351 | (CP) |
| 2nd Lt. | Robert W. Martin | O-733053 | (N) |
| 2nd Lt. | Burton W. Gross | O-668710 | (B) |
| T/Sgt. | George E. Larson | 16012219 | (E) |
| Sgt. | Hugh D. Jones | 14057749 | (AE) |
| S/Sgt. | Frank J. Scigliano | 17031441 | (RO) |
| Sgt. | Robert H. Albrecht | 16095747 | (AR) |
| Cpl. | Donald C. Stiens | 33457673 | (RV) |
| Sgt. | Leo P. Babik | 38057873 | (G) |
| M/Sgt. | George H. Langley | 14026489 | (CC) |
| Sgt. | Wallace N. Templeton | 14027684 | (ACC) |

### B-24D (Aircraft No. 42-40840)

| | | | |
|---|---|---|---|
| 1st Lt. | James A. Estes | O-430995 | (P) |
| 2nd Lt. | John T. Kelly | O-796400 | (CP) |
| 1st Lt. | Walter L. Garnett, Jr. | O-724308 | (N) |
| 2nd Lt. | Orrin Brown, Jr. | O-733020 | (B) |
| M/Sgt. | Edwin L. Johnson | 17021589 | (CC) |
| T/Sgt. | Russell R. Hancock | 17027284 | (E) |
| S/Sgt. | George B. Kirkpatrick | 38057883 | (RO) |
| S/Sgt. | Albert L. Krasevac | 39076124 | (AR) |
| Sgt. | Harry E. Siewart | 18037807 | (AE) |
| Cpl. | Lawrence G. Dana | 39827090 | (G) |
| Cpl. | John P. Myers | 37211953 | (ASV) |

### B-24D (Aircraft No. 42-40944)

| | | | |
|---|---|---|---|
| 1st Lt. | Lyman A. Sanders, Jr. | O-431532 | (P) |
| F/O | Wade A. Carpenter | T-60253 | (CP) |
| 2nd Lt. | Lonnie Hammond, Jr. | O-800715 | (N) |
| 2nd Lt. | Fred M. Burk | O-733022 | (B) |
| T/Sgt. | James H. Mays | 14026554 | (E) |
| T/Sgt. | Armond C. Hartzie | 17018056 | (RO) |
| S/Sgt. | Joseph W. Canfield | 12170678 | (G) |
| Sgt. | Clarence L. Johnson | 14059730 | (AE) |
| Sgt. | Willard T. Killip | 17011857 | (CC) |
| Cpl. | Robert L. Henry | 32444600 | • (RO) |
| Pfc. | Eden C. Burris | 38130795 | (AR) |

The above list of twelve crews was taken from records that are fifty years old. The paper is very yellow and the copy capability we had in 1943 was anything but perfect. Many letters and numbers did not come through the copy very well. Please accept my apology for any errors.

The squadron's key NCOs followed the crews to England by Air Transport Command aircraft. Some of these were: Drasher, Seegars, Van-DeeVenter, Herron, Braudt, White, and Wills.

Most of the men listed above are those who started, and many who also completed, the Carpetbaggers project. Some were transferred before the project started because their ability was required at other bases. Many of the above completed a tour of combat, took thirty days' leave in the U.S. and returned for another tour. This fact speaks well for the group leadership and the camaraderie that existed among members.

There is so much more I would like to write about the members of the 22nd Anti-sub Squadron. Those who worked hard together, played hard together, and yes, died together. But since most of the stories have "gone with the years" and my recall button does not seem to work anymore, let's just say it's time to call the tower for "landing instructions" and get this flying machine on the ground.

In addition to those listed in this article, I wish to thank Patty Elliott, daughter of Colonel Heflin, for her help with the information on her dad. Also, Marguerite Sanders, widow of Lyman Sanders, who found in "Sandy's" old military papers the missing information I needed so badly to complete the above.

— Bestow R. (Rudy) Rudolph

## Corrections, Additions, and Elaborations

Capt. James A. Estes was KIA on the night of November 3/4, 1943, while flying with an RAF crew of the 138 Squadron from Tempsford on an SOE mission to France. Their airplane, a Halifax bomber (serial number 726), struck high ground in fog at Marcols-les-Eaux (Ardeche) at a place called Col des Vios. He is buried in the Rhone American Cemetery at Draguignan in Var. Captain Estes was from Kentucky.

The mission was to supply the "Temple" DZ near Allex

(Drome). The RAF crew and Estes were all killed instantly; however, an RAF tail gunner who apparently was on temporary duty with the crew survived the crash. There is a commemorative plaque on "Rocher de Bourboulas," where the bomber hit a rock wall.

Lt. Burton W. Gross was KIA on the night of November 10/11, 1943, while flying on an SOE mission to France with an RAF crew of the 161 Squadron from Tempsford. The airplane was a Halifax B.V. (serial number EB 129). The airplane crashed at Brunelles (Eure-et-Loir) at a place called Saint Gilles, possibly after being shot down by a German night fighter.

The mission was to supply a "Pennyfarthing" party. All crew members and Gross were killed. Lieutenant Gross is buried in the Saint Desir Cemetery, a British cemetery, at Lisieux in Calvados. Lieutenant Gross was from California.

—S. Blandin via Si Sizemore

---

B-24D 42-63792 flown by Lt. Frank W. McDonald and crew crashed on the night of March 2/3, 1944, at Fienvillers (Somme) after being hit by heavy fire from antiaircraft guns mounted on railway cars. The prop on No. 1 engine was hit, No. 2 engine was on fire, No. 3 engine was hit and out, the tail turret was out, and numerous flak holes were through the fuselage with the left wing totally on fire. McDonald took violent evasive action and maneuvered the aircraft away from the fire of the German guns. The order to evacuate the aircraft was given. However, as McDonald attempted to gain an altitude safe for bailing out, he realized that the fire had now engulfed both wings and that a midair explosion was threatening. There was only one chance—to crash land in an open area he had spied.

In the nose, bombardier Shelvin, sensing the rapid descent, turned to see trees rapidly approaching. As the aircraft smashed into the trees he was catapulted through the broken plexiglass nose, followed by navigator Kendall. Both were knocked unconscious as they went out. The aircraft continued on its fiery path to the ground.

McDonald successfully set the airplane down in a crash landing. As it touched down the airplane began an uncontrolled slide, gouging a deep rut in the earth, snapping off the tail turret as its progress slowed, and finally coming to a grinding stop in front of some trees lining a French highway. The interior was a raging inferno. Copilot Kelley followed McDonald out a cockpit window. Tail gunner DeCoste and dispatcher Goswick exited through the opening which once housed the tail turret. Radio operator Ross, who was initially knocked out by the brutal impact, struggled to free himself from the mass of wreckage, guns, ammunition belts, and other debris which had buried him. Then he, too, went out through a cockpit window.

McDonald, Kelley, DeCoste, and Goswick gathered near the flaming aircraft looking for other survivors until the intense heat forced them to retreat only minutes before the fuel tanks exploded with a tremendous roar. They then walked in a southeasterly direction and found a deep gully, where they spent the night. Ross crawled and stumbled away from the wreckage until he came upon a fenced corner of a field, which he was unable to climb over. He could go no further.

Kendall regained consciousness lying on the ground under the trees and could see the burning airplane in a distant field. He soon found Shelvin unconscious a short distance away and managed to shake and talk him back to consciousness. Shelvin was in bad shape — really busted up. Unable to move, Shelvin told Kendall to leave the area. Kendall then made his way to the flaming wreckage, where he found no sign of life. Believing that he and Shelvin were the only survivors, he dragged himself in what he took to be a southerly direction. Unknown to all of them at the time, engineer Gellerman had been killed in the crash. His body was recovered by the Germans during the salvaging of the wreckage.

McDonald, Kelley, Goswick, and DeCoste walked at night and spent the days hiding in any safe shelter away from the Germans. After the fourth night a farm worker was approached by DeCoste, who could speak some French, and the farmer told them to stay hidden until he returned.

About two hours later he returned with an eighteen-year-old girl in tow. She spoke English very well. She asked to see their dog tags, what day they were shot down, and asked them to surrender their weapons. Unknown to the evaders, the French underground routinely contacted England and confirmed that the evaders were who they said they were. About dark the little French girl returned with two other Frenchmen with the news that their identity had been confirmed and asked that the airmen please follow them. Their destination turned out to be a milk barn converted to living quarters occupied by Pauline Delplanque, where they remained in hiding for quite some time.

In the meantime, the little French girl and her mother brought civilian clothes and identification papers in preparation for the trip south to the Pyrenees. After a two-week stay, an elderly woman and her twelve-year-old grandson picked them up, along with two B-17 gunners, and traveled by bus and train to Paris, then by train to Bordeaux. There they found that their underground contacts had been arrested by the Germans. They decided to continue on their own by train to Dax, then by foot the rest of the way.

It soon became apparent that they would have to split up in two groups of three to have any hope of evading the Germans while on their way. Since McDonald and Kelley were the only two officers, they drew straws and each chose two others. Kelley, with DeCoste and Goswick, decided to head straight south along the coast. McDonald with the two B-17 gunners decided to head southeast to avoid the congested area.

For three days McDonald's group followed a southeasterly direction until they arrived at Lacq. There McDonald approached a lone Frenchman. McDonald said that they needed his help to walk over the mountains, and asked if he would help. They then spent two weeks in the home of the farmer Marcel Trubert, in the village of Lendresse. On May 4, 1944, while waiting for their guide, the Gestapo dropped in and arrested Madam Trubert, McDonald, and the two B-17 gunners.

Kelley, with his group, also were in sight of the Pyrenees when they were betrayed by a man and wife who turned them in to the Germans in order to collect a reward. Only Kelley, who was walking far behind the others when they were taken, managed to get away, cross the Pyrenees, and return to England.

Shelvin and Ross were taken by the Germans shortly after the crash. Kendall was sheltered by the French underground until April 8, when he was taken by the Gestapo. McDonald, Kendall, Shelvin, Goswick, DeCoste, and Ross all spent the rest of the war in POW camps.

—McDonald

Lt. Wade A. Carpenter and crew crashed in B-24D 42-63789 on the night of March 3/4, 1944, at Humbercourt (Somme) after being hit by flak while flying at a low altitude. Burris (radio) was seriously wounded in the airplane by a flak burst prior to the crash. Dudley (tail gunner) bailed out at very low altitude and landed safely. The shock of the crash was brutal. Carpenter (pilot), Herdman (waist gunner), and Nesbitt (flying a buddy mission) were not injured. Eshleman (copilot) was wounded in the neck and foot, Burris lost his left eye, and Johnson (engineer) suffered a broken ankle during the crash. Hammond (navigator) was killed in the crash, and Rees (bombardier) was trapped under heavy metal in the airplane with both legs crushed.

Carpenter and Eshleman walked to the village at the bottom of the hill to get help. Dr. Jacquemelle was summoned from a nearby village, Lucheux, and after some time arrived to render all possible aid to the injured. However, they could not get Rees out of the wreckage. Part of the metal of the airplane had to be cut away before he was finally pulled out. Rees and five of the crew were taken to a farm home in the village of Humbercourt for care.

All eight of the fliers were taken by the Germans about noon on March 4. Hammond was buried on March 5 in the cemetery at Meharicourt. Rees was transferred to the hospital at Amiens, where both legs were amputated on March 5. Unfortunately, he was not able to take the shock and died the same day. Johnson and Burris were also hospitalized for their injuries. Carpenter, Eshleman, Nesbitt, and Herdman were taken to POW camps in Germany. Dudley managed to evade capture for a while with the help of the Bordeaux-Loupiac escape network before being taken by the Germans.

—Burris, Dr. Ducellier

On the night of March 3/4 1944, Capt. Gerald S. Wagstad and crew, flying in B-24D 42-72863, failed to return from their assigned mission and no word was ever received as to their fate. Those who have researched the records believe that the men were lost in the channel, off the French coast.

Blandin, a serious student of the wartime activities of the

Carpetbaggers, recently discovered that Wagstad (pilot), Walsh (copilot), Underwood (engineer), and O'Leary (radio) are all buried in the U.S. Military Cemetery at Epinal, in France. In his opinion, they were probably hit by flak over Somme and were the victims of a midair explosion when over the sea. Their remains could have been recovered by the Germans or, more probably, by the French after the war. He is of the opinion that the remains of the other four men in the crew were probably returned to the States for reburial.

— Blandin

Harold Van Zyl remembers Gerald Wagstead:

He was indeed a good friend of both my wife and myself. We flew together in our advanced cadet class in Lubbock, Texas, and were in the 2nd Air Corps high altitude crew training mission at the same time before joining the anti-sub group together with Willie Staple, that was stationed in Wilmington, North Carolina.

Gerald Wagstad was supposed to be the best man at our wedding in April of 1943 but wasn't able to make it, so Willie Staple was in our wedding party instead of Wag.

— Van Zyl

Blandin also had this to say about Lt. William W. Nicoll and crew in B-24D 42-72870, who crashed on the night of April 4/5, 1944, at Truttemer le Grand (Calvados) in France:

An important point is to correct the story of the Nicoll crew on page 31 [of *Carpetbaggers,* 1st ed.]. According to all reliable eyewitnesses — including the man who took the bodies to the local cemetery — four bodies were found in the wreckage of their B-24: those of Nicoll (pilot), Davis (bombardier), Bindell (engineer), and Brewer (radio). They were buried on April 5. A fifth body was found under part of the wreckage the next day; this should have been Harris, the navigator. He was buried separately. The sixth man — most probably Kittrell (tail gunner) — was found the morning following the crash, hanging in his parachute harness. The chute was caught in a tree about 80/100 yards from the burning plane. (The plane burned for hours.) It is supposed that he bailed out too low and was killed on impact. The evidence could

indicate a coup de grace by some angry German officer. This
was later confirmed by another witness, but we have no real
proof and such a cold-blooded action is still a matter of con-
jecture. Other reports said he was seriously wounded but we
have no proof of this, too. Anyway, *no* American airman was
shot or interned at nearby Château de la Rochelle. This is absolutely certain.

---

The George W. Ambrose crew crashed at Saint Cyr de
Valorges (Loire) in B-24D 42-40997 on the night of April 27/28,
1944, as reported in chapter 4 (*Carpetbaggers,* 1st ed.). In
April 1964, James J. Heddleson revisited the village of Saint Cyr
de Valorges at the request of the French citizens to participate
in ceremonies honoring the 20th anniversary of the tragic
crash of the Ambrose crew and to represent the crew as a survivor. Thousands of local people attended the occasion, with
the local French government, the French military, and the vice-
commandant of the U.S. Air Force Base at Chateauroux all participating.

Heddleson was presented a medallion by the local ex-
Maquis organization, a small box containing parts of the
crashed airplane, and the leather jacket he was wearing the day
of the crash. He was also made an honorary citizen of the village of Tarare and an official member of the French Maquis.

Later, in 1974, a square in the village of Saint Cyr de
Valorges was renamed "James Heddleson Square" in his honor.
It is believed that he is the only American enlisted man in
World War II to be so honored. He was told that he was one of
only a very few people who had flown the parachute drops
from England, participated in the drops on the ground, fought
with the Maquis and participated in sabotage work, and then
escaped back to England. He was told that this was one of the
reasons for renaming the square in his honor.

In 1981, Heddleson was again honored by being made an
honorary citizen of the village of S. Germain Laval.

— Heddleson

---

Lt. Murry L. Simon and crew crashed in B-24D 42-63798
during the night of May 5/6, 1944, at Mably (Loire). Simon's
crew this night was originally the crew of Capt. John A. Lucey
of the 406th Squadron. Lucey was promoted to a staff position

and Simon took over the crew. The picture of the crew (identified as the Simon crew) in the first edition of *Carpetbaggers* includes Lucey in the top row, center.

Lt. Henry W. Wolcott III and crew crashed on the night of May 28/29, 1944, near Burst (Belgium) in B-24D 42-40550.

Lt. Ernest B. Fitzpatrick and crew crashed in B-24D 42-40478 during the night of May 29/30, 1944, at Sart Saint Laurent (Belgium). Dogrothy (from Dillon's crew and on a buddy ride) was taken by the Germans and spent the rest of the war in a POW camp.

B-24D 42-63784, flown by the Lt. Kenneth Pratt crew, crashed at La Hulpe (Belgium) on the night of June 5/6, 1944.

Lt. John R. McNeil and crew crashed on the night of June 18/19, 1944, at Ferrieres (Loiret). Their airplane was B-24H 42-51124.

Lt. John J. Meade and crew, in B-24H 42-95317, crashed during the night of July 4/5, 1944, near Autruy sur Juine (Loiret) after an attack by a night fighter. German records indicate that Lovelace (copilot), Mitchell (navigator), and Syra (tail gunner) were all buried at Autruy sur Junie cemetery.

B-24D 42-50386, flown by Lt. Charles R. Kline and crew, crashed on the night of July 4/5, 1944, between Senlis and Dammartin en Goële (Sein et Marne). After an attack by a night fighter, the airplane exploded in midair. German records indicate that all members of the crew except Abate (tail gunner), who is shown as MIA in a missing air crew report, were buried in a French cemetery at Criel.

Lt. John C. Broten and crew in B-24H 42-72873 were shot down on the night of July 4/5, 1944, by a night fighter at Trancrainville (Eure et Loir).

Lt. David A. Michelson and crew crashed on the night of July 18/19, 1944, at Mazignien (Nièvre). Their B-24H 42-51187 crashed after a collision with Halifax II LL 364 of RAF 138 Squadron. Blandin says:

> A Halifax of the 138 Squadron RAF from Tempsford and a B-24 from Harrington were dispatched that night to supply presumably two different Maquis camps in the area, these being separated by only a short distance. It seems something went wrong with the marking of one of the drop zones and one of the aircraft had to go around again for another pass while the

other was now homing in on the Rebecca. In the darkness both planes collided sideways. Being very low over a hilly ground, both crashed almost immediately with all crews being killed instantly.

Lt. Robert C. McLaughlin and crew in B-24D 42-50584 crashed during the night of August 5/6, 1944, near Wihéries/ Dour (Belgium). Lt. Richard Norton, Jr., and crew crashed on the night of August 14/15, 1944, at Duerne (Rhône). Their airplane was B-24J 44-40172. The crew member who could not be saved was Moncy (radio). Two members of the Resistance risked their lives to pull him from the burning wreckage.

Lt. James M. McLaughlin and crew crashed during the night of September 16/17, 1944, between Lebeville and Charmes (Vosges) after being hit by friendly fire of Battery A, 115th AA Gun Battalion. Their airplane was B-24J 42-50693.

Mellicent S. Moorhead knew Lt. James M. McLaughlin when they were flying with the old 492nd BG at North Pickenham and knew him to be a competent pilot and a good instrument man. While flying with Major Hurley as his copilot, Moorhead considers that he became a capable pilot and under his tutelage became a first pilot. However, because he had minimal instrument time and lacked the formal transition training in the B-24, he didn't relish the idea of flying in the left seat at night on such missions.

I know that luck has a part in survival in flying missions but the odds were more favorable if each pilot was competent in his respective job, so McLaughlin and I got together somehow and I flew as his copilot. Mac and I made a good team. Our communication usually consisted of glances and hand signals. I had flown 27 high altitude missions with the old 492nd and so had eight more to go. I was one mission ahead of Mac. I flew my last mission and offered to go with Mac on his last one. He was happy to have me since we worked so well together. He came to me later after he thought it over and said (and I remember this well): "Buck, you're finished. Don't take the chance." I took his advice since I really had had enough. All these years I often thought if I had been along maybe things would have ended differently. So the paragraph about Lt. McLaughlin and his bad luck struck home. Even through the mist of four and a half decades I can still see the oil pressure, the oil temperature, and the cylinder head pressure. I watched them carefully since they were usually the first indication that a problem might develop and we would be ready for the emergency. Sometimes a simple adjustment of the mixture or the cracking of the cowl flaps would alleviate a potentially dangerous situation. I also remember well the hypnotic effect of the radar altimeter flashing green, yellow, and red as we flew around the foothills of the Alps.

— Moorhead

In November 1943, after flying to Nutts Corner, Ireland, via Gander, Newfoundland, Don Fairbanks was on one of the first newly assigned crews to the Carpetbaggers at Alconbury. His crew consisted of Bill McKee (pilot), Everett Harwell (copilot), Norman Stoll (navigator), Robert France (bombardier), Don Fairbanks (tail gunner), Joe Saylor (dispatcher), Don Fogelsoneer (radio), and Edd Cuplin (engineer). (In the *Carpetbaggers*, 1st ed., the McKee crew photo is mistakenly identified as the McKenny crew.)

Fairbanks recalls:

Since this was an outfit shrouded in secrecy, we got the shock of our lives when Lord Haw Haw, a German propagandist on the German radio (with the best music from home), welcomed us over the radio and told us they would be waiting for us to show up over the continent. Imagine how new, green soldiers would feel knowing that our enemy was looking over our shoulders, watching our every move, when GIs we knew did not know our mission. Very nerve-wracking.

We were assigned "C" for Charlie, a B-24D painted a dull matte black. The "C" and the serial number were about the only markings on it. There were no large emblems on the wings or fuselage. Later, about halfway through our tour, we were given B-24Js with the nose and ball turrets removed, and they were painted a glossy black.

On a mission one clear night the full moon was about my tail gunner's position, twelve to one o'clock high, when all at once I noticed an aircraft approaching from my right to left. It was a twin-engine, twin-tail Messerschmitt Me 110, and I could see both the pilot and the person in the rear cockpit very clearly in silhouette. We were down moon and slightly lower, so they never saw us; they just floated by. We had orders not to shoot unless we were fired on, as we were trying to sneak in and back out unnoticed. They just disappeared and never came back.

On our combat missions we each carried an "escape kit" which contained maps, food, money, and several compasses. Each kit was personalized for each crew member by having two "civilian" photos of the individual in a civilian shirt with a necktie that was knotted in the European fashion. We found out after the war that German Intelligence could tell which outfit we were in when captured and they saw the photos in our escape kit since everyone wore the same necktie. Each squadron or group had a different tie that was used in all the pictures.

Since we flew during the full moon, we normally received time off during the dark, moonless time of each month. When we first started going to London, everybody in the U.S. Army – everybody – wore flight crew wings. It seemed that by wearing wings you announced that your pay was fifty percent greater than the rank you wore indicated, which apparently gave you a better chance with a better class of girls. Sometime about spring of 1944 the U.S. Army announced that flying crew members would sew a blue patch over the left breast pocket and the wings would be pinned to the blue patch. Going to London after that, it was surprising how few wing wearers there were. The merchants that sold wings must have noticed a sharp drop in sales.

After a while of flying at night, our outfit (36th Bomb Squadron, 801st Provisional Group) moved from Alconbury to Watton near Norwich, an ex-RAF base with permanent buildings, an excellent perimeter taxiway, but no paved runways. Our engineers placed PSP (pierced steel planking) over the grass to provide us with runways to allow heavier aircraft to take off and land. However, since our loaded B-24s could not operate from it, as it tended to retard our takeoff speed, we had to go back to Alconbury for TDY. We then moved from Watton to Harrington and into quonset huts with all the aircrew enlisted men back together (about six crews to a hut).

Strange things happen during wartime, and there are no explanations. We were in the mess hall/barracks at Alconbury, getting ready to go on a mission, when the flight engineer on one of the crews we had been with since training back at Casper, Wyoming, started telling us what we could have of his equipment, an indicaiton that he was not coming back. That night their aircraft went down. It was too low to bail out when hit, so the pilot landed it in the darkness. The plane broke up, but everyone survived except the flight engineer.

We finished our tour on July 1, 1944. We were sent home on a thirty-day leave and were to return for a second tour. It was great to be home and to eat home-cooked meals again. When the time came to report back to Atlantic City for orders to return back to our outfit for a second tour, it was decided that only the officers would return and the enlisted men would be reassigned to Training Command to teach the newcomers.

— Fairbanks

---

Donald L. Taylor stayed in the Air Force after World War II. He flew B-29s in Korea and B-52s in Viet Nam. He retired in 1969 as lieutenant colonel to Washington state, where he died a few years ago.

Oliver W. Chapman, navigator on Taylor's crew, on Taylor and the crew:

Toward the end of my tour in the ETO I was a Carpetbagger, in late 1944. I am very proud to have had the opportunity to be a part of the 801st/492nd BG.

Donald L. Taylor, known to all his friends and crew as "Herk," started his flying career in the Army Air Force as a staff sergeant pilot. I believe he enlisted in 1939. By the time he became first pilot of Crew 73 (staging designation) he was a flight officer and had nearly 2,000 hours of time behind the controls of almost every type of aircraft the Army Air Force had at the time. Every member of our crew attribute our safe return to civilian life to the skill and good judgement of "Herk" Taylor.

The story of how he became our first pilot is strange and amusing. Crew 73 was assigned a first pilot in Salt Lake whom every member of the crew knew to be incompetent, uncoordinated, and unqualified to fly — let alone command an aircraft and crew. Morale was terrible. We knew that there was no way to survive with the problems we were having with this first pilot. During "staging" he never left the base with the rest of the officers and enlisted men — except once! Fortunately for Crew 73, he contracted a severe "social" disease on that occasion and was removed to the hospital for an extended stay.

For about two weeks the crew enjoyed the entertainments available in Colorado Springs. All good things come to an end and at a briefing one morning we met our new first pilot, "Herk" Taylor. He was not impressive — about 5'6" tall, weight about 135 pounds and an officer's hat (with a grommet in it — no sloppy Air Force hot-shot) placed squarely on his head. He was a perfect size to be a fighter jockey. What was he doing in a B-24? And only a flight officer at that.

We all wondered and we felt that we had gone from the frying pan into the fire. Not for long! We knew that we had a real pilot the first time he took our plane up. This guy could fly and he knew his plane inside and out. He had to sit on a parachute or two to reach the controls, but he was smooth! Morale rose and, all of a sudden, we had a team. Everyone worked together without having to be told what to do.

The old 492nd BG had preceded us overseas by about a week. We did not have a group assignment so we flew independently to the ETO via South America and Africa. We had a nice trip. Loaded the plane with rum and Canadian Club at Puerto Rico. Some of the enlisted men "acquired" a couple of MPs' bicycles in Trinidad. They didn't know that our aircraft would be taken away from us when we reached Blackpool, as was our booze and the bicycles! A sad ending to a good trip.

Our crew was then sent to North Ireland for further combat training. We were then assigned as the first replacement crew to the 492nd BG at North Pickenham. The 492nd had flown about thirteen missions when we arrived, and already they were getting the reputation of being a "hard luck" outfit. During our tour with the group they sustained the greatest losses to any group in the Eighth Air Force during a ninety-day period.

During our assignment to the 492nd BG at North Pickenham we lost five of our crew's airplanes. It seemed every time we stood down for a mission and another crew flew our plane, it — and they — didn't come back. We were juggled from one squadron to another and finally wound up in the 859th Squadron. Our crew flew twenty-five high-altitude daylight bombing missions and by that time there were few familiar faces in the whole group left. We started our missions on May 30, 1944, and flew all of the tough ones 'til August 10, 1944, when the 492nd BG was dismantled because it could no longer function. We were shipped to Cheddington and from there to the 801st BG at Harrington. We had not suffered a single injury to the crew!

Upon leaving the 492nd BG we were so elated that we fired-off all of the flares in the plane in celebration of surviving the 492nd. Two days later at Harrington the 801st BG was redesignated the 492nd BG!!! We were not happy.

Our crew, now down to eight men, flew eight Carpetbagger missions and six Trucking missions (five-man crew) hauling gasoline to Patton. So, in addition to twenty-five missions out of North Pickenham we flew fourteen out of Harrington. No record, I'm sure, but we attribute our success and survival to Donald L. "Herk" Taylor and a very fine crew of good men: Taylor (pilot), Hunt (copilot), Chapman (navigator), Hollopeter (bombardier), McCrory (radio), Jaroz (engineer), Fisher (ball turret), Samuels (top turret), Evans (waist gunner), and Suddath (tail turret).

— Chapman

———————————————

Jim McCrory, radio operator on Taylor's crew, kept a brief diary while on twenty-five high-altitude daylight bombing missions with the old 492nd BG at North Pickenham:

Arrived at 492nd Bomb Group (Heavy), 856th Bombardment Squadron, AAF Station 143, North Pickenham, on Thursday, May 25, 1944 (APO 558). Completed final training on May 29. Flew first combat mission on Tuesday, May 30, 1944.

Squadron flying silver B-24s with tail of white background with diagonal black bar, with squadron letter in white on black bar. Our first plane went down with Lt. Haag at Bernberg during a fighter attack on his twenty-second mission. Our second plane went down with Lt. Ives at Kiel when hit by flak. Ives was on his second mission.

Excerpts taken from McCrory's diary while on his twenty-five missions:

One plane went into a spin and crashed while assembling in clouds — five ground men killed attempting to rescue crew. One plane lost at enemy coast on return.

One plane down over enemy territory — another crew bailed out over North Sea — three of crew found by Air-Sea Rescue. One dead, other two unconscious.

Enemy fighters in large numbers attacked few minutes before target time. Whole squadron of 11 planes down in approximately 30 seconds. Apparently out of ammo when they reached us. Squadron leader down, two more crippled by flak over target. Tail guns out, right waist and ball turret knocked out by flak. Also elevator controls and trim tabs, hydraulic system out.

Enemy fighters attacking Wing over target directly ahead of us. Two of our bombs exploded by flak immediately after bombs away. Several B-17s crippled seen on return to coast.

Nine bombs dropped when bomb bay doors came open, 11 dropped on target. Most of others (100 lb. GP bombs) piled up loose in bomb bay. Kicked out over channel.

Several planes down, several badly damaged in 44th BG, high right on our squadron. One exploded from direct hit.

Extremely cold at altitude. Red almost froze in tail turret. Feathered No. 3 just past target.

No. 3 hit by flak. Vibrating badly but did not go out.

Taxied to take-off position. Found oil leak in No. 2. Changed planes and took off 45 minutes late. Unable to find our group — tacked on to 93rd BG at enemy coast. 93rd recalled over Belgium. Lost formation in solid overcast, returned alone.

Squadron leader's oxygen supply hit with flames coming out of waist windows.

ME109s attacked group directly behind us — driven off immediately by escort which stayed with us very close even through bomb run. Intense flak from Munich and target. Most of flak from 105s and 55s. B-17 exploded from direct hit, with only a puff of smoke left.

Near collision with plane pulling up from directly underneath. Solid wall of flak a half mile long over target. Some of it very close but missed most of it.

Hit on leg by piece of flak but unhurt.

Saw intense flak we had to go through — intense, very accurate box of flak, tracking very accurately for several minutes past bombs away. All large guns. Deputy group leader went down just past target — 10 parachutes.

— McCrory

In December 1943, M. T. Bowyer was shipped to the ETO as a casual via Stone, England, to Station AAF239 at Magha-

berry, North Ireland. Among the units stationed there was the
35th Complement Squadron. The 35th was a small squadron of
just under 100 men, having personnel to represent every function of an airfield. The squadron was supposed to follow the
invasion and set up and operate captured airfields for the use
of fighter planes. However, the development of drop-tanks increased the range of the P-47 and P-51 fighters and made this
plan moot.

About March 1944, the squadron was transferred to Station 179, Harrington, and quartered in one of the WAAF sites.
Personnel of the squadron were scattered among almost all
base functions while remaining in the 35th for administration.
Bowyer's duty was in the Court and Boards office, with Lt. William E. Lyons in charge.

                                                — M. T. Bowyer

_____

Frank J. Miller arrived at North Pickenham on June 5,
1944, after flying over via the northern route. Members of the
crew were: Bowland (pilot), Walton (copilot), Grossman (navigator), Puckett (bombardier), Albers (engineer), Jezior (radio),
Tosi (ball turret), Miller (waist gunner), Slater (waist gunner),
and Wells (tail turret). They were assigned to the 856th Squadron at North Pickenham and flew their first mission on June
11, 1944. Excerpts from his records:

> Todays mission was Politz, Germany. I was not scheduled to
> fly. All of the planes from the 856th Squadron except one
> (Valarde) did not return. We lost five members off our crew
> (Walton, Grossman, Puckett, Jezior, and Tosi) that were fly-
> ing as replacements on the other crews.
>     Flew as replacement on McMurry's crew.
>     (Two days later — Bernberg) McMurry and crew, after
> surviving their June 15 bailout, went down on this mission
> with no known survivors. We lost five more planes from the
> 856th Squadron today and one more crewman (Wells) off my
> original crew who was flying as a replacement.
>     Lt. Powers (pilot) and I assigned to what had been Lt.
> Graham's crew.
>     Two planes crashed into each other on landing (Pitzen-
> barger and Fleming) today.
>     Transferred to Harrington. Lt. Bowland, pilot on my

original crew, who had been flying as copilot on Capt. Valarde's crew, took over what had been the Craig Ladd crew. I rejoined Bowland. Now in 857th Squadron.

We were sent immediately on Detached Service to join Col. Balchen's Detachment 1 of the 1409th ATC at RAF Station Leuchars, Fife, Scotland. It was not unusual to see a person in Army uniform one minute and in civilian clothes the next, and there were people coming and going at all hours of the day and night.

Returned to Harrington about September 27, 1944.

My records indicate that I flew the last daylight mission for the 492nd Bomb Group out of North Pickenham and the first and last night bomb mission out of Harrington. They also reflect 10 daylight, 10 Carpetbagger and 10 night bombing missions.

I finished my missions and was at the port of debarkation on VE Day.

— Miller

---

Kenneth L. Driscoll started his tour as a pilot and flight leader of the 788th BS, 467th BG, at Rackheath, near Norwich, East Anglica.

After flying five high-altitude daylight missions, two as group lead (Maj. Robert Salzarulo, 788th Squadron CO, was flying off Driscoll's right wing as deputy group lead when he was shot down on Driscoll's fourth mission to Berlin), the 788th BS was transferred to the Carpetbaggers at Harrington via Cheddington in May 1944.

The Driscoll crew's success rate was superior in completing Carpetbagger missions; twenty-seven of twenty-nine drops were completed.

The crew flew four missions in April, three missions in May, and five missions in June. After volunteering to fly more frequent missions, they flew thirteen in July and ten in August to complete their tour on August 26, 1944.

It paid off, in their case, to be eager to fly as much as possible.

---

As radio operator, Russell K. Bond started flying at Boise, Idaho, on George Johnson's crew. Leaving Boise, the crew joined the 399th Bomb Group at Sioux City, Iowa, and flew a few night training flights with Capt. Jimmy Stewart. When the group shipped overseas, their crew stayed behind and via Pocatello, Idaho, joined the 467th Bomb Group at Wendover, Utah. After flight training, they flew out of Florida to Brazil, Dakar, Marakesh, Valley, Wales, and settled at Rackheath, Norwich, England. Shortly thereafter they were transferred to Harrington to join the 801/492nd (Carpetbaggers) group:

> I flew seven heavy bombardment missions with the 467th, twenty-eight night missions and five "gas" missions with the Carpetbaggers. I had a total of forty missions and was sent home in late August of 1944. All of my "heavy" and several of my night missions were with George Johnson. My remaining missions were flown with Bill Dillon.
>
> I remember one episode very clearly. After a long mission we were returning from our drop and still rather far from the channel. It was already quite light with what had to be a full moon. We were all dead tired. I was sitting in the upper turret, just above my radio station, when I saw a JU-88 sitting about 100 yards off our left wing. Immediately the entire crew saw the plane and pilot. He sat there for about a minute or two, peeled off, and we saw no more of him. Now, we were all very wide awake and expecting a visit from fighters. Needless to say, no fighters appeared and we made it home. The JU-88 had to slip up on us from a low position or he would have been seen. We were sitting ducks had the pilot wanted to shoot us down. We had other very close ones during the "heavy" raids, but this encounter will be long remembered.
>
> — Bond

---

Garth Bowen, copilot on Capt. Robert W. Bronar's crew which was shot down by British antiaircraft fire near Namur, Belgium, on the night of January 4, 1945, believes, in retrospect, that some of the crews assigned to the 856th Squadron were more experienced than the average:

> In my case I was shanghaied. I was a happy instructor pilot at Perin Field, Sherman, Texas, and volunteered for a shipment to P-38 school. I had about 800 hours of flying time, the second best skeet shooting average on the base, when my squadron commander, who had the best skeeting average on the base, gave me an inside tip. I wound up in the right seat of a

B-24. At each base I would scream. They would tell me, "Oh, you'll be sent to first pilot transition school." Lincoln, Nebraska; Colorado Springs, Colorado; Mountain Home, Idaho, and all the way to England they'd say, "Just be ready and keep your bags packed." Shortly after arriving in England I did check out as first pilot. Soon after that I made a pact with Bob Bronar. Bob was a stern taskmaster. After a couple of rough missions he lined the crew up for inspection, so he was easy to dislike but an excellent pilot. He invited me over to his room and suggested that we team up and work to fly together as he liked my flying. I had to admit to myself that he was a superior pilot. He had been an instructor in the States and probably had nearly 2,000 hours. After a couple of missions, his crew, who began by hating his guts, wouldn't have transferred off the crew if they lost their stripes. Thirty missions, shot down once and crash landed or landed on three engines or less three times.

We didn't feel like we were very effective in the leaflet-dropping action. We frequently flew when all other night operations were scratched. Many times the weather was so bad that the weather officer couldn't assure us that there would be a single base open in England when we got back. At one time we flew nine missions in ten nights and slept in our own beds once. We'd come back and be diverted to a remote base where the weather wasn't so bad that we could get in. As we wouldn't tell their intelligence what we were doing, we got treated like the enemy. We couldn't go into the officers mess as we didn't have on class A uniforms. The best treatment was when we would go into an English base. They didn't ask any questions and respected us as night fliers.

A number of us pilots spent quite a bit of time in a room where you could lean your elbow on a wood elevated device and have a mug of harf 'n harf in your other hand debating the merits of the B-24. We came to the conclusion that it was designed by a Nazi spy. The early B-24Ds were the best. We had excellent maintenance on our base. The later planes had so much crap, turrets, armour plating, etc., hung on them that there was constant trouble. It seemed that when you would have a little trouble it was just the start of a chain reaction.

When I finished my tour, the only way I could have a shot at making captain was to put in for a second tour, which I did in A-26s as we all thought it was the ultimate airplane.

When the first A-26 mission from the base failed to return, with Major Tresemer, I just screamed, "I want to go home."

— Bowen

---

As mentioned in *Carpetbaggers* (page 125), Maj. Edward C. Tresemer, Jr., 492nd Group navigator, was lost on the first A-26 mission to Germany. Major Tresemer was a well-respected officer of the Carpetbaggers, held in high regard both by his fellow officers and the enlisted men who knew and worked with him.

Major Tresemer was born in Verona, North Dakota, on February 9, 1920. He joined the Army Air Corps as an enlisted man (ASN 17025584) and reapplied at Fargo, North Dakota, for flying status as a lieutenant, Air Corps. He attended navigation school at the Pan American Airways School in Miami, Florida. Tresemer was assigned to the 46th BS of the 41st BG at Muroc Dry Lake, California, early in December 1941, and became Lt. Robert W. Fish's B-18 crew navigator. In that capacity he navigated the B-18 aircraft which was used to calibrate the newly installed RADAR system on the U.S. West Coast.

Maj. Edward C. Tresemer, Jr. (O-434010) was confirmed as KIA over Germany on March 19, 1945, while on a secret mission (delivering a spy). His hometown was listed as Temple City, Los Angeles County, California. Records indicate he was an only son of Edward C. and Ida May Tresemer, and was survived by his mother and a sister. Major Tresemer is buried in Lot B-40, Row 17, in the Ardennes American Cemetery and Memorial at Neupre (Neuville-es-Condroz) Belgium, which is near Liege, Belgium. He wore the Distinguished Flying Cross with Oak Leaf Cluster, the Air Medal with six Oak Leaf Clusters, and the French Croix de Guerre.

— Igor "Pete" Petrenko,
Col. Robert W. Fish,
Willis H. Beasley

---

John K. Lancaster flew at Harrington as copilot on Lt. Eugene "Hank" Polansky's crew that went down in the Orkney Islands off Scotland on March 31, 1945. (On page 132 of the first edition of *Carpetbaggers,* the pilot is incorrectly shown as Eugene Polinsky.)

This was the first mission they flew after I was transferred to the Lt. Robert H. Fesmire crew. All of the crew perished, except for the copilot who replaced me. He bailed out over the North Sea and was rescued. Also, the four or six men of the Norwegian operations group, who died in this crash, were probably the same people we failed to drop because we could not find the lake bed drop area, on the previous and the last mission I flew with Hank.

I flew three missions to Stockholm with Lt. Fesmire before the war was over. We flew these missions dressed in a "Sport Coat" issued in London. I remember Lt. Colonel St. Clair very well, as I shot skeet for his team. In fact, I give him credit for my life because of the transfer to Lt. Fesmire's crew a few days before the ill-fated Polansky mission.

> — Lancaster (From the "Carpetbagger" Newsletter,
> March 1992)

---

When is impossible possible? John Lancaster's story in the last Carpetbagger bulletin proved that you have to think about the impossible as an answer if you want an explanation. Who'd ever think of a Eugene Polansky as well as a Eugene Polinsky in as small an outfit as ours? Is there a Sebastian Carriere as well as a Sebastian Corriere in the Carpetbaggers? Impossible. But Polansky and Polinsky? Both Eugene? Not impossible.

I never even heard of him, let alone knew him. I had finished my 35 missions and was back in the States by September '44. Polansky went down in March of '45. The only time I flew to Norway was about a year earlier, on an orientation flight. We went in full moonlight because that was all we knew how to do at that time. It was quite a while before we got to flying in the dark of the moon. That night, the moon was so bright and the snow so white we felt like a sitting black duck. Worse, we had trouble at the rendezvous — there were trucks with headlights on down there — which made the drop moot. What was mooter was that one of the bomb-bay doors came off its tracks and started flapping in the wind. It was making so much noise we thought the entire German army of occupation was being alerted. The pilot — I can't remember who it was right now but my pilot, Neil Ellis, was flying copilot on this orientation flight — decided to get rid of the bomb-bay door. Which meant kicking it off. Which somehow ended up as my job. Did we tie me to anything? *No.*

Moose Martin—I'll never forget him—held on to me while I hung out over the white Norwegian terrain and eventually got the door off. I don't know who held on to him. But this Eugene Polinsky was luckier over Norway than that Eugene Polansky.

Norm Stoll led that mission on which Polansky was lost. Get him to tell you his account of it. Norm and I stay in touch once he found me again about six years ago. I like it that way. Wish we all did. There's lots of stories still not told.

— Polinsky (From the "Carpetbagger" Newsletter,
September 1992)

---

Bill Dillon remembers an ill-fated mission he flew into France. His crew was assigned a target east of Bordeaux, deep into France. The load included one "Joe." Later they found out that he was a paymaster for the FFI and was carrying several million dollars in French francs. However, they had to scrub the drop after making three passes over the target and getting a different signal from the target ground each pass. After narrowly missing getting coned by three searchlights, they escaped by lying into heavy fog, then landed at a Navy base in southern England for fuel. There they were treated with plenty of hostility upon landing in their black painted B-24, with no flight plan, a motley looking crew, and a "Joe" in his jumping gear. They never did find out exactly what went wrong at that target in Bordeaux.

Norman Stoll recalls a mission in his second tour that he will never forget. It certainly was the longest. In addition, they were assigned to a plane in which he had never flown. This meant that they had to swing the compasses, and calibrate the air speed indicator, which took several hours.

The target was a frozen lake in northern Norway, approximately a thousand yards from the Swedish border. Since he was the senior navigator on the mission, he was given the honor to lead it and was given a head start of thirty minutes so that the agents they were dropping could set up their signals for the rest of the group who were following them.

There were two routes to get to the target: To fly to northern Norway via the sea, make landfall and fly east; or, they could make landfall in southern Norway and use recognizable landmarks to pinpoint their position. They elected to do the latter.

The trip north was without incident. They found the target and made the drop, then set course for the coast (due west). Stoll estimated that they would be there in about twenty to twenty-five minutes. About fifteen minutes later, Stoll asked the bombardier if he could pick up the coast, and when he replied that all he could see was land, Stoll jumped out of his seat and pulled the curtain from the astral hatch to look at the sky. Polaris (the north star) should have been at three o'clock, directly off the right wing. Instead, it was at five o'clock. He told the pilot to turn sixty degrees to the right and dive. Just then they spotted flak exploding above them. For some strange reason, they were near the heavily guarded submarine base near Trondheim. He later discussed this phenomenon with several other navigators. They came to the conclusion that since they had been flying at sixty-seven degrees North latitude they were affected by a magnetic pole.

They returned to Scotland, where the first person to greet them was Ernie Holzworth, the squadron air exec who had come up to brief them and get their reports. They learned later that all the crews found the target, which was personal gratification. If they had made an error in the drop, those following might not have found those who were in their plane. However, about four crews were lost in Norway after making their drops. He surmised that they had been drawn off course the way his crew had been. By the time Stoll and crew returned to the base, they had flown about twenty hours.

---

Douglas D. Walker was dispatcher on Lt. Robert J. Swarts' crew. Four of the crews in his training class were assigned to the Carpetbaggers at Harrington, including his crew at the time, Lt. Roger McCormick's crew. When McCormick was reassigned to the 14th Air Force in the C-B-I theater in March 1945, Walker was ordered to report to Lieutenant Swarts' crew. Swarts' crew was already a veteran one with twenty-four missions behind them. He moved into the enlisted men's Nissen hut, which they shared with Lieutenant Hudson's crew:

> I quickly resumed my friendship with them (having attended air gunnery school at Harlingen, Texas, with various enlisted men of Hudson's crew). A few nights later, Lt. Hudson's crew and our crew took off on a dual mission to drop American

commandos of Norwegian descent together with munitions and supplies into the Jaevsjo Lake area northwest of Trondheim, Norway. We first flew to Scotland, where we picked up the commandos and refueled, then headed for Jaevsjo Lake, which was located in a very mountainous area of Norway. As we neared the drop zone we encountered severe thunderstorms and turbulence. After flying on for over an hour, the decision was made by Lt. Swarts to turn back. We couldn't possibly locate the drop zone in that miserable weather, let alone fly low enough to parachute the commandos to an accurate landing. After our arrival back at our base, we waited for Lt. Hudson's aircraft to appear, but to no avail. Finally, we learned what had happened to them. The Norwegian underground forces had radioed that their Liberator had crashed into a mountain in the blizzard!

Two of the men on Lt. Hudson's crew were Angelo Santini (tail gunner) and Jack Spyker (dispatcher). About two weeks after this tragedy, we were awakened in our quarters about midnight by an apologetic voice asking, "Angelo, are you here?" We switched on the light to reveal Angelo Santini's brother, in England on a furlough from his infantry outfit in France. He hadn't heard about his brother's death.

Then, about the middle of June when we were getting things ready to fly home, the war finally over, we had another saddened visitor. It was Jack Spyker's father. He had pulled some strings and managed to persuade the government to allow him to fly to England. He wanted to know as much about Jack's last days as possible and explained that he was on his way to Norway to claim Jack's body to return him to America for reburial in the family plot. His grief was great. Jack was an only son.

— Walker

Walker had other interesting experiences. One was dispatching a French girl in January 1945. Another was dispatching a former POW German Army sergeant. He was warned by an OSS captain that, "They weren't sure if the guy would spy for our side or was looking for a free ticket back home!"

In September 1987, Walker, as vice-president of the 801/492nd Bombardment Group Association, saw the fruition and completion of several years of effort toward building a memorial at Foxhall Farm, Harrington, England. The other officers of the Association said, "He planned it, organized it, and made it happen." Walker is now deceased.

## OSS Operations from Leuchars Field, Scotland

The Office of Strategic Services conducted a series of operations out of Leuchars Field, Scotland, under the command of Col. Bernt Balchen. Balchen was a naturalized citizen of the United States, born in Norway.

The first of these operations was known as "Operation Sonnie," which was set up under the auspices of the Air Transport Command to transport 2,000 Norwegian male subjects from Stockholm to England by air and was to be completed as soon as possible after March 17, 1944. Seven crews from Heflin's Carpetbaggers flew war-weary B-24s which had been modified at Burtonwood by sealing the bomb bays, installing seats for thirty-five passengers, painting out the army insignia, and installing special navigational equipment. The crews wore civilian clothes and the B-24s were not armed. The first flight was made on March 31, 1944. Many complications were overcome to carry out this operation, including the necessity of obtaining passport visas for each flight. Even though their agreement with Sweden allowed only three flights in any twenty-four-hour period, about 5,000 individuals were brought out of Sweden in this operation.

The "Ball Project" began in July 1944, with one modified B-24 painted a dull anti-searchlight black and equipped with special navigational instruments. A Joe-hole was used for dispatching agents, and the planes were fully armed. These crews wore USAAF uniforms and were trained by the Carpetbaggers at Harrington. When fully equipped with aircraft and combat crews, the unit was split into two groups: black-painted airplanes were used to fly agent and supply drops into Norway and green-painted airplanes made the civilian flights from Sweden. The civilian flights soon began carrying cargo for OSS to Sweden, consisting of small white sacks of a newly perfected plastic explosive which were consigned as medical supplies. When the final mission was flown on September 27, 1944, sixty-four missions had been flown in the "Ball Project."

A short-lived operation was called "Sea Otter," with the intent of kidnapping Wolfgang Fehmer, called "the most hated man in Norway." Fehmer was head of the Norwegian Gestapo. For this operation, a Navy PBY was brought into Leuchars with a Carpetbagger crew trained for night landings on water. However, it was decided that many, many Norwegians would be murdered by the Nazis in reprisal and the mission was abandoned.

But all was not wasted. While Balchen was in Stockholm, working out the details of the Fehmer kidnapping, it was learned that a couple of experimental German V-2 rockets had landed intact in Sweden and one was available to the Allied for examination if they could fly it out. Lt. Col. Keith Allen flew it out in a war-weary C-47.

Three airplanes and two crews were lost in operations from Leuchars. Lt. Col. Keith Allen and crew were shot down in Murmansk with Allen killed; Capt. Truett Bullock and crew crashed into a mountain between Stockholm and Goteborg with all killed; and Lt. John O'Hara with crew flew into a mountain in southern Norway with all killed.

Balchen also conducted two special operations from Stockholm after September 1944. The first was the "Where and When Project" to transport Norwegian Police troops and to fly war materiel and food into the Norwegians when the Germans moved out. The second was the "Sepal Project," utilizing C-47s to carry saboteurs and equipment into Norway in February 1945.

———————————————

A. L. Sharps, a gunner on Lt. Howard Davis' Carpetbagger trained crew, was sent north to Leuchars. He flew seven missions on the "Ball Project" from July 31 to September 21, 1944. He recalls:

> I doubt if the Colonel ever thought of himself as "old." I still recall him as the best flier, the best navigator, and the most deadly soldier I ever knew. Balchen had a built in compass in his brain which worked when the regular compass went crazy.
>
>    Leuchars is more than a mile north of Edinburg. You'll find it across the river Tay from the city of Dundee. We did not fly under cover of darkness, for that far north it doesn't get dark in July and August. We flew at fifty feet altitudes and

ducked in and out of fjords. Canisters were dropped at 100 feet altitude and agents at 400 feet.

— Sharps

## Carpetbagger Operations From Italy

On December 17, 1944, the entire 859th Bombardment Squadron (H) flew to Brindisi Airfield, located outside the port of Brindisi, Italy. Involved in the movement were eighteen B-24 "Organic Aircraft" with approximately fifteen personnel on each and sixteen C-47 "Transport Aircraft" with approximately thirteen personnel aboard.

The squadron staff included the following:

| | |
|---|---|
| Lt. Col. Leonard M. McManus | Commander |
| 1st Lt. William J. Carey | Executive Officer |
| Capt. James A. Seccafico | Operations Officer |
| Capt. James P. Stewart | Intelligence Officer |
| 1st Lt. Russell P. Knott | Adjutant |
| Capt. Kenneth L. Bechtold | Engineering Officer |
| Capt. James T. Dresser | Flight Surgeon |
| 1st Lt. Leo F. Johnson | Supply Officer |
| 1st Lt. Herbert Kahn | Communications Officer |
| 1st Lt. Carl F. Johnson | Transportation Officer |
| 1st Lt. Philip C. Vogel | Radar Officer |

The B-24 aircraft flown to Italy by the 859th Squadron were as follows:

| | | | |
|---|---|---|---|
| B-24 42-50393 | B-24 42-50447 | B-24 42-51208 | B-24 42-7563 |
| B-24 42-95259 | B-24 42-95262 | B-24 42-52711 | B-24 42-50377 |
| B-24 42-50428 | B-24 42-95152 | B-24 42-50380 | B-24 42-94763 |
| B-24 42-95003 | B-24 42-95131 | B-24 42-7612 | B-24 41-29163 |
| B-24 42-51201 | B-24 42-50331 | | |

At Brindisi, the operations of the 859th were joined with those of the 885th Bombardment Squadron (H), which had also recently arrived from England. The two B-24 squadrons formed the basic tactical elements of the 15th Special Group (Provisional) commanded by Col. Monro MacCloskey.

The move from Harrington, England, to Brindisi, Italy, was viewed as somewhat of a disappointment. Not only did everyone have to live in old barracks, but also the December weather was uninvitingly cold and damp. Unlike the sociability encountered at Harrington, the local populace in Brindisi kept behind closed doors and shuttered windows to avoid unnecessary contact with the Americans, whom many looked upon as strangers and intruders.

On February 9, 1945, a B-24 piloted by Lt. Robert W. Maxwell on a mission to Yugoslavia was reported by two other B-24 crews from the squadron as having exploded in the air, presumably from enemy fire. The four officers and three enlisted members of the crew on board were subsequently reported as "Killed in Action."

On February 17, the 859th and 885th squadrons dispatched a total of twenty-six B-24s for missions covering ten different target areas in Northern Italy. All aircraft returned safely after successfully completing their missions. Subsequently, the 2641st received a Unit Citation from Headquarters, Fifteenth Air Force.

On March 6, 1945, the 15th Special Group (Provisional) was given the new designation of 2641st Special Group (Provisional). The commanders of the organizations concerned and the mission remained unchanged.

On March 24/25, 1945, 112 officers and 388 enlisted men of the 859th BS flew in their squadron aircraft 400 miles north to Rosignano Airfield. Again they joined with the 885th BS, which had arrived a few days earlier. Tents became living quarters for the bulk of the men. The tents were strewn around an estate surrounding a large castle, old, vacant, but habitable. It had once been occupied by German troops. The castle became the offices of the group and squadron headquarters. Key personnel working in the offices were billeted on the top floor of the castle.

During April, Resistance groups in the Po Valley, Austria, and Czechoslovakia were scheduled for support by the 2641st Special Group (Prov.). On April 19, one of the B-24s from the 859th BS piloted by Capt. Walter L. Sutton was shot down by fighters over Northern Italy. All crew members bailed out. Captain Sutton and three crew members were captured and taken prisoner, only to be rescued by Allied troops shortly thereafter. Four of the crew were picked up by Italian Partisans, who returned them to the Allies.

On April 25, a B-24 from the 859th piloted by Lt. Edward

F. Reilly, Jr., departed on a mission to Austria and failed to return. All efforts to locate the plane, which carried four officers and four enlisted men, were futile. Subsequently, the crew was reported as "Missing in Action."

Most of the men in the 859th correctly sensed that the war in Europe was drawing to a close and that they would soon be on the way home to the United States.

On April 29, upon completion of his combat tour, Lieutenant Colonel McManus returned to the United States. Capt. Albert J. Beller assumed command of the squadron. Tactical operations had ceased. On May 20, with the exception of the rear echelon motor convoy, the entire squadron flew in its B-24s on a two-and-one-half-hour flight to Gioia del Colle Airfield for the purpose of securing needed maintenance facilities to pre-flight and test-hop the squadron's aircraft in preparation for return to the United States. The squadron was relieved from its assignment to the 2641st Special Group (Prov.) and attached to the base at Gioia del Colle.

On July 2, Captain Beller completed his flying tour and returned to the United States. The executive officer, Capt. William J. Carey, was appointed 859th commander.

On July 20, except for a small cadre left behind to assist in salvaging aircraft, the squadron departed Gioia del Colle by truck to what was to become its final relocation. It arrived in Bari, Italy, on the same day. By the end of September, all personnel except Captain Carey had returned to the United States. Aircraft had been flown back by the 859th aircrews or salvaged. Equipment and supplies had been disposed of through base facilities.

On October 1, with heavy heart, Captain Carey signed the last "Morning Report," thus terminating the existence of the 788th/859th Bombardment Squadron (H). Then, he too flew home to the United States.

Military historians and researchers will attest to the heroic achievements of the 788th/859th Bombardment Squadron (H) commander, Lt. Col. Leonard M. McManus, his chief of operations, Capt. James A. Seccafico, and the brave aircrews whose direct and obvious contribution to the defeat of the Axis warrant the gratitude of the free world.

William J. Carey, Executive Officer
788th/859th Bombardment Squadron (H)

## Night Bombing

William S. Bartholomew went through B-24 R.T.U. training at Chatham Field at Savannah, Georgia, and was assigned to Ralph B. Sampson's crew, No. 520. The crew consisted of Sampson (pilot), Bartholomew (copilot), Green (navigator), Shimkus (bombardier), Ford (engineer), Schiff (radio), Dunn (nose gunner), Wible (waist gunner), Bennett (tail turret), and Lindquist (ball turret).

The Sampson crew was one of fourteen aircrews shipped out of New York harbor on November 30, 1944, on the HMS *Louis Pasteur,* landing in Liverpool, England, on December 7, 1944. They were sent by bus to Harrington and were assigned to the 858th Bomb Squadron of the 492nd Bomb Group.

Sampson and I had completed a lot of night flying and instrument time in our training. We spent several more weeks training for night high-altitude bombing missions in new B-24H type aircraft.

Our first high-altitude night bombing mission was on the 21st of February, 1945. I remember walking to our briefing with Shimkus at about 4:00 P.M. Our target assignment was the railroad marshalling yards at Duisburg in the Ruhr Valley of Germany.

As we climbed out we could see other bombers (RAF and U.S.) rising up off the dark land into the air. We soon lost track of the planes ahead of us and forgot about them. Green, our navigator, called us on the intercom and said that we had to lose one minute. That was easy — the quickest way to accurately lose one minute was to make a full, 360-degree (one needle-width) turn — it takes exactly one minute.

We had about three night fighter passes after leaving the I.P. Nearing the target, the flak became heavier. Searchlight beams were slowly sweeping the night sky over the target area. Now, we could see bomb strikes dead ahead. At this time two bluish colored searchlight beams coned an airplane about a mile ahead of us. He was sitting at the apex of the two light beams. Immediately a ring of about thirty searchlights were turned on, and the airplane was sitting in a one-quarter-mile-wide circle of light. They had our bombing altitude, now. Within a few seconds the entire lighted area was filled with flak. In a matter of ten to fifteen seconds the airplane exploded in a bright cloud of smoke and fire. Only the blue lights were left on, for us, as we approached the target.

Now we seemed to be at the same spot as the "unlucky plane" that was ahead of us. The bomb racks began clicking away as Shimkus called out, "Bombs away." Since we were to take an aerial photo of the target, we remained on course for several minutes (it seemed like a half hour). We cranked the airplane over in a steep, diving turn – spiraling 180 or 190 degrees to the left and lost 2,000 feet in the turn. Seven to eight minutes off the target, we seemed to be in the clear. Suddenly, there was a tremendous explosion under us. We noted that the altimeter gained about 300 feet. Wible (waist gunner) yelled, "Bart, we're on fire!" I said, "Say again!" "Dammit Bart, this is Wible in the waist – we are on fire!"

Ralph and I could feel the heavy drag on the port side and noticed the airplane was turning slowly to the left a few degrees per minute. Ralph decided to go back to the waist for a better look at our damage, where he found a tongue of fire about eight feet wide extending out past the vertical stabilizers. There was a hole about twenty to twenty-four inches in diameter located about two feet from the fuselage and one foot ahead of the flaps on the port side.

The plane was turning back into Germany, and it was important to get out of the plane before the tip tank blew. Ralph rang the bail-out alarm bell five long rings. Each man on the crew called on the intercom as they left the ship. All was clear for me to go next. I stepped off the right side of the bomb bay catwalk into the night sky. Our altitude was about 14,000 feet and our airspeed was about 190 mph. My helmet and goggles came off as I hit the slip stream. I planned to count up to ten to lessen the opening impact of my chute. But, when I got to three, that was it, I pulled the ripcord. Boy, it was sure taking a long time to open. Then, I realized that I was falling head down. The chute suddenly filled and I was sent to the bottom of the harness. I swung like a pendulum through 160 degrees for the first few swings. The chute was spilling air and the lower half of the canopy threatened to collapse as I reached the high point of the swing. I pulled on the opposite risers with each swing, and soon I had a comfortable descent. The next thing I noticed was that my big flying boots were hanging three feet below my feet on electrical wires that had been pulled out of the legs of my heated flying suit. Slowly and carefully I gently retrieved the dangling wires like an anxious fly fisherman.

I could hear people yelling and talking, dogs were barking and flashlights were bobbing about near a small village at a four-way road intersection. The village was Tinlot, Belgium, located about eighteen miles south and west of Liege, Belgium. While planning my escape route, I became aware that the ground was rushing up at me. I pulled up on my risers, put my feet together, and hit the ground. I got my flying suit off without too much trouble and buried it. I turned toward the highway and was startled to see a man standing on the center line about 100 feet away, watching me. I pointed my finger at him as if I had a pistol, and he turned quickly and walked very fast away from the village.

Now that I had been seen, I hurried toward the southwest to watch traffic on the road. About this time several GI trucks came by, headed toward Tinlot. The time was now about 10:00 P.M. I heard a jeep coming down the road with two soldiers talking loudly. I whistled as the jeep went by. It stopped quickly, and slowly backed toward me. I could see their rifles pointing at me as I came out of the trees next to the road.

They took me in to the Tinlot MP station. I signed the jeep operator's passes and they took me to the crash site and then in to Liege to the Red Cross Station. I then reported to a small fighter strip that we were shot down and they forwarded the message to Harrington. After resting a day or two in Liege, the other crew members drifted in, with eight of us collecting at the Red Cross Station. We were missing our bombardier, Shimkus.

The next morning a C-47 picked us up and flew us back to Harrington. Lieutenant Colonel Boone met our plane as we landed, and we reported that Shimkus was missing. Colonel Boone smiled and said that Shimkus had been flown back to Harrington two days earlier by a brigadier general in an L-5 "Spotter" aircraft.

— Bartholomew

## Flight to the China-Burma-India Theater

In November 1944 Maj. Bestow R. Rudolph departed from Harrington on a flight to New Delhi, India. Accompanying him and his crew were Lieutenant Colonels Gable and Chandler of the London OSS office, who were to discuss with OSS officials in the China-Burma-India Theater the feasibility of conducting operations there. B-24D No. 42-63980, *Playmate,* one of the oldest B-24s in Carpetbagger operations, was selected for the flight and would demonstrate the modifications and general appearance of Carpetbagger airplanes.

Leaving from Harrington, they stopped at Bovington to pick up the OSS officials, then flew to New Delhi via Naples and Cairo. At OSS Headquarters in New Delhi, meetings were held with other OSS people to determine the need for Carpetbagger operations in the C-B-I Theater. General Donovan was to arrive in a few days. Before his arrival, the crew and OSS officials inspected bases and facilities to get an all-around picture of conditions and to determine whether or not the operation could be carried out effectively. Sites were inspected in North Burma, Calcutta, and Dinjan, India. Colonels Gable and Chandler flew by ATC aircraft over the hump into China to complete the investigation and inspect conditions in the field, spending five days in China before returning to New Delhi.

General Donovan finally arrived with his staff, and the meeting began. It was decided that a Carpetbagger project was needed for the C-B-I Theater but that no part of the ETO group of Carpetbaggers would be sent to the C-B-I Theater unless the entire group was available, and as long as a part of the ETO group was needed in Europe a new group should be organized for the C-B-I Theater from units already in that theater.

*Playmate* returned to England on January 29, 1945, following the same route back, with the exception of a stop at Tel Aviv so that Capt. Emanuel Choper could enjoy a short visit with his grandfather whom he had never seen. The round trip covered 25,000 miles and took sixty days.

Although the 801st/492nd Carpetbaggers did not operate in the C-B-I Theater, the report of the investigation of facilities and the basic information and organizational procedures passed on from the ETO Carpetbaggers was of vital importance in starting the project in the C-B-I Theater.

Members of the crew making the trip with Rudolph were Choper (copilot); McGuire (navigator); France (bombardier); Fulton (engineer); Delano (crew chief); Lewis (radio).

On March 30, 1945, two Carpetbagger crews along with two Carpetbagger B-24s were transferred to the 14th Air Force and left Harrington on PSC to Kunming, China, to help start operations in the C-B-I Theater. One of the pilots was Lt. Roger B. McCormick from the 856th BS.

The records of the 801st/492nd Carpetbaggers do not give even an inkling of the C-B-I Carpetbaggers' successes and failures, or if they in fact even got organized after Lieutenant McCormick arrived there with the two modified B-24s from Harrington.

However, from other sources there is evidence that they were, indeed, organized and active during the last several months of the war with the Japanese. The following is taken from *The Doolittle Raid: America's Daring First Strike Against Japan,* by Carrol V. Glines.

On August 20, 1945, a coded message was tapped out on a portable high-frequency radio transmitter from Peking:

> Four Doolittle Raiders located in Military Prison Peking.
> Names are Lt. George Barr, Lt. Robert Hite, Lt. Chase Nielsen, and Cpl. Jacob De Shazer. Barr in poor condition. Others weak. Will evacuate these men first. Advise ETA of aircraft.

The locating of these men followed weeks of work by undercover OSS teams of five and six men each who had been searching behind Japanese lines for POW camps to prevent the Japanese from killing the prisoners as a last gesture of defiance. Some of these teams parachuted into Japanese strongholds in the dead of night; others walked through the Japanese lines.

One three-man team, with the code name "Magpie Mission," was sent into the Peking area in the early spring of 1945 and reported a large POW camp at Fengtai, just outside Peking. They reported that other Americans were being held in a military jail inside the city in Prison #1407. A report on August 6 gave size of cells, furnishings, and the daily routine of the prisoners. On August 9 the second and last atomic bomb of World War II was dropped on Japan from a B-29 of the 20th Air Force from North Field, Tinian.

On August 13 a six-man OSS team was dispatched from Chunking to liberate the Americans at Fengtai and from the military jail inside Peking. The team successfully parachuted onto a small Japanese fighter strip outside Peking from a B-24 with the ball turret removed. They carried a total of $100,000 in American cash and a letter from General Wedemeyer, commanding general of the U.S. Forces, Far East, addressed to the Japanese, stating firmly that no harm was to come to the team and that they were representing him until American troops arrived to take over the city.

On August 14 the unconditional surrender of Japan was announced by President Truman. All prisoners at the Fengtai camp had been released by the morning of the twentieth. The OSS team knew, however, that four of Doolittle's fliers were being held in special confinement in the military prison in the city. The Japanese believed that no one but themselves knew that the fliers were in prison in Peking and did not release them with the other POWs. Their plan was to keep them as prisoners forever, even if Japan lost the war.

The OSS team demanded that the four fliers be released immediately. The Japs were stunned, but within an hour the four Doolittle fliers were released from their cells. A few hours later the world learned for the first time the fate of two of Doolittle's B-25 crews that had gone down in enemy territory in April 1942.

## Special Services, AAF Station 179, Harrington

Special Services began to organize about April 1, 1944. Very little was offered at first, due to a lack of facilities and equipment, but movies were shown when film could be obtained and copies of *Stars and Stripes* were made available. An enlisted men's lounge was soon established in the buildings reserved for the future Aero Club to fill in until the American Red Cross could establish its Aero Club. A stage was built in the snack bar of the future Aero Club to handle all live entertainment.

During April, the first dance was sponsored on the base, attended by service girls from surrounding British military installations and with civilian girls from Northampton serving as hostesses. The affair was a success, with a buffet lunch being served to those attending.

A library, placed in the chaplain's office in the gym, proved to be very popular and was moved into the Aero Club when it was established. Numerous educational facilities were available, including British University and Armed Forces Institute courses, and French and German classes were held three times a week. Large-scale maps of all the war theaters and fronts gave the latest available status of the warring nations.

Lt. Charles L. Guimento arrived at Harrington in June and was assigned as athletic officer. He organized an athletic department and conducted organized athletic activities on the base. A gym with baskets and backboards for basketball, boxing equipment, weights, medicine balls, punching bags, and wrestling mats were provided. Musical instruments were made available, and a base dance band was formed. Organized athletics included baseball, softball, track, basketball, swimming, tennis, boxing, and tug-of-war.

In July, a popular feature known as Cabaret Night was started in the snack bar. Presented every Thursday night, this activity created an atmosphere found in a typical night club with dancing and floor shows.

Sgt. Carl Scherberle of the 352nd Service Squadron represented the base as a member of the Composite Command Swimming Team, participating in an Eighth Air Force Swimming Carnival in August. Among strong competition, he won three places in three events: first place in the 50-yard backstroke, third place in 150-yard medley (three men), and third place in the 200-yard free style relay (four men).

Also in August, members of two RAF Stations and two USAAF Stations participated in all events at a track meet. S.Sgt. Shirley Williamson of the 858th BS won the broad jump with 18'9", and took second place in the high jump with a jump of 5'7". Sgt. Jack Johnson of the 35th Station Complement Squadron placed third in the broad jump with a jump of 18'2", and placed third in the high jump with a jump of 5'5". The tug-of-war team of the 35th Station Complement Squadron, with an average weight of 201 pounds, won five of seven pulls to take first place. The track team earned a total of eighteen points to take third place in the meet. The tug-of-war team later participated in the Rothwell Holiday activities and won the first two pulls to take first place.

The 857th BS volleyball team was the winner of the base single-elimination tournament and represented the station in the Composite Command single-elimination tournament, losing to Alconbury in the first round. A boxing exhibition was held in the base gym before an audience of 400 officers and enlisted men. Cpl. Benny McColan of the 856th BS, former Pennsylvania State Bantam Weight Champion, AAU, was matched with a member of the Billy Conn troupe. Billy Conn gave a three-round exhibition with Cpl. Lee Matricianni, the Eighth Air Force Heavyweight Champion. Capt. Frank X. Shields and Sgt. Charles Hare, internationally known tennis stars, put on a singles exhibition at the Lancaster Estate tennis court before 200 officers and enlisted men. They then split up to team with two paratroopers from Market Harborough in tennis doubles.

The base football team was made up of members of all units on the base. Late in starting, a six-game schedule was arranged with two games being canceled. Of the remaining four games played, the base team tied two and lost two. Outstanding players, and named to the First Bombardment Division All Stars Team to play at Bedford on New Year's Day, were Cpl. James Matlock (858th BS); S.Sgt. Benjamin Street (856th BS); S.Sgt. Robert Weiss (856th BS); Pvt. Owen Moffit (857th BS); and Maj. Edward Tresemer (Hdg. 492nd BG).

---

Robert H. Sellers was "base safety officer, base mess officer, company commander, bomb reconnaissance officer all rolled in one."

I never saw Heflin, Dickerson or McManus smile. They had every reason to be serious. But I suspect Boone and St. Clair of slipping into Sullivan's room one night and snipping off one side of his beautiful, long, waxed moustache. Boone would have been a good salesman. He was a good listener and looked into your eyes, giving all attention to you and blotting out all else. Boone once owned a roadside tavern in Ohio. He sold the place after taking on Christ. He occasionally preached sermons in the base Chapel. He and crew went down into the Channel where one, if alive, on impact would

die in the cold water within minutes. You show a picture of
Captain Bell, the special services officer. He could break up a
crap game when called upon which resulted in his sending
home to his wife many thousands of dollars.

— Sellers

## Return to AAF Station 179, Harrington

Former airmen from the 801st/492nd Bombardment Association and their wives and associates returned to England on
September 19, 1987, to dedicate a permanent Memorial Monument to mark the Air Field on Foxhall Farm, Harrington, England, where they served their country in World War II and as a
tribute to their comrades who flew from there and were lost.
The monument was designed by a Carpetbagger, Douglas
Walker, and his wife, Jackie. The most outstanding feature of
the monument is an engraving of a black B-24 taking off from
the Air Field with the Foxhall cottage in the background. Members of the Carpetbaggers contributed the money needed to
construct the granite monument, which is located on privately
owned land. Lady Susan Glover gave the association the lease
covering the memorial site.

A time capsule was interred under the Memorial Monument containing the following:

FFI arm band; USA Flag patch worn on the shoulder; a book,
*Carpetbaggers,* written by Ben Parnell; a copy of the Lieces-
ter Evening Mail with the story of President Roosevelt's death
— April 5, 1945; a copy of the *Stars and Stripes* — April 5,
1945; a notice from the 406th BS bulletin board by Gen.
Eisenhower—February 25, 1944; one leaflet from SHAAF on
the end of the war; one wristwatch worn by S. Corriere
when in England; one package of assorted coins from Europe, circa 1940–1945; an assortment of leaflets dropped
over Europe; assorted francs and one American $2 bill; one
photograph of B-24 taking off with the Foxhall cottage in the
background; one package English humor cards — 1940; one
package of English scenery cards — 1930; copies of Group
Newsletters; one open letter to whomever opens the time
capsule; one private letter to whomever opens the time capsule; copies of the Group's History; copy of Group's Battle
Honors; actual stories of typical missions.

— From the 801/492nd Newsletter
December 1987

**Comments and corrections to *Carpetbaggers*, 1st ed., from Serge Blandin, French aviation historian, Lyon, France:**

Page

8   Allier Department: Allier is one of the French Départements. A "département" is one of the administrative divisions of France.

7   Annecy: Well-known city in Haute-Savoie (a department).

87   Belfort: City in Territoire-de-Belfort.

35   Mr. Benoît: A family name.

88   Besancon: City in Doubs.

64   Billay: Probably Belley, a city in Ain.

87   Birare: Briare, a city in Loiret, on Loire River.

50   Braine-le-Compte: Braine-le-Comte, a city twenty-five kilometers southwest of Brussels, Belgium. Not in France.

93   Bron: A suburb of Lyon (not Lyons, which is the English spelling). Airfield there.

32   Caen: City in Calvados.

53   Carentan: City in Manche.

85   Charmes: Spelling is correct, but there are many Charmes in France. Most probably Charmes in Vosges.

60   Chartres: City in Eure-et-loir.

31   Château de la Rochelle: No positive identification possible. Could be in Charente.

93   Château Marieux at Collonges-au-Mont d'Or: A large family house where Americans were billeted. Correct spelling is probably Merieux — a well-known family.

69   Château Percia: Probably a private place.

97   Château Rouge: Village in Moselle. Identification still doubtful.

87   Chatellaunt: Should be Chatellerault in Vienne. Still to be confirmed. "Mark 19" field code unknown to me.

45   Cheny-le-Chatel: Chenay-le-Châtel, a village in Saône et Loire.

60   Cherbourg: Well-known city in Manche.

110   Coubre Point: Pointe de la Coubre, a well-known cape northwest of Royan in Charente Maritime with strong German defenses at the time.

69      Dampierre: There are more than thirty Dampierre in
        France! Could be Dampierre-au-Temple, a village in
        Marne.

72      Department of Ain: Ain is a département just northeast
        of Lyon, not northwest.

128     Dijon: My hometown. A well-known city in Côte-d'Or,
        with big German air base and marshalling yards.

8       Dordogne Department: Dordogne had many drop zones
        during 1944.

99      Dunkerque: Most famous port and city in Nord.

56      Elbeuf: City in Seine-Maritime, on Seine River.

68      Guise: City in Aisne.

7       Hainault: A province of Belgium, not France.

75      Haute-Savoie Department: A département in Eastern
        France near Lac de Genève.

93      Hôtel Beau-Rivage: A well-known resort at Annecy
        where Americans were billeted.

8       Lacelle: Village in Correze.

82      Lake Annecy: Lac d'Annecy is the correct name in
        French.

47      Lae: Probably Lay, near Saint-Symphorien-de-lay in
        Loire.

37      Lanquait: Totally unknown. Could be the secret landing
        ground at Loyettes in Ain.

87      Laroche: La Roche. Positive identification impossible.
        Too many La Roche in France.

68      Le Château: Most probably Le Cateau-Cambrésis, a
        small town between Maubeuge and Guise in Nord.

53      Le Mans: Well-known city in Sarthe.

46      Le Palaiso: Lapalisse in Allier.

88      Limoges: Well-known city in Haute-Vienne.

46      Loddes: Village in Allier.

29      Loire River: Spelling is correct.

47      Lyon: Third French city in Rhône. Lyons in English.

93      Lyon-Bron: Prewar airport. Now a busy general aviation
        airport near city center.

46      Marcigny: Village in Saône-et-Loire near Charolles.

119     Marseilles: Mareseille in French. Well-known second
        city south of France.

68      Maubeuge: City in Nord, near Belgian border.

68    Mons: City in Belgium, not France. Between Brussels and French border. Also called Bergen in Flemish.

37    Montbrisson: Montbrison is correct spelling. Small town in Loire.

32    Normandy: Normandie in French. A province or region.

4     Orleans: Well-known city on Loire River.

63    Penvenan: Village in Britanny near Lannion.

46    Picuador: La Pacaudière, a village between Lapalisse and Roanne, in Loire.

11    Pyrénées: Mountain range between France and Spain.

88    Quarra: Could be Querré, a village in Maine-et-Loire. Code name Dick 35 is still unidentified. Quarra is not the right name. Does not exist at all.

137   Reims: Large city in Marne.

31    Renault: The Renault plant in Paris.

45    Roanne: Well-known city in Loire.

7     Rumilly: Town in Haute Savoie.

136   Saint-cyr-de-Valorges: Village in Loire.

36    Saint-Germain-Laval: Village in Loire.

53    Saint-Lo: Town in Manche.

41    Saint-Polgues: Village in Loire.

136   Tarare: City in Rhône.

81    Troarns: Troarn is correct spelling. Small town in Calvados.

69    Vallé Multria: Most probably La Vallée-Mulâtre, a village in Aisne, between Maubeuge and Guise.

8     Var Department: A département in southern France, on the Riviera.

37    Ville: Villefranche-sur-Saône, a town north of Lyon, in Rhône.

69    White Horse: Was in fact a secret landing ground near French-Belgian border. Correct name of the nearest hamlet is Le Cheval Blanc, just south of Rocroi in Ardennes.

xi    7,000 francs = 1,400 dollars.

*Memorial to the Ambrose crew at Saint-Cyr-de-Valorges (Rhône), France, April 28, 1944. Five killed, one POW, two evaded.*
— Courtesy: S. Blandin

*Monument to the McNeil crew at Le Pressoir, near Ferrières (Loiret), France.*
— Courtesy: S. Blandin/ J. F. Lafosse

*Monument to the Norton crew at Duerne, France.*
— Courtesy: S. Blandin

*Monument to the Michelson crew (and Royal Air Force crew) at Marigny l'Eglise (Nièvre), France. Text can be translated as follows: "Glory and gratitude to our friends the American and British airmen and to the gallant Russian soldier\* who fell gloriously on the soil of Marigny-l'Eglise on July 19, 1944 for our liberation."*
*\* An unknown Russian patriot was found dead by the local Maquis men on the same day.*
— Courtesy: S. Blandin

*Lieutenant Colonel Boone and partial staff and section heads..*
— Courtesy: Bestow R. Rudolph

*Lieutenant Colonel Dickerson and staff.*
— Courtesy: Ivon Ressler

*Lieutenant Colonel McManus and partial staff.*
—Courtesy: Leonard McManus

*Castle at Rosignano Airfield, 2641 Special Group Headquarters.*
— Courtesy: Leonard McManus

*Photo of Robert Sellers was made in Bournemouth, England, in 1944 by Edmund Lukar, Royal photographer.*
— Courtesy: Robert Sellers

*British Mosquito PR XVI at Harrington.*
— Courtesy: S. Blandin

*Maj. B. R. Rudolph (left, rear) and crew with passengers, just before taking off for India.*

— Courtesy: Bestow R. Rudolph

*Biarritz, France, 1944, after landing a C-47 behind the German lines. Front center: Colonel Fish.*

— Courtesy: Ron W. Clarke

*Archambault crew.*
— Courtesy: Bestow R. Rudolph

*Boone crew.*
—Courtesy: Bestow R. Rudolph

*Bowland Crew*

— Courtesy: F. Miller

*Berkoff crew.*

— Courtesy: G. Snyder

*Carpenter crew (formerly Sanders crew).*
— Courtesy: Burris/Sanders

*Dillon crew.*
—Courtesy: W. F. Dillon

*Ellis crew.*
— Courtesy: Bestow R. Rudolph

*Estes crew.*
— Courtesy: Bestow R. Rudolph

*Gilpin crew.*
— Courtesy: Leonard McManus

*McCormick crew.*
— Courtesy: D. Walker

*McDonald crew.*
— Courtesy: Frank McDonald

*Mulligan crew.*
— Courtesy: Leonard McManus

*Sampson crew.*
— Courtesy: Wm. S. Bartholomew

*Taylor crew.*
— Courtesy: Chapman, McCrory

*Laying the wreath on the memorial: Col. Robert Fish (left), Clive Bassett. Left side (back to front): 859th – Ed Albers, 857th – Charles Dee, 406th – Paul Kasza, 858th – Kevin O'Brien. Right side (back to front): 850th – John Carey, 788th – Bill Dillon, 856th – Bernard Beverly, 36th – Igor "Pete" Petrenko.*

— Photo by *Northamptonshire Evening Telegraph*, courtesy W. Shearsmith, via Si Sizemore

*Report of the month by Gen. H. H. Arnold from "The Thunderbird" newsletter.*

— Photo from "The Thunderbird" newsletter, Thunderbird Field, Scottsdale, Arizona, courtesy W. G. Arthur

*Carpetbagger Memorial, Harrington, England.*

— Courtesy: B. Dillon

THE UNITED STATES ARMY AIR FORCE
801st/492nd BOMBARDMENT GROUP (H)
CARPETBAGGERS
FLEW CLANDESTINE NIGHT MISSIONS FROM THIS SECRET AIRFIELD
DURING WORLD WAR TWO IN BLACK B-24 LIBERATOR BOMBERS
DROPPING MUNITIONS AND SUPPLIES TO UNDERGROUND RESISTANCE FIGHTERS
IN NAZI OCCUPIED EUROPE.
THEY PARACHUTED AND LANDED OSS AGENTS INTO BELGIUM, DENMARK,
FRANCE, THE NETHERLANDS, NORWAY AND GERMANY
TO CARRY OUT ESPIONAGE ACTIVITIES AGAINST ENEMY FORCES.
THEY ALSO FLEW NIGHT BOMBING MISSIONS.
208 AMERICAN AIRCREWMEN GAVE THEIR LIVES FLYING FROM THIS AIRFIELD.

# Appendix I

## War Log

### 1938–1939

British prepare two pamphlets: "The Art of Guerrilla Warfare" and "Partisan Leader's Handbook." This was the beginning of British SOE.

### 1942

*June:* By presidential order, OSS becomes federal agency responsible for American covert operations. SOE and OSS enter into agreement spelling out basic terms of operation.

### 1943

*July:* 4th Antisubmarine Squadron arrives in UK.

*August:* Air Echelon of 22d Antisubmarine Squadron arrives in UK.

*September:* SOE and OSS representatives discuss unification and issue joint statement of responsibility for D-Day procedure.

*24 October:* Key personnel of 22d AS Squadron meet at Bovingdon, where it is learned that the 22d AS Squadron will work in covert operations with British.

*25 October:* Select combat crews depart for Tempsford to observe RAF in covert operations.

*27 October:* Ground sections of 22d AS Squadron report at Alconbury; combat crews about a week later. Ground sections of 4th AS Squadron arrive at Alconbury in early November.

*2 November:* 36th and 406th BS designations assigned to Eighth Air Force, First Bombardment Division.

*3 November:* Pilots, navigators, and bombardiers of the 22d AS Squadron start making missions with British. First unit casualty: Capt. James E. Estes, MIA with British crew.

*7 November:* Training flights under way and crews checked out. Lack of modified B-24s holding up operations.

*9 November:* King and Queen of Great Britain visit Tempsford. Have tea at Officer's Club. Each combat crew personally introduced.

*11 November:* Lieutenant Gross reported MIA with British crew in Halifax.

*22 November:* Air Echelon of 22d AS Squadron and Ground echelon of 4th AS Squadron form nuclei of new squadrons, 36th and 406th, attached to 482nd BG (P) for administration.

*28 November:* 36th BS officially organized, Maj. Robert W. Fish, CO; 406th BS officially organized, Lt. Col. Clifford J. Heflin, CO.

*5 December:* Captain St. Clair, ops officer, and Lieutenant Shapiro, intelligence officer, 36th BS, return to Tempsford with several combat crews for training with British.

*9 December:* Capt. Ralph V. Everly transferred to 36th BS from 406th BS as squadron surgeon.

*14 December:* Lieutenant Colonel Heflin relieved of command, 406th BS. Major Fish relieved of command, 36th BS. Both transferred to Group Headquarters. Capt. Rodman A. St. Clair assumes command, 36th BS; Capt. Robert L. Boone assumes command, 406th BS.

*17 December:* Master Sergeant Girard, 36th BS, relieved and returned to States to enter school for advanced engineering leading to a commission. Lt. Glen C. Nesbitt, 406th BS, bails out of Halifax bomber over England with RAF crew.

*20 December:* Lieutenant Cosgrove, armament and chemical warfare officer, 36th BS, relieved and sent to States to enter aviation cadet program.

*22 December:* Maj. Marshall C. Edenfield assigned 406th BS as ground executive officer.

*25 December:* 36th and 406th BS play host to group of English children.

*27 December:* 36th BS sustains first crew loss: the crew of Capt. Robert L. Williams.

*28 December:* Lt. Benjamin A. Mead promoted to ops officer, 36th BS; Lt. Ernest S. Holzworth promoted to assistant ops officer.

## 1944

*4 January:* First operational mission. Flown from Tempsford, Bedfordshire, RAF base.

*6 January:* Lt. R. O. Barber, radar officer, 36th BS, sent on D/S to Tempsford.

*14 January:* 2d Lt. Charles E. Gibney joins 36th BS. Captain Boone returns with crew after intensive training with RAF.

*16 January:* Lt. Donald G. Brine, assistant intelligence officer, 36th BS, sent on D/S to Tempsford.

*18 January:* A new second lieutenant AWOL as of 17 January.

*19 January:* All personnel return from D/S to Tempsford.

*20 January:* Lt. Lyman A. Sanders, Jr., ops officer, 406th BS, promoted to captain.

*25 January:* Capt. Rodman A. St. Clair promoted to major; Lt. B. A. Mead to captain; Lieutenant Garnett to captain — all of 36th BS. Capt. Robert L. Boone promoted to major, 406th BS.

*31 January:* Captain Sanders takes temporary leave to Washington, D.C.

*1 February:* Master Sergeant Ontko, line chief, 36th BS, dies from injuries received when struck by jeep while bicycling the night before. Master Sergeant Turner succeeds to line chief.

*7 February:* 406th BS with thirty-nine officers and 326 enlisted men begin move to Watton by motor convoy.

*10 February:* The King and Queen of Great Britain, escorted by General Doolittle, visit Alconbury.

*14 February:* New second lieutenant in arrest in quarters at Alconbury.

*17 February:* 36th BS with fifty-eight officers and 317 enlisted men leave for Watton.

*18 February:* New second lieutenant absent in arrest at Alconbury.

*21 February:* 36th and 406th BS relieved assignment 482d BG effective 14 February. New second lieutenant back to arrest in quarters at Alconbury.

*26 February:* 36th and 406th BS relieved assignment, First Bombardment Division. Reassigned to VIII Air Force Composite Command.

*27 February:* Headquarters, 328th Service Group, designated acting Group Headquarters.

*28 February:* Capt. Arnold Fletcher, adjutant, 36th BS, relieved and transferred to Group to become adjutant. Lieutenant Madden promoted to adjutant, 36th BS.

*1 March:* Lieutenants Frank Silkebaken and Howard Bosworth assigned to Group as communications officer and statistical officer, respectively. Combat crews of 36th and 406th BS and some ground sections leave Watton on D/S to Alconbury to begin March moon-period operations.

*2 March:* First "Joe" dropped on operational mission. Major Edenfield, 406th BS, transferred to Group to become executive officer. Captain Gans transferred to Group to become group surgeon.

*3 March:* Captain Sanders, 406th BS, transferred to Group to become ops officer. Lts. Robert D. Sullivan and Samuel Wakefield, intelligence officers, Capt. Charles Teer, bombardirr, and Lt. Roy Cunningham, ordnance officer, 406th BS, transferred to Group. Lieutenant McDonald and crew MIA last night.

*4 March:* Lieutenant Carpenter and crew, and Captain Wagstad and crew, MIA last night.

*23 March:* Staff Sergeant Gordon, 406th BS, transferred to Group as section chief, intelligence.

*25 March:* Advance echelons, 36th and 406th BS, arrive Harrington, Northamptonshire.

*28 March:* 406th BS attached to 801st BG (P), new Group designation for Carpetbaggers; Lieutenant Colonel Heflin, CO.

*30 March:* Pvt. James McColgan, 36th BS, represents squadron at boxing match sponsored by Red Cross. KOed in first round.

*31 March:* Remaining personnel of 406th BS leave Watton by motor convoy for Harrington.

*4 April:* 36th BS attached to 801st BG (P).

*5/6 April:* Seventeen B-24s dispatched on operational missions. Lieutenant Nicoll MIA with crew night of 4/5 April.

*8 April:* Four crew chiefs, 36th BS, return to squadron. Orders halting aviation cadet candidates returning from ETO to States for training, changes their plans.

*9 April:* Capt. Bestow R. Rudolph assumes 406th BS Operations; Captain Love relieved.

*9/10 April:* Twenty-three B-24s out on operational missions.

*10/11 April:* Twenty-three B-24s on operational missions.

*11/12 April:* Twelve B-24s on operational missions.

*14 April:* Staff Sergeant Whittington, 36th BS supply sergeant, transferred to Group.

*15 April:* Lieutenants Deutsch and Cawthorne assigned 406th BS as assistant intelligence officers.

*16 April:* Major St. Clair on D/S to London for court martial of the new second lieutenant. Capt. B. A. Mead assumes temporary command, 36th BS.

*19 April:* Major St. Clair returns from London. Reassumes command, 36th BS.

*21/22 April:* Six B-24s out on operational missions.

*23 April:* Lieutenant Colonel Heflin, with Lieutenant Colonel Gable of OSS, fly in modified B-24 to Algiers, Africa, to confer with Algiers Squadron concerning Carpetbagger work there.

*23/24 April:* Nine B-24s on operational missions.

*24/25 April:* Eight B-24s dispatched on operational missions.

*25 April:* Sergeant Lasko and Corporal Thomas, 36th BS, transferred to 406th BS Ops Section.

*25/26 April:* Six B-24s dispatched on operational missions.

*27 April:* Brigadier General Hill, Commanding General VIII AF Composite Command, visits Harrington.

*27/28 April:* Twenty-one B-24s out on operational missions. Lieutenant Ambrose and crew MIA (B-24 42–40997).

*28 April:* Captain McClarren new executive officer, 406th BS.

*28/29 April:* Twenty-one B-24s dispatched on operational missions.

*29/30 April:* Fourteen B-24s on operational missions.

*30 April:* Major Fish, Deputy Group CO, promoted to lieutenant colonel.

*30 April/1 May:* Twenty B-24s dispatched on operational missions.

*1 May:* Deeds to Harrington airfield handed to Lieutenant Colonel Heflin by Squadron Leader E. D. King, representing the RAF, at flag-raising ceremony.

*1/2 May:* Twenty-five B-24s sent out on operational missions.

*2 May:* Sergeants Kuzmannovich, Johnson, Marks, and Corporal MacKenzie, 36th BS, come in a strong second in theatrical competition in Northern Ireland.

*3/4 May:* Nine B-24s dispatched on operational missions.

*5/6 May:* Twenty-one B-24s dispatched on operational missions. Lieutenant Simon and crew MIA (probably B-24 42–40798).

*6/7 May:* Twenty-two B-24s out on operational missions. Lieutenant Pipkin and crew MIA (B-24 42–63798SA).

*7/8 May:* Fourteen B-24s dispatched on operational missions.

*8 May:* Lieutenant General Koenig, highest ranking French general in the United Kingdom, visits Harrington airfield.

*8/9 May:* Fifteen B-24s dispatched on operational missions.

*9 May:* Lieutenant Bjorge, communications officer, 406th BS, promoted to captain. Word received that Lieutenant Kelly of Lieutenant McDonald's crew, MIA 3 March, on way back to England; Lieutenant Shelvin reported POW.

*9/10 May:* Thirteen B-24s sent on operational missions.

*11/12 May:* Four B-24s on operational missions.

*13 May:* Lieutenant Colonel Heflin promoted to colonel.

*15/16 May:* Five B-24s dispatched on operational missions.

*17 May:* Advance echelons of 788th and 850th BS join units at Harrington airfield.

*18 May:* New regulations issued covering site and airfield defense. Harrington airfield known to have high priority on enemy's list due to nature of Carpetbagger work. Believed that German paratroopers may try to drop on airfields in England. All personnel now armed.

*22/23 May:* Twelve B-24s dispatched on operational missions.

*23/24 May:* Seven B-24s sent on operational missions.

*24/25 May:* Three B-24s out on operational missions.

*27 May:* Lieutenant Holmes and Technical Sergeant Wengert, MIA with Lieutenant Pipkin's crew, return to England.

*28/29 May:* Twenty-two B-24s dispatched on operational missions. Lieutenant Wolcott and crew MIA (B-24D 42-40550).

*29 May:* Lt. John B. Mead, MIA with Lieutenant Simon's crew, contacted by 406th BS crew radio operator during mission to France. Reports all members of Simon crew safe and on way back to England. Gen. William "Wild Bill" Donovan, commanding general, OSS, attends night's interrogation of returning crews.

*29/30 May:* Twenty-three B-24s sent on operational missions.

*31 May:* Crews of lieutenants McNeil and Bales fly first 850th BS missions.

*31 May/1 June:* Twenty-two B-24s sent on operational missions. Lieutenant Fitzpatrick and crew MIA (B-24D 42-40478).

*1 June:* Lt. Robert D. Sullivan, group intelligence officer, promoted to captain.

*1/2 June:* Twenty-two B-24s out on operational missions.

*2/3 June:* Eighteen B-24s sent on operational missions.

*3/4 June:* Twenty-three B-24s sent on operational missions.

*5 June:* Lt. Wm. H. Seybold, adjutant; Lt. Ader, radar officer, 406th BS, promoted to captain. Capt. Oliver B. Akers, engineering officer, transferred to Group. Lt. Frank T. Castiglione promoted to 406th BS engineering officer.

*5/6 June:* Eleven B-24s dispatched on operational missions. Lieutenant Pratt and crew MIA, Belgium (B-24D 42-63784).

*6 June:* H-Hour of D-Day. The invasion of the Continent.

*7 June:* Lt. Joseph A. Bodenhamer joins 36th BS as adjutant. Captain Madden promoted to executive officer. Lieutenant Simon, MIA 5/6 May, returns to England.

*7/8 June:* Fourteen B-24s out on operational missions.

*8 June:* Lieutenant Kelly, MIA with Lieutenant McDonald's crew, returns.

*9 June:* 36th BS completes forty-four of sixty missions during eight-day moon period for 73% score.

*12/13 June:* Sixteen B-24s dispatched on operational missions.

*13/14 June:* Six B-24s dispatched on operational missions.

*14/15 June:* Twenty B-24s sent on operational missions.

*15 June:* Red Cross Aero-Club for Enlisted Men opens under direction of Miss Nelda Kurtz. Staff Sergeant Radthe, tail gunner, 406th BS, awarded Purple Heart.

*17 June:* Lt. David L. Kaplan, 406th BS, returns from POW Conference at RAF Station, Caen Wood Towers.

*18 June:* Master Sergeant DeLano, 36th BS, first crew chief of Group to be awarded Bronze Star.

*18/19 June:* Nine B-24s sent on operational missions. Lieutenant McNeil and crew MIA, France (B-24 42–51124SA).

*20/21 June:* Twenty-five B-24s dispatched on operational missions.

*21/22 June:* Twenty-one B-24s sent on operational missions.

*22/23 June:* Ten B-24s on operational missions.

*23/24 June:* Twenty-one B-24s sent on operational missions.

*24 June:* Master Sergeant Knierim, crew chief, 36th BS, awarded Bronze Star.

*25 June:* 3d Bomb Division sends 180 B-17s on daylight supply-dropping operation in order to arm rapidly growing resistance groups in Southern France. Two B-17s reported MIA.

*25/26 June:* Twenty-four B-24s dispatched on supply missions.

*27/28 June:* Sixteen B-24s out on missions. One B-24 MIA on training flight. Lieutenant Huenekens and crew attacked by enemy night fighter intruder.

*28/29 June:* Eighteen B-24s sent on operational missions.

*1 July:* Group staff officers promoted to ranks indicated: Captain Wakefield (S-2); Major Tresemer (S-3); Major Teer (S-3); Major Sanders (S-3); Major Fletcher (S-1).

*1/2 July:* Eighteen B-24s dispatched on operational missions.

*2/3 July:* Thirty-seven B-24s dispatched on operational missions.

*3/4 July:* Thirty-eight B-24s dispatched on operational missions.

*4/5 July:* Thirty-six B-24s out on operational missions. Lieutenant Meade and crew, 850th BS, MIA (B-24 42–50386SA). Lieutenant Kline and crew, 850th BS, MIA (B-24 42–72873SA). Lieutenant Carscaddon and crew, 850th BS, attacked by three JU-88s. Major battle damage suffered. Lieutenant Broten and crew, 36th BS, MIA (B-24 42–95317SA).

*5/6 July:* Eight B-24s dispatched on operational missions.

*6/7 July:* Twenty B-24s dispatched on operational missions. Colonel Heflin and crew land in Ain area in C-47. Group's first "Dakota" operation.

*7/8 July:* Nineteen B-24s dispatched on operational missions.

*8/9 July:* Seventeen B-24s sent on operational missions.

*9 July:* 2d Lt. French M. Russell, MIA 5/6 May, returns from France in C-47 with Colonel Heflin and crew.

*9/10 July:* Thirty-seven B-24s dispatched on missions.

*10/11 July:* Twelve B-24s sent on missions.

*13/14 July:* Twenty-eight B-24s out on operational missions.

*15/16 July:* Twenty-seven B-24s sent on operational missions.

*16/17 July:* Twenty-four B-24s dispatched on operational missions.

*17/18 July:* Sixteen B-24s dispatched on missions. Lieutenant Michelson and crew, 850th BS, MIA (B-24H 42-51187).

*20 July:* 2d Lieutenant Russell promoted to first lieutenant.

*20/21 July:* Twelve B-24s sent on operational missions.

*22/23 July:* Forty-four B-24s dispatched on operational missions.

*23/24 July:* Twenty-five B-24s dispatched on operational missions.

*24/25 July:* Six B-24s out on operational missions.

*25/26 July:* Seventeen B-24s out on operational missions.

*26 July:* Master sergeants Templeton, Perkins, and Johnson, crew chiefs, 406th BS, awarded Bronze Stars.

*26/27 July:* Nine B-24s dispatched on operational missions.

*29/30 July:* Forty-four B-24s dispatched on operational missions; twelve aborts.

*30/31 July:* Thirty-one B-24s dispatched on operational missions.

*31 July/1 August:* Thirteen B-24s sent on operational missions.

*2 August:* Captains Shull, Garnett, and Stapel with crews dispatched on Dakota missions to France.

*2/3 August:* Forty-two B-24s dispatched on operational missions.

*4/5 August:* Corporal Michalak, dispatcher on Lieutenant Gilpin's crew, 788th BS, MIA after falling from B-24 over the English Channel.

*5/6 August:* Thirty-six B-24s sent on operational missions. Lt. Robert C. McLaughlin and crew, 788th BS, MIA, along with Lt. Wm. F. Reagan, pilot of a 850th BS crew, flying "buddy ride" with McLaughlin crew (B-24D 42-50584).

*7 August:* Captain Stapel returns from successful Dakota mission.

*9 August:* B-24 of Captain Bales and crew, 850th BS, received major battle damage last night while on mission to Belgium. Over 1,000 flak and cannon holes in airplane.

*10 August:* M/Sgt. Samuel D. Brandt, crew chief, 406th BS, awarded Bronze Star. Sergeants Henderson and Heddleson, MIA 27 April with crew of Lieutenant Ambrose, return to England and report that they and Sergeant Mooney, injured and taken POW, only survivors.

*11 August:* Lieutenant Callahan and Lieutenant Carscaddon, 850th BS, awarded Silver Stars.

*11/12 August:* Thirty-one B-24s dispatched on operational missions.

*13 August:* Major shake-up: 492d BG (H) designation absorbs Carpetbagger personnel at Harrington with new unit designations. 788th BS designation rejoins 467th BG. 850th BS designation rejoins 490th BG. 36th BS becomes 856th BS. 850th BS becomes 857th BS. 406th BS becomes 858th BS. 788th BS becomes 859th BS. 36th BS and 406th BS designations transferred to Cheddington. 858th BS designation rejoins 492d BG. Colonel Heflin officially assumes command of 492d BG (H).

*13/14 August:* Thirty-six B-24s dispatched on operational missions.

*14 August:* 121 enlisted men of 856th BS awarded Good Conduct Medals.

*14/15 August:* Thirty-seven B-24s dispatched on operational missions. Lieutenant Norton and crew, 856th BS, MIA (B-24J 44-40172).

*15/16 August:* Twelve B-24s sent on operational missions.

*16 August:* Promoted to lieutenant colonel: Major St. Clair, CO, 856th BS; Major Dickerson, CO, 857th BS; Major Boone, CO, 858th BS. Four new combat crews join 857th BS. Lieutenant Tappan, MIA with Broten crew 4/5 July, returns to England as only survivor.

*17/18 August:* Thirty-three B-24s dispatched on operational missions.

*23 August:* Paris liberated by FFI.

*24 August:* Pfc. Robert L. Goodson, 857th BS, killed after accidentally hit in back by .50-caliber machine gun fire.

*25/26 August:* One C-47 dispatched on operational mission to France.

*26 August:* Lt. Col. Robert W. Fish assumes temporary command of 492d BG. Col. Clifford J. Heflin on leave to States.

*28 August:* Capt. B. A. Mead, 856th BS ops officer, promoted to major.

*31 August/1 September:* Thirty-seven B-24s and C-47s dispatched on operational missions.

*1/2 September:* Forty-four B-24s sent on operational missions; three abort.

*2/3 September:* Two C-47s dispatched on operational missions.

*3 September:* Lieutenant Bodenhamer, 856th BS adjutant, promoted to captain.

*4/5 September:* Forty B-24s, four C-47s dispatched on operational missions.

*5/6 September:* Forty-six B-24s, two C-47s dispatched on operational missions.

*7/8 September:* Forty B-24s dispatched on operational missions.

*8/9 September:* Lieutenant Berkoff and crew, 859th BS, crash while en route to target. Lieutenant Berkoff KIA; others bail out safely. One C-47 dispatched on operational missions.

*9 September:* Colonel Heflin awarded French Croix de Guerre and Legion of Honor in Paris by General Koenig of France.

*9/10 September:* Forty B-24s and C-47s dispatched on operational missions.

*10 September:* Lieutenant Pratt, MIA 5/6 June, returns to England. Lieutenant Leindorf and Sergeant Warren are POWs, no information on others.

*10/11 September:* Thirty-five B-24s and C-47s dispatched on missions.

*11/12 September:* Thirty-eight B-24s dispatched on operational missions.

*12/13 September:* Thirty-six B-24s and C-47s dispatched on missions.

*14 September:* Only daylight Carpetbagger operation for Group. Four airplanes and crews completed drops on targets in heart of Paris.

*15 September:* Top secret classification removed from history of 492d BG. Reclassified secret. Lt. Ivon Ressler promoted to adjutant, 857th BS.

*16 September:* All of France liberated. Carpetbagger operations are finished. OSS recalls detachment from Harrington airfield.

*16/17 September:* Thirty-two B-24s and C-47s are dispatched on final night of Carpetbagger operations. Lt. James M. McLaughlin and crew MIA (B-24J 42-50693).

*17 September:* Preparations begin to haul tank fuel to Belgium.

*18 September:* Final C-47 operational mission. Personnel at Harrington deluged with fruit being brought back by crews flying to Belgium and France.

*21 September:* Captain Everly, 856th BS surgeon, and five enlisted men, leave for bases in Belgium. First flights with tank fuel dispatched.

*22 September:* Personnel of original Carpetbagger units presented Croix de Guerre by General Koenig of France at formal ceremony attended by Lt. Gen. James Doolittle, General Partridge, and Brigadier General Sanford. Lieutenants Callahan and Carscaddon, 850/857th BS, presented Silver Stars. Maj. B. A. Mead assumes temporary command of 856th BS while Lieutenant Colonel St. Clair takes leave in States.

*24 September:* Capt. James A. Darby assumes temporary command of 857th BS while Lieutenant Colonel Dickerson takes leave in States.

*30 September:* Fuel-hauling duties completed. Resume C-47 "Dakota" operations to Southern France.

*1 October:* 492d BG relieved from assignment to VIII AF Composite Command and reassigned to VIII Fighter Command. APO changed to 637.

*9 October:* Lieutenant Pitsenbarger and crew crash at Holme in Yorkshire (B-24 42-94841).

*22 October:* 492d relieved from assignment to VIII Fighter Command and reassigned to USSTAF, First Bomb Division, APO 557. All C-47s in Group transferred to 856th BS; 857th, 858th, and 859th BS to begin training for medium-level night bombing operations. Colonel Heflin assigned to War Department in Washington, D.C. Lieutenant Colonel Fish assumes command of 492d BG. Lieutenant Choper promoted to captain and assistant ops officer, 856th BS.

*5 November:* Crews of lieutenants Kuntz, Lemke, Bronar, Borden, Seger, Walling, and Abernathy, 856th BS, sent on D/S to Cheddington with 406th Night Leaflet Squadron.

*10 November:* Personnel turn in all field equipment. Needed at front lines.

*12 November:* Lieutenant Colonel Boone transferred to headquarters, 492d BG.

*18 November:* Lieutenant Lemke and crew, on temporary D/S with 406th Night Leaflet Squadron, crash at Oulton, instantly killing six of crew (B-24 42-94775).

*27 November:* 108 personnel, 856th BS, donate blood to 8th AF Blood Bank drive.

*29 November:* Personnel leave on mission to investigate possibilities for Carpetbagger operations in CBI Theater.

*30 November:* Lieutenant Colonel St. Clair reassumes command of 856th BS.

*1 December:* Lieutenant Bradley returns to 856th BS as survivor of Lemke crash. Lt. Col. Robert L. Boone, Deputy Group CO, 492d BG, on leave to States. Lt. Col. Jack M. Dickerson, former CO, 857th BS, appointed Deputy Group CO.

*2 December:* 856th BS personnel donate sixty-five pounds toward the Group's effort to adopt three war orphans.

*5 December:* Lieutenants Kuntz, Borden, and Walling, with crews, report back to 856th BS from D/S at Cheddington.

*6 December:* Maj. B. A. Mead, ops officer, 856th BS, relieved and sent to States. Capt. Ernest S. Holzworth promoted to ops officer, a job which he has been performing since 22 September. Lt. Ross D. White new assistant ops officer and gunnery officer.

*7 December:* Capt. John Madden, executive officer, 856th BS, appointed Assistant Group adjutant, and assumes duties of adjutant in absence of Major Fletcher, who was hospitalized 6 December. Group acquires P-47 to be used in training.

*9 December:* Lieutenant Connett and Staff Sergeant Abelow placed on D/S in France.

*11 December:* Lieutenant Abernathy and crew, on D/S at Cheddington, crash at Woodbridge.

*16 December:* S/Sgt. Samuel Abelow, historian and 856th BS Intelligence, awarded Bronze Star for producing history of 492d BG.

*17 December:* Col. Hudson H. Upham assumes command 492d BG. Lieutenant Colonel Fish resumes former duties of Deputy Group CO. 859th BS sent on D/S to Brindisi airfield in Italy. Lieutenant Abernathy and crew, 856th BS, return from D/S at Cheddington.

*19 December:* 856th BS operations and intelligence sections move into ops block of their own.

*20 December:* Lieutenants Hudson, Heran, McCormick, and Friberg, with crews, arrive from States and join 856th BS.

*24 December:* Eighth Air Force dispatches largest armada of warplanes in history. First night bombing missions of "Black Liberators" on coastal batteries.

*25 December:* Christmas activities combined with coldest weather in forty years of English history.

*26 December:* Lieutenants Abernathy and Yancey granted seven days' leave. Lieutenant Salomone relieved and sent to States. Other members of Abernathy crew granted seven days' leave at Sunnyside Mansions.

*28 December:* OSS personnel set up office in 856th BS ops block. "Black Liberators" dispatch sixteen B-24s on night bombing mission, same target as night of 24 December.

*31 December/1 January 1945:* Carpetbagger operations begin again. Crews of Lieutenants Thompson, Swarts, and Heaberlin set pace with 100% performance.

### 1945

*4/5 January:* Twelve B-24s bomb coastal batteries.

*5 January:* Lt. John H. Singleton on D/S to France to assume intelligence duties. Captain Bronar and crew shot down by British ack-ack batteries over Brussels last night. All crew members bail out safely.

*12 January:* Captain Bronar and crew granted seven days' leave at combat crew rest home. Lt. Eugene V. Connett, 856th BS intelligence officer, returns from Lyon-Annecy operation.

*21 January:* Lieutenant Thompson and crew fly first Carpetbagger mission from advanced base at Lyon, France, into Germany. Lieutenant Walling and crew depart for Italy carrying OSS personnel.

*23 January:* 859th BS attached to 15th AF in Italy to carry out Carpetbagger special operations there.

*29 January:* Maj. Bestow R. Rudolph and crew return from New Delhi, India. Colonel Upham, Group CO, Lieutenant Colonel St. Clair, Captain Choper, Captain Bodenhamer, Major Tresemer, Major Messer, Major Fletcher, Staff Sergeant Leinninger, Staff Sergeant Scozzavava, and Corporal Johnson depart on D/S to France.

*29/30 January:* Two B-24s dispatched on Carpetbagger missions to Norway.

*1 February:* Lieutenant Blume and crew down on training flight (probably B-24 44–49476). Lt. Abe M. Thompson, 856th BS, promoted to first lieutenant and recommended for DFC.

*11 February:* 856th BS receives instructions to train bombardiers and navigators in high-altitude work. Captains Shull and Garnett are relieved and sent to States. Lieutenant McGuire and Lieutenant France appointed 856th BS navigator and bombardier, respectively.

*17 February:* Annecy operation ends.

*20 February:* Lieutenant Seger and crew relieved and sent to States.

*20/21 February:* Twenty-six "Black Liberators" bomb Neustadt.

*21/22 February:* Twenty-nine "Black Liberators" bomb Duisburg, with crew of Lieutenant Wiebe MIA (probably B-24 44–49500). One B-24 and crew lost over continent, one receiving battle damage.

*22/23 February:* Seven B-24s dispatched on Carpetbagger missions.

*23/24 February:* Twenty-seven "Black Liberators" bomb Neuss marshalling yard. Two B-24s sent on Carpetbagger missions to Norway.

*25 February:* 2d Lieutenant Bass, and 2d Lieutenant St. Martin of Lieutenant Thompson's crew, 856th BS, promoted to first lieutenants.

*26/27 February:* Five B-24s dispatched on Carpetbagger missions.

*27/28 February:* Twenty-six "Black Liberators" bomb Wilhelmshaven marshalling yard.

*28 February/1 March:* Twenty-five "Black Liberators" bomb Freiburg rail depot.

*2/3 March:* Four B-24s sent on Carpetbagger missions.

*3/4 March:* Twenty-four "Black Liberators" bomb Emden railroad docks.

*4 March:* Lt. Col. Earle J. Aber, Jr., CO, 406th Night Leaflet Squadron, KIA (B-17 43-37516).

*5/6 March:* Twenty-four "Black Liberators" bomb Wiesbaden rail station. One B-24 dispatched on Carpetbagger mission to Denmark.

*6/7 March:* Five B-24s dispatched on Carpetbagger missions.

*7 March:* Captain Holzworth, 856th BS ops officer, promoted to major. Maj. Robert H. Gaddy assumes command, 406th BS.

*7/8 March:* Twenty-one "Black Liberators" bomb Dortmund marshalling yard. One airplane and crew MIA with one other receiving major battle damage.

*8/9 March:* Fifteen "Black Liberators" bomb Dortmund marshalling yard again. Seven B-24s dispatched on Carpetbagger missions.

*9 March:* Lieutenants White and Heaberlin, 856th BS, promoted to captain.

*9/10 March:* Nine B-24s dispatched on Carpetbagger missions.

*10 March:* Major Daby, Captain King, Captain Klinger, Lieutenant Shackel transferred to Group Headquarters from 857th BS.

*10/11 March:* Thirteen "Black Liberators" bomb Munster marshalling yard again.

*12 March:* Most personnel and all aircraft of 857th BS absorbed by Group Headquarters and 856th and 858th BS; 857th BS designation and some personnel absorb First Scouting Force at Bassingbourn.

*12/13 March:* Ten B-24s dispatched on Carpetbagger missions.

*13 March:* Lieutenant Colonel Dickerson transferred to Group Headquarters from 857th BS. Major Akers, group engineering officer, sent to 4203 US Army Hospital for treatment. Detachment "A," all personnel and equipment, move from Lyon, France, to Dijon, France.

*14 March:* 856th BS loses independent status. Merges again with Group. 406th BS (NL) joins 492d BG at Harrington airfield.

*14/15 March:* Seven "Black Liberators" bomb Wiesbaden marshalling yard.

*15 March:* Captain Madden, executive officer, 856th BS, promoted to major. Major Scheafer appointed Group assistant ops officer; Lieutenant Schackel to assistant equipment officer; Captain Klinger to assistant intelligence officer; Captain King to Group engineering officer; Major Daby to air inspector.

*15/16 March:* Sixteen "Black Liberators" bomb Munster rail station.

*16/17 March:* Twenty-two B-24s sent on Carpetbagger missions.

*18 March:* Lieutenant Sheppard and crew, 856th BS, crash on mountainside near Llangying, North Wales, while on training flight.

*19/20 March:* First Mosquito "Red Stocking" mission dispatched.

*20 March:* Major Sanders relieved assignment to 492d BG.

*20/21 March:* Major Scheafer appointed Group ops officer. One Mosquito, two A-26s dispatched, with one A-26 MIA.

*21 March:* Captain Heaberlin, Lieutenants Webb, St. Martin, and Clarke relieved from assignment 856th BS and transferred to 7th Photo Group. Major Tresemer MIA as of 20 March on mission over Germany (A-26 43–22524).

*22/23 March:* Two Mosquitos dispatched on "Red Stocking" missions.

*23 March:* First agent team successfully dropped into Austrian Alps.

*23/24 March:* Nineteen B-24s dispatched on Carpetbagger missions to Denmark.

*24 March:* Capt. Laurence Rivkin transferred from 858th BS to become Group navigator. Major Tresemer relieved.

*24/25 March:* One "Red Stocking" Mosquito dispatched. Twenty-four Carpetbagger B-24s dispatched on missions to Scandinavia.

*25 March:* Lieutenant Bradley, survivor of Lemke crash, relieved and sent to States.

*26/27 March:* One "Red Stocking" Mosquito dispatched.

*27/28 March:* One "Red Stocking" Mosquito dispatched.

*29/30 March:* Two "Red Stocking" Mosquitos dispatched.

*30 March:* Lieutenants Bennett, McCormick, Hallburg, Clark, and Sergeants McCarthy, Nightingale, Thomas, and Williams relieved assignment to 856th BS; transferred to 14th AF with two Carpetbagger B-24s at Kunming, China, to establish Carpetbagger operations in that theater. Lt. Richard A. Dennis assigned to Group as adjutant. Major Fletcher relieved.

*30/31 March:* Nineteen Carpetbagger B-24s dispatched on missions to Norway. Lieutenant Polinsky and crew, 856th BS, crash on Orkney Islands, Scotland.

*1/2 April:* One "Red Stocking" Mosquito dispatched.

*2/3 April:* Twenty-four Carpetbagger B-24s dispatched to Denmark. One "Red Stocking" Mosquito dispatched.

*3/4 April:* One "Red Stocking" Mosquito and two A-26s dispatched.

*4/5 April:* Eleven Carpetbagger B-24s dispatched on missions to Denmark.

*5/6 April:* One "Red Stocking" Mosquito dispatched.

*6/7 April:* One "Red Stocking" Mosquito dispatched. Three B-24s dispatched on Carpetbagger missions to Norway. Lieutenant Hudson, 856th BS, MIA with full crew.

*8/9 April:* Twelve "Black Liberators" bomb Travemunde Port area. One Mosquito "Red Stocking" mission completed.

*9/10 April:* Fourteen "Black Liberators" bomb Stade airfield. Two A-26s dispatched on Carpetbagger missions. One Mosquito dispatched on "Red Stocking" mission.

*10/11 April:* Fourteen "Black Liberators" bomb rail depot at Dessau. One Mosquito dispatched on "Red Stocking" mission. 856th BS takes part in their first high-altitude night bombing mission. Most of personnel from newly assigned crews from old 857th BS.

*11/12 April:* Eleven Carpetbagger B-24s dispatched on missions to Denmark. One Mosquito dispatched on "Red Stocking" mission.

*12/13 April:* Six Carpetbagger B-24s sent on missions to Denmark. Two Mosquito "Red Stocking" missions completed.

*13 April:* FDR dead. Harry S Truman assumes office of president and commander in chief.

*13/14 April:* Twelve "Black Liberators" bomb Beizenburg rail junction. Four Carpetbagger B-24s sent to Denmark. One "Red Stocking" Mosquito dispatched.

*14 April:* Lt. Robert R. France, 856th BS navigator, promoted to captain.

*14/15 April:* Four Carpetbagger B-24s dispatched on missions to Denmark. One Mosquito dispatched on "Red Stocking" mission.

*15/16 April:* One Mosquito and nine "Black Liberators" dispatched to bomb Lechfeld airfield; mission aborted. One "Red Stocking" Mosquito sent on operational mission.

*16/17 April:* One Mosquito sent on "Red Stocking" mission.

*17 April:* Flight Leader Abe M. Thompson and 856th BS Bombardier Charles W. McGuire promoted to captains.

*17/18 April:* Twenty Carpetbagger B-24s dispatched on missions. Two "Red Stocking" Mosquitos dispatched on missions.

*18/19 April:* Eighteen Carpetbagger B-24s sent to Denmark and Norway. One Mosquito dispatched on "Skywave" mission to Italy.

*19/20 April:* Sixteen Carpetbagger B-24s dispatched to Norway, two MIA. Two "Red Stocking" Mosquitos dispatched on missions.

*20/21 April:* Two Mosquito "Red Stocking" missions completed. Twelve Carpetbagger B-24s dispatched to Norway. Lieutenant Keeney and crew MIA. Lt. Norman C. Stoll, 856th BS, relieved and sent to States, having completed his second tour.

*21/22 April:* Two "Red Stocking" Mosquitos dispatched to Germany.

*22/23 April:* Twelve Carpetbagger B-24s dispatched to Norway.

*23/24 April:* Two "Red Stocking" Mosquitos dispatched. Fourteen Carpetbagger B-24s dispatched to Denmark. Lieutenant Brenner and crew, 856th BS, struck by light AA fire with three of crew injured.

*24/25 April:* One "Red Stocking" Mosquito dispatched; crashed at Winchfield on return.

*25/26 April:* Twelve Carpetbagger B-24s sent on missions to Norway. One "Red Stocking" Mosquito dispatched to Germany. 492d BG receives letter of commendation for operations at Dijon, France.

*26/27 April:* One "Red Stocking" mission dispatched.

*28/29 April:* One "Red Stocking" Mosquito dispatched. Late in month, Lt. Col. Robert W. Fish again assumes command of 492d BG. Col. Hudson H. Upham transferred to 40th Combat Wing in France.

*29/30 April:* One "Red Stocking" Mosquito dispatched. Lt. Peter C. Pulrang receives Purple Heart.

*2/3 May:* One "Red Stocking" mission dispatched.

*7 May:* Victory in Europe.

*5 June:* Lieutenant Colonel Fish relieved of command, 492d BG, transferred to 41st Combat Wing in France. Lieutenant Colonel Boone relieved of command, 858th BS, to assume temporary command of 492d BG in absence of Lieutenant Colonel Dickerson, who was appointed to assume command of the Group but was on leave.

*6 June:* Maj. Ernest S. Holzworth, 856th BS ops officer, transferred to 858th BS to assume command. Capt. Ross D. White continues as gunnery officer and Capt. William McKee becomes ops officer, 856th BS.

*7 June:* Lieutenant Colonel Dickerson returns from leave and assumes duties as CO of 492d BG. Lieutenant Colonel Boone to Group executive officer.

*11 June:* Capt. Milton Shapiro, 856th BS intelligence officer, awarded Bronze Star for outstanding work at Dijon.

*14 June:* 1st. Lt. Albert R. Habney granted seven days' leave following his wedding. Detachment "A" officially discontinued as of 2400 hours, 21 May, 1945.

*30 June:* Capt. Roscoe E. Klinger becomes assistant adjutant, 492d BG.

*1 July:* Early in month Maj. Ernest S. Holzworth appointed CO, 492d BG. Captain Klinger becomes adjutant.

*7 July:* Air Echelon, 492d BG, leaves Harrington for Z of I.

*16 July:* Ground Echelon, 492d BG, relieved assignment Eighth Air Force. Assigned to

VIII Fighter Command.

*4 August:* Ground Echelon leaves WAAF Site I, Harrington, at 0140 hours for Gurrock, Scotland, to embark on Queen Elizabeth for Z of I.

*11 August:* Ground Echelon arrives NY Port of Entry at 0830 hours. Arrives Camp Kilmer, NJ, at 1930 hours.

*14 August:* Ground Echelon arrives Sioux Falls Army Airfield, South Dakota, at 1630 hours.

*17 August:* All personnel of air and ground echelons, 492d BG, transferred to Squadron S (Pool) 211 AAFBU (AS) Sioux Falls, SD. Organization left for Kirtland Field, Albuquerque, NM, arrives at 2400 hours. No personnel, assigned, attached unassigned, or attached from other organizations, effective 2400 hours, 17 August, 1945.

*29 August:* Organization redesignated from Heavy to Very Heavy. Group headquarters opened at Kirtland Field with one officer, Lt. Col. George E. Bergstrom, executive officer.

*30 August:* Lt. Col. Dalson E. Crawford assigned to 492d BG as commanding officer.

*30 August to 15 September:* Approximately forty-five officers and 1,120 enlisted men assigned to organization. Majority were transferred to other units in preparation for inactivation of 492d BG (VH).

*17 October:* Group inactivated.

# Appendix II

## Combat Crew Roster

Available records indicate that the following pilots and their crews flew months as shown. However, the list probably is not complete, particularly during April, May, and June of 1945. The unit to which the crew was attached is shown in parentheses; months are indicated by number; the year was 1944 unless otherwise shown.

Abernathy (856) 9, 11, 12
Alford (788) 6, 7, 8
Ambrose (36) 4
Archambault (406) 2, 3, 4, 5, 6
Bales (850) 5, 6, 7, 8; (857) 9
Beard (858) 9
Beller (788) 7, 8; (859) 9
Berkoff (856) 9
Bledsoe (858) 3 (1945)
Blume (858) 9

Boone (406) 1, 2, 3, 4, 5, 6, 7, 8; (858) 2 (1945)
Borden (856) 9, 11, 12; 1, 2, 3 (1945)
Boswell (859) 9
Bronar (856) 11, 12; 1 (1945)
Broten (36) 6, 7
Byerly (850) 7, 8; (857) 9
Carpenter (36) 2, 3
Carscaddon (850) 7, 8; (857) 9
Cassedy (36) 3, 4, 5, 6
Choper (36) 2, 3, 4, 5, 6, 7

Sandberg (850) 7, 8; (857) 9
Sanders (406) 1, 5, 6, 8; (856) 2 (1945)
Schaefer (857) 9; (856) 2, 3 (1945)
Schreiner (36) 1, 2
Seccafico (788) 7, 8; (859) 9
Seger (856) 9, 11, 12; 1 (1945)
Simon (406) 4, 5
Smith, A. (36) 3, 4, 5, 6, 7
Smith, W. (850) 6, 7, 8; (857) 9
Stamler (788) 7, 8; (859) 9
Stapel (36) 1; (406) 2, 3, 5, 6, 8; (858) 9
St. Clair (36) 5, 6, 7, 8
Stinchcomb (406) 6, 7, 8
St. Martin (856) 2 (1945)
Swarts (36) 8; (856) 9; 1, 2, 3 (1945)

Taylor (859) 9
Thompson (856) 9, 11, 12; 1, 2, 3, 4, 5 (1945)
Van Zyl (406) 1, 2, 3, 4, 5, 6
Velarde (858) 9
Wagstad (36) 1, 2, 3
Walling (36) 7, 8; (856) 9, 11, 12
Ward (36) 5, 6, 7, 8
Warn (36) 8; (856) 9
White (856) 2, 3, 4 (1945)
Wiebe (857) 9; 2 (1945)
Wills (788) 6, 7, 8
Wilson (788) 6, 7, 8; (859) 9
Wolcott (406) 2, 3, 4, 5
Wonnell (857) 9
Wood (788) 6, 7, 8
Wright (850) 6, 7, 8; (857) 9
Zink (36) 8; (856) 9
Ziringer (850) 8; (857) 9

# Endnotes

Chapter 1.   THE 36TH AND 406TH SQUADRONS: GETTING STARTED

1. Bestow R. Rudolph, letter to author, July 17, 1984.

2. Wilmer L. Stapel, letter to author, May 3, 1984.

3. Members of the crew were Williams, pilot; Lt. Joseph W. Hanley, copilot; Lt. Milton L. Remling, navigator; Lt. Louis F. Peterson, bombardier; T.Sgt. Jesse A. Wallace, engineer; T.Sgt. Glen O. Wichner, radio operator; S.Sgt. Henry D. McMillan, gunner; and S.Sgt. Eddie P. Rush, gunner.

4. Wilmer L. Stapel, letter to author, May 3, 1984. Among the pilots at Tempsford were Lt. Wilmer L. Stapel, Lt. Harold Van Zyl, and Lt. Gerald S. Wagstad. After their graduation in Pilot Class 42-I in December 1942, their crews had been formed at Salt Lake City. The three had been based in Arizona and New Mexico for high-altitude bomber training. While awaiting assignment overseas as replacement crews, they received orders to report to Langley Field, Virginia, for training as antisubmarine crews. They were assigned in May 1943 to the 22d Antisubmarine Squadron at Wilmington, North Carolina. In August, with Colonel Heflin and twelve crews, Stapel, Van Zyl, and Wagstad were sent to Dunkeswell, England, and then in November to Alconbury. Now, in January 1944, they were flying from Tempsford.

5. Stapel's crew consisted of Stapel, pilot; Lt. Hal M. Harrison, copilot; Lt. Milton S. Popkin, navigator; Lt. Glen C. Nesbitt, bombardier; T.Sgt. James B. Elliott, engineer; Sgt. Wallace R. Goodman, radio operator; S.Sgt. Leo C. Roettger, dispatcher; and S.Sgt. Eugene J. Wozniak, tail-gunner.

6. Lieutenant Wagstad and crew flew two missions, but both were noncomplete. An agent in the field reported that the lack of reception was due to German patrols on the grounds. Lieutenant Rudolph and Lt. David H. Schreiner each flew noncompleted missions on the night of January 4. It was later learned that the reception was not out that night because of Gestapo activity. Captain Boone flew two missions, completing both. A few nights later, Lieutenant Rudolph flew another noncomplete mission. Lt. Claude H. Cummings and Lieutenant Schreiner each flew a completed mission, and Lieutenant Stapel flew a noncompleted mission on the night of January 6. In a few days an agent on the ground reported that they had not been on the drop grounds that night because the Gestapo occupied the area after a member of the Secret Army turned traitor. Lieutenant Mead and Lieutenant Sanders each flew two missions, each completing one. Lieutenant Van Zyl flew one completed mission, and Colonel Heflin completed one of two missions.

7. Lt. Wade A. Carpenter and crew flew three missions, completing one. Lt. Emanuel Choper flew two, completing neither. Lt. Marvin L. Fenster completed one of two missions; Lieutenant Harrison completed one of three. Captain Mead and Lieutenant

259

Harrison each flew a mission to the same site on the night of February 8, with both called noncompleted. (Later, a message from the field declared both complete.) Lt. Frank C. McDonald completed three of four on first report. Lt. William G. McKee flew four missions, with one complete, while Lt. Earl F. McKenny flew three with all noncomplete. A message from the field reported on the drops made on the night of February 8 by McKee and McKenny on the same site: "Most of the material was taken by the Germans." Lieutenant Schreiner flew two missions, completing both. Lieutenant Smith's single mission was noncomplete. Lieutenant Wagstad flew two, completing one.

Lt. Charles E. Archambault and Major Boone each flew one completed mission. Lt. Jerome Crance flew three missions, completing one on the night of February 8. Lt. Ernest B. Fitzpatrick flew three missions, with one complete, on the night of February 10. Lt. John T. Kelly flew two missions, both noncomplete; Lt. John A. Lucey flew one called noncomplete.

Lt. Jack H. Munn and Lt. Volney T. Peavyhouse each flew three missions with all called noncomplete. Lt. George Pipkin and Captain Rudolph flew two missions each, with one each called complete. Captain Stapel flew two, completing both. Lieutenant Van Zyl flew two noncomplete missions. Lt. Henry W. Wolcott flew two, completing one. Colonel Heflin flew one completed mission, and Major Fish flew one, which was called noncomplete.

8. *History of the 856th Squadron,* on microfilm at Maxwell AFB, Alabama.

9. Wilmer L. Stapel, letter to author, May 3, 1984. Stapel's crew was as follows and remained the same through their thirtieth mission: Stapel, pilot; Lt. Russell C. Rivers, copilot; Lt. Milton S. Popkin, navigator; Lt. Hubert A. Bowen, bombardier; T.Sgt. James B. Elliott, engineer; Sgt. Wallace R. Goodman, radio operator; Sgt. Charles J. Roth, dispatcher; and S.Sgt Eugene J. Wozniak, tail-gunner.

10. The crew consisted of McDonald, pilot; Lt. Frederick C. Kelly, copilot; Lt. Thomas H. Kendall, navigator; Lt. Edward F. Shevlin, bombardier; S.Sgt. Leroy S. Goswick, dispatcher; T.Sgt. Warren L. Ross, radio operator; Sgt. Norman R. Gellerman, engineer; and S.Sgt. Edward H. DeCoste, tail-gunner.

11. The crew consisted of Carpenter, pilot; Lt. Bernard M. Eshleman, copilot; Lt. Lonnie Hammond, Jr., navigator; Lt. William D. Rees, bombardier; Lt. Glen C. Nesbitt, bombardier (406th Squadron); T.Sgt. Clarence L. Johnson, engineer; T.Sgt. Eden C. Burris, Jr., radio operator; Sgt. Edward Herdman, dispatcher; and S.Sgt. John H. Dudley, tail-gunner.

12. Members of the crew were Wagstad, pilot; Lt. Henry W. Walsh, copilot; Lt. Edward Martinez, navigator; Lt. Joseph P. Connor, Jr., bombardier; T.Sgt. Earl W. Underwood, engineer; T.Sgt. Cornelius P. O'Leary, radio operator; S.Sgt. Leo C. Roettger, dispatcher; and S.Sgt. Frederick M. Wagner, tail-gunner.

13. Lt. James A. Cassedy flew two missions, one complete. A later message from the field confirmed the success of the mission called noncomplete. Lieutenant Choper flew five missions, completing three; Lieutenant Cummings flew one noncompleted mission; Lieutenant Fenster completed two out of four; and Captain Rudolph completed three of three. Lieutenants Harrison and Pipkin and Captain Rudolph all dropped on the same site on the night of March 4. Lieutenant Pipkin completed three of four successfully. A message from the field reported, "No parachutes opened on night of March 4/5 and consignment was practically totally destroyed. Nobody was hurt — hope to be able to obliterate all traces and save the remains."

Captain Mead flew one mission, called noncomplete. Lieutenant McKee flew four, with all completed. Messages from the field confirmed the success of drops made on the nights of March 2 and 6. Lieutenant McKenny completed one of three successfully; Lieutenant Smith one of two.

Lieutenant Archambault flew one noncompleted mission; Major Boone completed one of two; Lieutenant Fitzpatrick completed two of four successfully. Fitzpatrick's mission of the night of March 6 was confirmed by the field, and the pilot was congratulated for "wonderful drops from a very low altitude. All the material was recovered in spite of a violent wind." Lieutenant Crance flew two missions, completing one. Lieutenant Kelly flew three, one completed, with a message from the field confirming the drop on the night of March 5. Lieutenant Lucey flew three with two completed; Lieutenant Munn flew five, completing two. Munn's mission on the night of March 6 to the same site as Fitzpatrick's was confirmed in the message confirming Fitzpatrick's.

Lieutenant Peavyhouse completed one of four; Lieutenant Van Zyl completed one of two. Lieutenants Lucey and Van Zyl dropped on the same site on the night of March 6; the message from the field confirmed the receipt of twenty-four containers and seven packages, which was five packages short of the number dropped. Lieutenant Wolcott flew three, completing two. On the mission of the night of March 2, the pilot reported bad weather which made site identification very difficult, but a message from the field reported the success of the operation. Captain Stapel flew two missions, completing neither. Colonel Heflin flew two completed missions. His mission on the night of March 6 marked the first agent-dropping operation for the units. The field confirmed that two agents and all material had arrived safely.

14. *History of the 856th Squadron*, on microfilm at Maxwell AFB, Alabama.

Chapter 3. THE CREW AND ITS MISSIONS

    1. Joe Milliken, letter to author, August 9, 1982.
    2. Robert L. Stroud, letter to author, November 12, 1984.

Chapter 4. EARLY MISSIONS RECOUNTED

    1. *History of the 406th Squadron*, on microfilm at Maxwell AFB, Alabama.
    2. The crew consisted of Nicoll, pilot; Lieutenant Kalbfleisch, copilot; 2d Lt. William G. Harris, navigator; Lt. Thomas F. Davis, bombardier; S.Sgt. Richard C. Bindell, engineer; S.Sgt. Warren A. Brewer, radio operator; S.Sgt. Ralph L. Kittrell, tail-gunner; and Sergeant Porter, dispatcher.
    3. Other members of the Ambrose crew were: Lt. Robert H. Redhair, Lt. Arthur B. Pope, Lt. Peter Roccia, and S.Sgt. Charles M. Wilson.
    4. James J. Heddleson, letter to author, May 15, 1984.

Chapter 5. INTO THE DARKNESS: THE 858TH (NIGHT LEAFLET) AND THE 788TH AND 850TH SQUADRONS

    1. *History of the 788th Squadron*, on microfilm at Maxwell AFB, Alabama.

Chapter 6. EVASIVE ACTION IN ENEMY TERRITORY

    1. Members of the crew were: Simon, pilot; Lt. French M. Russell, copilot; Lt. John B. Mead, bombardier; Lt. John A. Reitmeier, navigator; T.Sgt. Leo F. Dumesnil, engineer; T.Sgt. Phillip B. Latta, radio operator; S.Sgt. Graham S. Hasty, gunner; and S.Sgt. Homer C. Collier, tail-gunner.

2. Members of the crew were Pipkin, pilot; Lt. Israel M. Barron, copilot; Lt. Clair D. Vander Schaef, navigator; Lt. Floyd N. Holmes, bombardier; T.Sgt. Dale Helmer, engineer; T.Sgt. Jack C. Wengert, radio operator; S.Sgt. James F. McCaskey, dispatcher; and S.Sgt. Vincent Galiozzi, gunner.

3. The crew consisted of Wolcott, pilot; Lt. Robert F. Auda, copilot; Lt. William G. Ryckman, navigator; Lt. Wallis O. Cozzens, bombardier; S.Sgt. Frederick A. Tuttle, engineer; T.Sgt. Dale S. Loucks, radio operator; T.Sgt. Dervin D. Deihl, dispatcher; S.Sgt. Richard G. Hawkins, tail-gunner; and Lt. Carmen T. Vozzella, who was a navigator from the 788th Squadron flying a check-out mission.

4. Henry W. Wolcott III, letter to author, June 1985.

5. Members of the crew were Fitzpatrick, pilot; Lt. Richard V. Theriot, copilot; Lt. James S. Sherwood, navigator; Lt. Joseph J. Lasicki, bombardier; S.Sgt. James E. Williams, gunner; T.Sgt. Paul P. Kasza, radio operator; S.Sgt. Walter W. Swartz, engineer; S.Sgt. William Schack, tail-gunner; and Lt. Cornell Dogrothy, a 788th Squadron navigator flying a check-out mission.

6. The crew consisted of Pratt, pilot; Lt. Ralph Leindorf, copilot; F. O. Russell J. Pyrne, navigator; F. O. Carlo C. Starkovich, bombardier; S.Sgt. Ollie Warren, dispatcher; T.Sgt. Joseph A. Caren, radio operator; S.Sgt. Roy C. Koons, engineer; and S.Sgt. James Warner, tail-gunner.


Chapter 7.   D-Day and Beyond: The Events in Normandy

1. Brig. Gen. Brian S. Gunderson (Ret), letter to author, March 29, 1985.

2. The crew consisted of McNeil, pilot; Lt. Glen O. Thompson, copilot; Lt. Joseph P. Bova, navigator; Lt. Robert F. Siebert, bombardier; S.Sgt. Henry H. Ricard, dispatcher; S.Sgt. Jerome J. Hummel, radio operator; Sgt. Fred H. Lowery, engineer; and Sgt. Fred Monico, tail-gunner.

3. The crew consisted of Huenekens, pilot; Lt. John M. Cronan, copilot; Lt. Robert Callahan, navigator; Lt. Robert L. Sanders, bombardier; S.Sgt. Carl R. Adams, engineer; and Sgt. Randall G. Sadler, tail-gunner.

4. Members of the crew were Carscaddon, pilot; Lt. Otis W. Murphy, copilot; Lt. Joseph C. Denaro, navigator; Lt. William L. Cranbery, bombardier; T.Sgt. Charles E. Cernik, radio operator; T.Sgt. Franklin J. Hasty, engineer; S.Sgt. Paul A. Stralka, Jr., dispatcher; and S.Sgt. Laurie A. Salo, tail-gunner.

5. Members of the crew were Kline, pilot; Lt. Clyde H. Schultz, copilot; Lt. Richard J. Brace, navigator; Lt. Jesse H. Snider, Jr., bombardier; T.Sgt. Floyd A. Lauletta, engineer; T.Sgt. Dana R. Wemette, radio operator; S.Sgt. Warren L. Rock, dispatcher; and S.Sgt. Arthur G. Abate, tail-gunner.

6. The crew consisted of Broten, pilot; 2d Lt. Edward Tappan, copilot; 2d Lt. Roy C. Gehue, navigator; 2d Lt. Alfred C. Emert, bombardier; Sgt. Jesse R. Ellis, radio operator; S.Sgt. Harry L. Sparks, engineer; and Sgt. Michael J. Pranzetelli, tail-gunner.

7. The 850th Squadron crew consisted of Meade, pilot; Lt. James L. Lovelace, copilot; Lt. Gerald E. Mitchell, navigator; Lt. John D. Bonnin, bombardier; S.Sgt. William R. Dubois, Jr., waist-gunner; T.Sgt. Edward J. Jones, radio operator; T.Sgt. Frank F. Hines, engineer; and S.Sgt. Ellis H. Syra, tail-gunner.

Chapter 8.   C-47 "DAKOTA" AND CONTINUED SUMMER MISSIONS

1.  Wilmer L. Stapel, letter to author, May 3, 1984.

2.  The crew consisted of Michelson, pilot; John P. Shaw, Jr., copilot; Lt. Donald C. Boyde, navigator; Lt. Melvin Weiss, bombardier; S.Sgt. Arnold Marinoff, dispatcher; S.Sgt. William J. Hovanec, radio operator; T.Sgt. Duncan L. Patterson, engineer; and S.Sgt. Enoch K. Wooten, Jr., tail-gunner.

3.  The crew members were McLaughlin, pilot; Lt. Daniel G. Olenych, copilot; Lt. Bertram D. Knapp, bombardier; Lt. Leo O. Arlin, navigator; T.Sgt John Y. Bear, engineer; S.Sgt. Fred H. Heath, dispatcher; T.Sgt., Donald C. Adamson, radio operator; 2d Lt. William F. Reagan, a passenger from the 850th Squadron on a "buddy ride"; and S.Sgt. Warren H. Lee, tail-gunner.

4.  Conversation with William L. Bales, October, 1983.

Chapter 9.   OBTAINING — AND CONCEALING — INFORMATION

1.  *History of the 492d Bomb Group,* on microfilm at Maxwell AFB, Alabama.

2.  *Ibid.*

Chapter 10.   THE ILL-STARRED ORIGINAL 492D; NEARING FRENCH LIBERATION

1.  I have never seen in print that what followed was ordered to be that way, but it certainly is logical and the way it happened.

2.  The 36th Squadron designation was given to the radio countermeasures operation, and the operation moved from Oulton to Cheddington. The 406th Squadron designation absorbed the operations of the 858th Night Leaflet Squadron based at Cheddington. The other two squadron designations formerly attached to the 801st Bomb Group rejoined their original groups. The 788th Squadron designation went back to reform in the 467th Bomb Group (H) at Rackheath, and the 850th Squadron designation left Harrington to reform in the 490th Bomb Group (H) at Eye.

3.  They were the crews of Lt. James M. McLaughlin, Lt. Charles W. Beard, Lt. Robert K. Doyle, Capt. Armando C. Velarde, Lt. Ross D. White, Lt. Stanley A. Seger, Flight Officer Abe M. Thompson, Jr., Lt. Harold F. Powers, Lt. Elmer D. Pitsenbarger (sometimes spelled Pitzenbarger), Lt. Mellicent S. Moorhead, Lt. Wilfred B. Boswell, and Flight Officer Donald L. Taylor. In addition to these twelve crews, it is known that at least another four pilots went from North Pickenham to Cheddington, then to Harrington on August 17, some with partial crews. They were Lt. James G. Kuntz, Lt. Orrin T. Bowland, Lt. Ernest C. Skwara (sometimes written Earnest C. or Ernest G.), and Lt. Curtis A. Abernathy (sometimes spelled Abernethy). All these crews and pilots had served for varying lengths of time in the 492d at North Pickenham.

Velarde, Powers, Beard, McLaughlin, Doyle, Moorhead, and it is believed Kuntz, were all pilots of the original 492d crews who had begun operations from North Pickenham on May 11, having come all the way from the States with the original group. Velarde had been a flight officer, the only pilot of that rank, when the 492d had left the States. His copilot was Powers; his crew was No. 615.

Beard's crew was No. 603; Doyle's, No. 808; and McLaughlin's, No. 811. Moorhead was copilot on crew No. 604 (Hurley's crew).

Bowland and his crew had joined the 492d on June 5 as a replacement crew, as did Abernathy and crew on June 24. White and Seger, with crews, joined on July 11, and

Thompson and crew on July 13. On July 18, Boswell and crew had joined; Skwara joined on August 6. All of these crews flew missions with the old 492d, with the exception of the crew of Lieutenant Skwara. Pitsenbarger and his crew had joined on July 4.

On June 19, Taylor and crew had transferred to the 857th Squadron from the 858th when that designation left North Pick. Then, two days later, they were transferred to the 856th Squadron. Obviously, the Taylor crew joined as a replacement crew, but nothing has been found indicating when they joined the 492d at North Pickenham.

4. Velarde was appointed assistant operations officer of the 856th Squadron on July 27, and the 492d's final mission — No. 67 to Ostend, Belgium — was led by Velarde on August 7. He had just made captain.

5. There is some confusion over the name Kuntz. Lt. James E. Kuntz, 0808563, was pilot of crew No. 616 on April 1, Lt. James G. Kuntz, 0808562, moved from North Pickenham to the Carpetbagger project on August 17. Perhaps this was a series of clerk-typist's errors in the middle initial and last digit of the serial number.

6. Because the 406th Squadron designation was given to the night leaflet operation at Cheddington, the 858th Squadron designation left Cheddington and rejoined the 492d Bomb Group at Harrington. There, personnel of the old 36th Squadron became the 856th Squadron; personnel of the old 850th became the 857th; personnel of the old 406th became the 858th; and personnel of the old 788th became the 859th Squadron.

7. Wilmer L. Stapel, letter to author, May 3, 1984.

8. The crew consisted of Norton, pilot; 2d Lt. Connie L. Walker, copilot; 2d Lt. Benjamin Rosen, bombardier; 2d Lt. Lloyd L. Anderson, navigator; S.Sgt. James H. Husbands, engineer; S.Sgt. William H. Moncy, radio operator; S.Sgt. Wayman B. Skadden, tail-gunner; and Sgt. John W. Gillikin, dispatcher.

9. Members of the crew were Berkoff, pilot; 2d Lt. John H. Webb, copilot; 2d Lt. Vincent D. Woods, navigator; 2d Lt. George M. Snyder, bombardier; Sgt. Alphonso J. Rinz, engineer; Sgt. George F. Williams, radio operator; Sgt. Daurel Transtrum, dispatcher; and Sgt. John D. Duer, tail-gunner.

10. The crew consisted of McLaughlin, pilot; Lt. Carl L. Lee, copilot; Lt. George F. Bradbury, navigator; Lt. Ernest G. Skwara, bombardier; T.Sgt. Alforne A. DeVries, engineer; T.Sgt. Henry Stee, radio operator; S.Sgt. James G. Pirtle, tail-gunner; and S.Sgt. Merrill G. Brewer, dispatcher.

11. The crew consisted of Seger, pilot; Lt. George J. Carter, copilot; Lt. Ralph Mack, navigator; Lt. Andrew Torado, bombardier; Sgt. Robert E. Marvel, engineer; Sgt. John D. Craig, radio operator; Sgt. Earl V. Wood, gunner; Sgt. Leon C. Yates, gunner; Sgt. Gordon J. Gillette, gunner; and Sgt. Stanley B. Richardson, gunner.

12. Stanley A. Seger, conversation with author, August 1983.

13. Ralph P. Beaman, letter to author, June 2, 1982.

14. Stanley A. Seger, letter to author, March 2, 1980.

15. Wilmer L. Stapel, letter to author, May 3, 1984.

Chapter 11.   FUEL FOR PATTON — AND OTHER SPECIAL MISSIONS

1. *History of the 492d Bomb Group*, on microfilm at Maxwell AFB, Alabama.

2. Abe M. Thompson, letter to author, April 1, 1984.

3. Forrest S. Clark, letter to author, March 28, 1984.

4. Ralph P. Beaman, letter to author, December 4, 1984.

5. B. Blunt, letter to author, September 15, 1984.

6. Others killed were Lt. Elmer D. Pitsenbarger, pilot; Lt. James D. Nendel, co-

pilot; F. O. Jack M. Bliss, navigator; T.Sgt. Presley E. Farris, engineer; T.Sgt. Joseph W. Zwinge, radio operator; S.Sgt. Frank A. Villelli, gunner; Cpl. Charles T. Lowblad, tail-gunner; and Clarence Watson, who apparently was a passenger.

7. Stanley A. Seger, letter to author, March 2, 1980.

8. The crew consisted of Lemke, pilot; Lt. Frederick C. Bofink, copilot; Lt. Henry E. Salmons, navigator; Lt. Daniel A. Bradley, bombardier; Sgt. Leslie C. Cazzell, engineer; T.Sgt. Gordon W. Elmore, radio operator; S.Sgt. James K. Albright, waist-gunner; S.Sgt. John Koliada, waist-gunner; and S.Sgt. Garrett C. Parnell, Jr., tail-gunner. Sergeant Parnell was on temporary detached service with the Lemke crew; his regular crew was that of Lt. Abe M. Thompson.

9. Garth Bowen, letter to author, April 6, 1984.

10. James K. Albright, letters to author, July 5, 1980, and July 22, 1980.

11. Don Prutton, letter to author, June 22, 1980.

Chapter 12. NIGHT BOMBING OPERATIONS

1. The 859th Squadron was to distinguish itself in the new assignment: Among crews flying missions on the night of February 17, 1945, which resulted in the award of a second unit citation to the 2641st Special Group (Prov.) to which they were attached, were the 859th Squadron crews of Lt. E. F. McKenny, Lt. H. E. Gilpin, Lt. J. S. Mulligan, Lt. A. J. Hunter, Jr., Lt. R. C. Robins, Maj. C. H. Cummings, Lt. J. W. Fox, and Capt. J. A. Seccafico.

2. A 1934 graduate of the United States Military Academy, Colonel Upham had attended advanced flying school and was rated as senior pilot. He served at various stations, including Randolph and March fields, studied French in Canada, and taught at West Point. After A-20 training at Will Rogers Field, B-17 transition courses at Hendricks field, and combat crew training at Ardmore, Oklahoma, he was assigned in November 1944 to the European Theater of operations.

Chapter 13. RENEWED CARPETBAGGER OPERATIONS

1. The crew consisted of Thompson, pilot; F. O. Donald A. St. Martin, copilot; 2d Lt. William K. Clarke, navigator; 2d Lt. David C. Groff, bombardier; S.Sgt. Harold E. Parvi, engineer; S.Sgt. Louis W. Meyer, radio operator; Sgt. Robert J. Osborne, waist-gunner; Sgt. Walter N. Rohde, waist-gunner; Sgt. Garrett C. Parnell, Jr., ball-turret-gunner; and Sgt. Johnnie L. Page, tail-gunner.

2. Telephone conversation with William K. Clarke, May 1981.

3. Telephone conversation with Robert W. Bronar, May 1984.

4. Members of the crew were Bronar, pilot; Lt. Garth Bowen, copilot; Lt. Henry T. Dixon, navigator; Lt. William H. Kibbie, bombardier; T.Sgt. Presley W. Smith, engineer; S.Sgt. Thomas Braswell, Jr., radio operator; Sgt. Robert C. Nelson, waist-gunner; and Sgt. Robert C. Willems, tail-gunner.

5. Abe M. Thompson, letter to author, July 13, 1979.

6. Robert J. Osborne, letter to author, April 19, 1980.

7. The crew consisted of Aber, pilot; Lt. Maurice J. Harper, copilot; Capt. P. S. Stonerock, navigator; Lt. C. R. Morton, bombardier; T.Sgt. C. P. Valley, radio operator; T.Sgt. M. Silber, top-turret-gunner; S.Sgt. S. Dombrowski, ball-turret-gunner; S.Sgt. J. A. Trexler, waist-gunner; S.Sgt. F. W. Thomas, waist-gunner; S.Sgt. R. W. Ramsey, tail-gunner; and Lt. R. W. Billings, a new navigator on a training flight.

8. Ivon R. Ressler, letter to author, May 1983.

Chapter 14.   To Berlin and the Alps

1. P. Petrenko, letter to author, November 18, 1984.
2. The crew consisted of Lt. Oliver H. Emmel, pilot; Maj. John W. Walsh, navigator; Major Tresemer, bombardier; and S.Sgt. Frederick J. Brunner, Marine Corps, gunner.
3. Ross D. White, letter to author, October 1984.
4. The crew consisted of Sheppard, pilot; Lt. Julian W. Bradbury, copilot; Flight Officer John A. Rogers, navigator; Lieutenant Shaefer, bombardier; Sgt. James R. Green, engineer; Cpl. John F. Mattingly, radio operator; Sergeant Kouser, waist-gunner; Private Holata, waist-gunner; and Sgt. David U. Blanton, tail-gunner.

Chapter 15.   Victory in Europe: Mission Completed

1. William E. Colby, letter to author, February 15, 1985.
2. Donald F. Heran, letter to author, May 10, 1984.
3. Members of the crew were Hudson, pilot; the substitute copilot, Lt. Leon G. Dibble, Jr.; F. O. Arthur H. Bardknecht, navigator; Lt. Richard A. Bosch, bombardier; Sgt. Gilbert L. Magruder, radio operator; Sgt. Angelo Santini, engineer; Sgt. Jack H. Spyker, gunner; and Sgt. Fayette Shelledy, gunner.
4. William E. Colby, letter to author, February 15, 1985.
5. Donald F. Heran, letter to author, May 10, 1984. Members of Heran's crew were Heran, pilot; Lt. William T. Wright, copilot; Lt. Clayton S. Berger, navigator; Lt. Donald A. Fischer, bombardier; Cpl. Calvin D. Johnson, gunner; Cpl. J. C. McBrayer, gunner; Cpl. Donald J. McHale, radio operator; and Cpl. Alfred W. Nowaczyk, engineer.
6. Members of the crew were Keeney, pilot; Lt. Hayden R. Parker, copilot; Lt. Jack L. Divine, navigator; Lt. Stephen J. Marangus, Mickey operator; S.Sgt. R. L. Broaddus, engineer; S.Sgt. H. H. Brabec, radio operator; S.Sgt. C. McClure, gunner; S.Sgt R. P. Beard, gunner; S.Sgt. A. L. Greenwood, gunner; and S.Sgt. R. L. Haussen, gunner.
7. Abe M. Thompson, letter to author, July 13, 1979.
8. Bestow R. Rudolph, letter to author, February 2, 1984.
9. Robert W. Fish, letter to author, January 4, 1984.

# Bibliography

*Aerospace Historian* (Official Journal of the Air Force Historical Foundation).

Angelucci, Enzo, and Paolo Matricardi. *World War II Airplanes*. Vol. 2. Chicago: Rand McNally, 1978.

Asprey, Robert B. *War in the Shadows*. Garden City, NY: Doubleday, 1975.

Birdsall, Steve. *The B-24 Liberator*. New York: Arco, 1968.

Blue, Allan G. *The Fortunes of War*. Fallbrook, CA: Aero, 1967.

Bowman, Martin. *Fields of Little America*. Norwich, England: Wensum Books, 1977.

Carter, Kit C., and Robert Mueller. *The Army Air Forces in World War II: Combat Chronology, 1941–1945*. Prepared by Albert F. Simpson Historical Research Center, Air University, and Office of Air Force History: U.S. Government Printing Office, 1973.

Cave Brown, Anthony. *The Secret War Report of the OSS*. New York: Brandt, 1976.

Churchill, Winston S. *The Grand Alliance*. Boston: Houghton Mifflin, 1950.

Consolidated Aircraft Company and L. Kohn. *Flight Manual for B-24 Liberator*. Appleton, WI: Aviation Publications, 1977.

Craven, Wesley Frank, and James Lea Cate. *The Army Air Forces in World War II, Volume Three*. Chicago: The University of Chicago Press, 1951.

Eisenhower, Dwight D. *Crusade in Europe*. New York: Hearst, 1948.

Foot, M. R. D. *SOE in France*. London: HMSO, 1966.

Freeman, Roger A. *The Mighty Eighth*. Garden City, NY: Doubleday, 1970.

———. *Mighty Eighth War Diary*. New York: Jane's, 1981.

Jablonski, Edward. *Flying Fortress*. Garden City, NY: Doubleday, 1965.

Knight, Clayton, and Robert Durham. *Hitch Your Wagon*. Drexel Hill, PA: Bell Publishing Co., 1950.

Koch, R. W. *The FP-45 Liberator Pistol, 1942–1945*. Private Publication, 1976.

MacCloskey, Brigadier General Monro. *Secret Air Missions: Counterinsurgency Operations in Southern Europe*. New York: Richards Rosens Press, 1966.

Meyer, Robert, Jr. *The Stars and Stripes Story of World War II*. New York: David McKay, 1960.

Piquet-Wicks, Eric. *Four in the Shadows*. London: Jarrolds, 1957.

Pogue, Forrest C. *George C. Marshall: Organizer of Victory*. New York: Viking, 1973.

Pyle, Ernie. *Here is Your War*. Cleveland and New York: World, 1945.

Smith, Ben, Jr. *Chick's Crew*. Waycross, GA: Yarbrough Brothers, 1978.

*War Report of the Office of Strategic Services*. Prepared by Kermit Roosevelt. OSS, declassified
     1976.

In addition to the specific sources listed above, many squadron and group records,
available on microfilm at the Albert F. Simpson Historical Research Center, Maxwell
AFB, Alabama, have been consulted. Correspondence with former Carpetbagger personnel
has provided otherwise unrecorded information.

# Index

92$^{d}$ Bonb gp

Bovington

Pg.
2 Alers